Financin

2012 Election

FINANCING THE 2012 ELECTION

David B. Magleby

editor

BROOKINGS INSTITUTION PRESS
Washington, D.C.

Library of Congress Cataloging-in-Publication data
Financing the 2012 election / David B. Magleby, editor.
     pages   cm
  Includes bibliographical references and index.
  ISBN 978-0-8157-2563-3 (pbk. : alk. paper)   1. Presidents—United States—
Election—2012—Finance. 2. United States. Congress—Elections, 2012—
Finance. 3. Campaign funds—United States. I. Magleby, David B., author,
editor of compilation.

  JK19682012 .F56 2014
  324.973'0932—dc23   2014017120

9 8 7 6 5 4 3 2 1

Printed on acid-free paper

Typeset in Sabon

Composition by R. Lynn Rivenbark
Macon, Georgia

Contents

List of Tables and Figures

Preface

$\mathbf{M}$uch has changed since Herbert Alexander published a book summarizing how the 1960 election was financed. Since that 1960 volume, we have seen major federal legislation on the rules of campaign finance, important court cases on the constitutionality of those reforms, and creative political professionals testing the limits of what can be done in raising and spending money to elect or defeat candidates. The pace of change in campaign finance has accelerated and the ability of the participants to adapt to new rules has been remarkable. Despite these significant changes, the importance of money in our democracy has remained constant. *Financing the 2012 Election* is the fifteenth book that continues Alexander's commitment to document and analyze how American elections are financed.

During the 2012 election cycle we saw a new entity emerge in a presidential election, the independent expenditure-only committee or Super PAC, which grew out of court cases and Federal Election Commission rulings. We also saw growth in the Section 501(c) committees, which are not required to disclose their donors. In some respects, 2012 was reminiscent of the 1996 and 2000 election cycles where interest groups and party committees spent money for and especially against candidates, but technically not in coordination with them. In each of these elections some of the sources of these funds were not disclosed. The expanded array of ways participants could legally spend money in the 2012 elections makes campaign finance more complex because different rules apply to different participants and to different recipients of contributions. Some have contributions limits while others do not; some must disclose their donors while others are not required to do so. Some types of coordination are allowed while others, such as coordination with candidates or party committees, are not. In this volume we have attempted to make these distinctions clear and explain their consequences.

The role of individual donors has been enhanced by the 2002 campaign finance reforms in the Bipartisan Campaign Reform Act, which doubled the individual contribution limit and indexed those limits to inflation. In 2012 we saw contrasting strategies by the two major party presidential nominees in response to these changes. Barack Obama cultivated both large and small donors. Mitt Romney placed primary emphasis on donors giving the maximum allowable contribution. Obama's success among small donors was most notable. Individuals were also the most important source of funding for Super PACs, but in this case the contributions were unlimited and a small number of donors gave the most money. While political parties and interest groups continue to play important roles, especially in congressional elections, a big part of the story in the 2012 presidential election was the extent to which candidates were reliant on Super PAC help—something that may become more common in congressional races as well.

As in prior editions, chapter authors bring a wealth of expertise to their chapters. Anthony Corrado provides an insightful summary of campaign finance law and administrative rulings that set the stage for the 2012 election. The presidential nomination phase in 2012 had an unchallenged incumbent seeking renomination but a contested battle for the Republican Party nomination. John Green, Michael Kohler, and Ian Schwarber examine this phase, showcasing the relative success of the candidates in fundraising but also the role played by Super PACs. Though the Democratic primary was uncontested, both the Obama campaign and Obama's Super PAC were active in raising money and advertising during that cycle. Candice Nelson's chapter on the presidential general election insightfully highlights the contrast between the two candidates in campaign strategy. For instance, Romney relied more on large donors, his party, and his Super PAC while Obama had greater success with individual donors at all levels, and especially small donors. Nelson emphasizes the likely continuing role of Super PACs as a replacement of public financing, which no major candidate accepted for the 2012 election cycle.

Congressional elections feature wide variation in the ability of challengers to mount visible campaigns. In their chapter, Paul Herrnson, Kelly Patterson, and Stephanie Curtis provide data and analysis on how incumbents, challengers, and open seat candidates financed their campaigns. Outside groups were also part of the story in congressional races in 2012, including substantial activity by party committees through independent expenditures in battleground races. Some had speculated that by banning soft money, the Bipartisan Campaign Reform Act of 2002 would greatly reduce the role parties play in elections. However, party committees have substituted hard-money funded independent expenditures for much of what they once did with soft money. Diana Dwyre and Robin Kolodny then assess the role of party committees in 2012 and also the possible further expansion of parties thanks to the recent *McCutcheon* v. *Federal Election Commission* decision in 2014. Long before the advent of Super PACs, interest groups were important in funding elections. Jay Goodliffe and I discuss the role of traditional PACs as well as Super PACs and Section 501(c) organizations in our chapter on interest groups in 2012. Finally, Tom Mann concludes the book by looking at lessons for reformers that can be drawn from the 2012 election.

I am grateful for the financial support provided to this project by the John D. and Catherine T. MacArthur Foundation where program officer Jeff Ubois was most helpful. Financial support for the project also came from Brigham Young University. Once again this volume greatly benefited from the assistance of Stephanie Perry Curtis who is skilled at navigating the complex data sets at the Federal Election Commission. The project also benefited from a capable team of BYU undergraduate research assistants, specifically Troy Anderson, Zachary Barrus, Ethan Busby, Geoff Cannon, Kenneth Daines, Bree Gardner, Kirsten Hinck, Katie Kleinert, Luke MacDonald, Robbie Richards, and Tessa Sheffield. At BYU, editorial assistance was provided by Kim Greenberg, and grant management support was provided by Gary Reynolds at the Office of Research and Creative Activity, Kathleen Rugg in Research Accounting, Marilyn Webb in the College of Family, Home, and Social Sciences, and Kellie Daniels in the Department of Political Science.

The professionals at Brookings were helpful and patient with us as we produced this volume. We express appreciation especially to Chris Kelaher, Janet Walker, and Valentina Kalk. Katherine Kimball provided a thorough copy edit. We also express appreciation to the two anonymous reviewers whose comments and suggestions improved the book.

Finally, I would like to dedicate this volume to my four children, Joseph, Kathryn, Daniel, and Benjamin, all of whom have taken a keen interest in our government. Their support and encouragement I greatly appreciate.

DAVID B. MAGLEBY

ONE

The 2012 Election as
a Team Sport

DAVID B. MAGLEBY

Continuing a trend, the 2012 federal election saw more money raised and spent than any other election in U.S. history. Although not all expenditures are reported, our best estimate is that at least $8 billion was spent in the 2012 federal elections. This estimate includes what we know from candidate, party committee, and interest group disclosure reports to the Federal Election Commission (FEC), the Internal Revenue Service (IRS), and interviews we conducted with several interest groups active in 2011 and 2012.[1] The $8 billion spending estimate for federal elections constitutes a more than $1.6 billion increase in inflation-adjusted dollars over 2008 (a 25 percent rise) and a more than $3 billion increase over 2004.[2]

The substantial increase of spending in 2012 when compared to 2008 and 2004 is all the more noteworthy given that the country had experienced a major recession and that only one party had a contested presidential nomination. Part of the rise in overall spending was attributable to increased spending in congressional elections in 2012 over previous years. Contrary to these trends, spending by presidential candidates was down by $455 million in 2012 compared with 2008, in part because only one party had a contested nomination and the cycle was slower to start than in 2008. However, the dip in presidential candidate spending was largely invisible to voters because outside groups and the national party committees more than made up the difference. Looking just at the spending in the presidential race in 2012, we estimate a total of more than $2.3 billion was spent by candidates, parties, individuals, and groups, with Mitt Romney and allies at near parity in spending with Barack Obama and allies.

The most important change in the way the 2012 election was financed was the return of outside money on a large scale to federal elections. Outside money is campaign spending by individuals, groups, or parties done outside the control of the candidates or their campaigns. In 2012, groups and parties acting independently spent at least $1.7 billion in support of or opposition to federal candidates.[3] Spending by groups other than the candidates and parties was subject to fewer restrictions than in previous elections. As Anthony Corrado explains in detail in chapter 2, the regulatory environment going into the 2012 election had been reshaped both legally and psychologically by the Supreme Court rulings in *Citizens United* v. *Federal Election Commission* and *SpeechNow.org* v. *Federal Election Commission*.[4] These two cases, combined with the court's 2007 decision in *Federal Election Commission* v. *Wisconsin Right to Life, Inc.,* in which the court reversed its decision in *McConnell* v. *Federal Election Commission* regarding electioneering communications, or what are often called "issue ads," meant individuals and groups had much greater latitude in spending money to influence the outcome of federal elections.[5]

Presidential contests traditionally take center stage in presidential election years, and this was again true in 2012. Owing in part to the slow economic recovery the country was experiencing, Republicans were optimistic about winning back the White House, and some pre-election modeling projected that the GOP would quite likely win the presidency.[6] It was also uncertain whether a second Obama candidacy could achieve the same level of grassroots enthusiasm and fundraising success as it had experienced in 2008.[7] Despite these possible limitations, the Obama campaign was expected to spend in excess of $1 billion in the 2011–12 cycle.[8] At the time, some questioned whether that would be possible given the struggling economy and some evidence of a demoralized base in the Democratic Party.[9]

In congressional contests, most attention was focused on a few high-profile U.S. Senate races. Given that the Democrats were defending twenty-three seats, several of which were in historically Republican states, there was a real possibility that the Democrats could lose their majority. Accordingly, some interest groups such as the League of Conservation Voters (LCV), an environmental group that supported Democrats, made Senate races their highest priority for independent expenditures in 2012.[10] If Obama were to be defeated, these interest groups sought to build a "firewall" of forty-one Democratic Senate votes, which would be enough to block filibusters designed to weaken environmental laws or regulations. As it turned out, the LCV and other pro-Democratic groups not only helped reelect Obama but also helped Democrats win a net gain of two Senate seats, giving the Democrats fifty-five senators, well above the forty-one-seat firewall.[11]

The GOP went into the 2012 election with 242 U.S. House seats, while the Democrats held 193 seats, meaning the Democrats would need a net gain of twenty-five seats to retake the majority. Democrats had suffered major losses in 2010, with Republicans picking up a net gain of sixty-three seats and the majority.[12] Redistricting following the 2010 census had also hurt Democrats. Republicans did well in state legislative and gubernatorial races in 2010, allowing them to control the redistricting process in eighteen states[13] while Democrats had control in only in six. As the political scientist Gary Jacobson has written, "After redistricting, there were 11 more Republican-leaning districts, 5 fewer Democratic-leaning districts, and 6 fewer balanced districts."[14] Given these factors, few prognosticators saw the Democrats as having a serious shot at winning a House majority in 2012.[15] Republicans had a net loss of 8 seats but were able to retain a 234-201 seat majority in the House after the election.

Republicans' success in House elections in 2010 and 2012 has meant that they have controlled at least one congressional chamber during more than half of the Obama presidency. In an era of a sharply polarized Congress, the sense that control of Congress is possibly up for grabs has been a frequent refrain in fundraising appeals to supporters of both parties.

Given the competitive nature of presidential contests since at least 2000 and the possibility of a change in party control of one or both houses of Congress, how did 2012 compare with earlier cycles in overall spending? Figure 1-1 plots the inflation-adjusted candidate expenditures in presidential, House, and Senate elections by election cycle.

Inflation-adjusted spending by presidential candidates rose only gradually between 1976 and 2000, in part because of public financing. Campaign finance reforms in the 1970s established a system of partial public financing of presidential nomination contests through a system of partial matching funds to candidates participating in the system and full public funding of party nominees through a grant, which if accepted, meant that candidates would cease raising money for their campaigns. The widespread candidate acceptance of public funding appears to have had the effect of constraining expenditures by candidates in presidential races. In

Figure 1-1. *Inflation-Adjusted Congressional and Presidential Candidate Campaign Expenditures, 1976–2012*

Millions of 2012 dollars

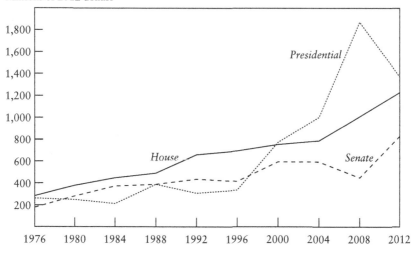

Sources: 1972–98 data from *Financing the 2008 Election*, edited by David B. Magleby and Anthony Corrado (Brookings, 2011); 2000–12 data from the Center for Responsive Politics (www.opensecrets.org).

2008 and 2012, as presidential candidates abandoned public funding and its accompanying spending limits, their combined presidential candidate spending exceeded House candidates' spending, something that had not been true before 2008. Spending by House candidates roughly doubled between 1976 and 2000, and spending by Senate candidates showed more variability, in part owing to the different mix of states that held Senate elections in different cycles.

It is important to note that party soft money (the unlimited but disclosed contributions parties could raise and spend, banned after the 2002 elections) and so-called interest group "issue advocacy" spending, as well as independent expenditures in presidential and congressional races, are not included in this figure. Interest groups and individuals have long spent money in federal elections beyond their contributions to candidates, party committees, and political action committees (PACs). They have done this by making expenditures themselves independent of the candidates. Between 1996 and 2002 they also exploited an unrealistic definition of electioneering to claim that expenditures they were making were about issues and not elections and therefore not subject to disclosure. This latter type of spending was called "issue advocacy."

In the 2011–12 election cycle, $1.224 billion was spent by House candidates, a 29 percent increase over 2008. Aggregate spending by House candidates increased in 1992, after which it leveled off, only to rise again in 2000 by about $100 million. A similar increase occurred in 2004. The 2008 cycle saw a 43 percent increase in House candidate expenditures, with $948 million spent by House candidates. Thus the trend is clearly for House candidate spending in a presidential election year to rise substantially over the previous cycle.

Aggregate spending by Senate candidates shows more ups and downs, which is not surprising given the different mix of states with Senate races in any given election cycle. But spending by House and Senate candidates in the aggregate was at an inflation-adjusted all-time high in 2012 of $2.059 billion, nearly double the $1.097 billion spent in 2000.

Compared with spending in House and Senate contests, spending in presidential races shows quite a bit of stability between 1976 and 2000, with aggregate expenditures in real dollars ranging from $225 million to $452 million in 2012 dollars. As presidential candidates abandoned public funding and the spending limits that came with those funds, presidential candidate spending nearly doubled between 2000 and 2004 and nearly doubled again between 2004 ($863 million) and 2008 ($1.7 billion). Presidential candidate spending in 2012 was $1.418 billion.[16] As noted, this dip in 2012 occurred because only one party had a contested nomination and not due to presidential candidate spending, which was up in 2012.

The money spent by federal candidates was raised under the contribution limits of the Federal Election Campaign Act (FECA), which were in place from the 1970s through the 2002 election cycle. Those individual contribution limits were raised by the Bipartisan Campaign Reform Act (BCRA) and took effect in the 2004 election cycle. BCRA essentially doubled the individual contribution limits and indexed them to inflation while leaving PAC contributions unchanged and not indexed to inflation. Table 1-1 shows the contribution limits in place for the 2011–12 election cycle.

One reason why candidate expenditures have risen since 2000 is that BCRA doubled contribution limits and indexed them to inflation, permitting candidates to raise more money from donors who want to give more than $2,000, the pre-BCRA limit, in an election cycle. As we

Table 1-1. *Individual Campaign Contribution Limits over Two-Year Election Cycle, Pre-BCRA and Post-BCRA*
2012 dollars

Year	Pre-BCRA	2004	2006	2008	2010	2012
Recipient						
Any candidate committee (per election)[a]	1,000	2,000[b]	2,100[b]	2,300[b]	2,400[b]	2,500[b]
Any national party committee (per year)	20,000	25,000[c]	26,700[c]	28,500[c]	30,400[c]	30,800[d]
Any state or local party (per year)	5,000	10,000[e]	10,000[e]	10,000[e]	10,000[e]	10,000[e]
Any PAC or other political committee (per year)	5,000	5,000[b]	5,000[b]	5,000[b]	5,000[b]	5,000[b]
Aggregate total per election cycle						
Candidates	25,000	37,500	40,000	42,700	45,600	46,200
To parties and political committees	25,000	57,500	61,400	65,500	69,900	70,800
		(37,500)[f]	(40,000)[f]	(40,000)[f]	(45,600)[f]	(46,200)[f]
Overall	25,000	95,000	101,400	108,200	115,500	117,000

Source: Adapted from Center for Responsive Politics, "Campaign Contribution Limits" (www.opensecrets.org/big picture/limits.php).
a. Primary, general, or runoff election.
b. Subject to aggregate limit.
c. Per party committee.
d. Per party committee; subject to aggregate limit.
e. Levin funds, subject to state law but not subject to the aggregate limit.
f. Figure in parentheses is maximum amount of larger total to political committees.

demonstrate in this book, maxed-out donors, each of whom could give up to $5,000 to a candidate in 2012, have become an increasingly important element in building a viable candidacy for the presidency—and, increasingly, for the U.S. Congress. These maxed-out donors are likely to play an even greater role in the future, as the Supreme Court in 2014 declared unconstitutional the aggregate candidate and party contribution limits in *McCutcheon* v. *Federal Election Commission*.[17]

The contribution limits for PACs have remained unchanged since 1974. Under FECA, PACs were allowed to contribute five times as much to a candidate as an individual was allowed to contribute. But since the 2002 BCRA doubled individual contribution limits and indexed them to inflation, an individual could contribute half as much as a PAC in 2012. Yet contributions to candidates by individuals and PACs, while important, are only part of how elections are financed. Of the $8 billion spent on federal elections in 2012, only 40 percent was raised and spent by candidates, the remainder being raised and spent by party committees and outside groups acting independently of the candidates.[18]

Money raised for campaigns is not of equal value. This is true not only when the money is spent but also in how it can be spent. As Charles R. Spies, general counsel to and treasurer of the pro-Romney Super PAC Restore Our Future, observed, "The timing of money can be more important than the amount."[19] Early money is, generally speaking, more valuable to a candidate than late money. Early money can be invested in campaign infrastructure, which takes time to develop and cannot be done as effectively late in the campaign. Early money may also help to reinforce the impression of candidate viability, as John Green discusses in chapter 3. In 2011–12 the Democrats had an incumbent candidate for president seeking an uncontested nomination. Republicans, on the other hand, had a multicandidate field, and Romney was not the presumptive winner until former Pennsylvania senator Rick Santorum dropped out in April.[20] Candidates are preferred recipients of contributions because they can spend more efficiently and because their spending is part of a campaign strategy and focused message. As we discuss in this book, candidates and party committees working in coordination, like candidates on their own, are eligible for more favorable rates for television ads, and party committees are eligible for more favorable mail rates. Had the *McCutcheon* v. *Federal Election Commission* ruling been in effect in 2012, an individual could have given $5,000 to all general election federal candidates and $30,800 to each of the three party committees, plus $10,000 to each state party, $2,500 to other primary election candidates, and $5,000 to each PAC. That is, an individual could give in excess of $800,000 to candidates and parties alone and much more than that if the donor also wanted to give to multiple PACs.[21]

How the Money was Raised in 2011–12

How was the $8 billion raised to finance the 2012 election? Most of the money to fund federal elections comes from individuals. In aggregate figures, in 2012 individuals gave 64 percent of all funds contributed to federal candidates, compared with 53 percent in 2000, the last presidential election before passage of BCRA.[22] Individuals play an even larger role in funding presidential candidates. Of all money raised by the presidential candidates in 2011–12, 72 percent came from individuals. This compares with 77 percent in 2008 and 73 percent in 2004. President Obama, who set records for fundraising from individuals in 2007–08, ran uncontested for the Democratic nomination in 2012. His receipts from individuals in 2012 were $715 million compared with $656 million in 2008. However, in 2008 all other Democratic candidates seeking the nomination raised $256 million from individuals. More broadly, the amount of money raised from individuals has risen dramatically since passage of BCRA in 2002. That legislation, by increasing the amounts individuals could give while holding PAC contributions constant, was intended to increase the role played by individuals in funding federal elections.[23] The act was successful in this regard, as the number of reported contributions to the FEC has risen from 1.6 million in 2000, the last presidential election before BCRA took effect, to 2.5 million in 2004, 3.4 million in 2008, and 3.5 million in 2012.[24]

In addition to doubling the individual contribution limit, BCRA banned party soft money, which had become a way for candidates to circumvent individual contribution limits by encouraging donors to give unlimited amounts to their party committees. In the 2000 election, for example, the party committees collectively spent nearly $500 million in soft money on party activity in presidential, congressional, and state and local races.[25] Since BCRA the party committees have exploited the higher individual contribution limits and raised substantially more hard-money contributions, which are limited as to source and amount, than they had before (a $129 million difference). Contrary to the predictions of some that banning soft money was a form of "suicide" for party committees because they were giving up their soft-money pipeline, the two national party committees raised as much in 2012 in hard money as they did in 2000 in hard and soft money combined.[26] In 2000 the Democratic National Committee (DNC) and Republican National Committee (RNC) raised $956 million in inflation-adjusted hard and soft money, compared with $942 million raised by the two committees in 2012 ($403 million by the DNC and $539 million by the RNC). This includes money raised in joint fundraising with their presidential nominees.[27] The law allows presidential nominees to form joint fundraising committees, which in turn may raise funds jointly from individuals wishing to give to the candidate and national party committee.

Party committee fundraising success extends to the party congressional campaign committees. In 2012 the Democratic Senatorial and Democratic Congressional Campaign Committees raised two to three times the amount they raised in hard money in 2000, and they raised more in hard money in 2012 than they did in hard and soft money in 2000. On the Republican side the increase has not been as high or as consistent. Although spending by party committees has been outstripped by their candidates and by outside groups, party committees have successfully substituted hard money for soft money. Party committees provide an important broader perspective on politics than do particular interest groups or individual candidates. Party committees have proved themselves able to adapt to new fundraising rules, which has kept them in the game with candidates and interest groups.

Under the law in place in 2012, an affluent person wishing to give the maximum allowable to federal candidates ($45,600 in 2011–12) could give $69,900 to some combination of party committees, with no more than $30,800 going to any single party committee. A maxed-out donor must thus decide either to allocate less to candidates or to one or more party committees. This results in some competition between the party committees, as most maxed-out donors give the maximum allowed to candidates.

The dominant role of individual donors in funding presidential candidates is also evident in the funding of Super PACs, the independent expenditure–only committees that were a major development in 2012. In *Citizens United* v. *Federal Election Commission,* the Supreme Court ruled that these committees were not subject to the contribution limits of other PACs. Subsequent court decisions and FEC rulings opened the door to unlimited individual, corporate, and union contributions to Super PACs, which in turn could spend that money advocating for or against federal candidates. Although much of the initial interest in Super PACs derived from their possible funding by corporations and unions, 93 percent of Super PAC receipts come from individuals.[28] While individual donors may be more or less motivated by an issue or a candidate, participants on both sides have noted that the general pattern was for individual donors to give first to the candidates, then to the party committees, and lastly to Super PACs. Spencer Zwick, who directed the Romney campaign's fundraising in 2012, stated, "If you talk to Karl Rove, Ben Ginsberg, or Steve Roche, or anyone that has great insight into a Super PAC, they will tell you that they always tell donors, 'Go max out to the campaign before you give any money to the Super PAC.'"[29] Candidate campaigns have advantages in terms of advertising rates for TV ads, and to the extent possible candidates can best manage the message of the campaign with resources they control.

Candidates routinely seek the maxed-out donor, who in 2011–12 gave $2,500 for the nomination phase of the campaign and $2,500 for the general election phase. These donors also are more likely to have the financial capacity to contribute to the national party committee for joint presidential campaign and party committee spending, and in 2012 these individuals were also prime targets for fundraising by Super PACs. In the 2011–12 election cycle, the Romney campaign had 26,172 maxed-out donors in the primary and general elections combined, and Obama had 21,880 maxed-out donors for both the primary and general elections.[30] These donors donated 7 percent of Romney's total itemized candidate receipts and 3 percent of Obama's total itemized receipts. It is important to note that these percentages include only contributions from itemized donors, that is, donors whose contributions were reported to the FEC because they gave more than $200. Obama made up for this gap in maxed-out donors by having far more donors who did not max out. Obama had 644,106 donors who gave more than $200 but not the maximum, and Romney had 351,312. Maxed-out donors to the Obama and Romney campaigns gave about the same proportion to their national party committees in 2011–12. Twenty-three percent of Romney's maxed-out donors gave to the RNC, and 22 percent of Obama's gave to the DNC.[31]

The Romney campaign placed a priority on large donors, and especially maxed-out donors, because as Matt Waldrip, the deputy national finance director for the Romney campaign, put it, "That's the biggest bang for your buck."[32] Although these donors could assist the campaign by contributing to the joint RNC-Romney account beyond the $5,000 candidate contribution limit, they could not donate more money directly to the Romney campaign. This meant that to raise additional contributions for his campaign in the critical May to August 2012 period, Romney could not go back to these donors for more money and instead needed to find new donors who had not maxed out. An advantage to donors of giving to candidates and joint fundraising committees is that the candidate's campaign can direct how these funds are spent, something that could be done with a Super PAC.

Small donors were also an important part of the story of financing the 2012 election. Small donors are conventionally defined as individuals who in the aggregate do not give more than $200 to a candidate, party committee, or PAC. The FEC does not require that the names of these donors be disclosed; only the aggregate number of dollars raised from this group must be disclosed. In total dollars Obama raised $233,215,440 from 3,646,949 small donors in 2012, compared with Romney, who raised $80,005,536 from 1,483,203 small donors.[33]

In 2008 Obama enjoyed similar success in soliciting contributions from small donors, in addition to those who gave "at or near the maximum allowed."[34] The 2008 Obama campaign reported that it raised $114 million from 3,216,039 small donors.[35] In contrast, the McCain campaign raised $32 million from 613,385 small donors through June 30, 2008, not long before the McCain campaign accepted public funding and ceased fundraising for the campaign.[36] Reasons for Obama's success among small donors include the importance the campaign placed on this group, the Obama campaign's superior use of social media, and success in obtaining contributions from younger, new, and female donors, all of whom were less likely to be represented among donors.[37]

Going into the 2012 election cycle, it was unclear whether Obama could retain the same level of small-donor support he had in 2008, and it was also unclear whether the Republicans could close the small-donor gap with the Democrats. The funds Obama raised from small donors in 2012 represented an increase of 430,910 small donors over 2008.[38] Moreover, Obama more than doubled the funds raised from small donors in 2012 over his strong showing among this group in 2008. Thus the answer to the question of whether Obama could match his 2008 success among small donors in 2012 was a resounding yes. In 2012 the Romney campaign reported it had raised more than $80 million from 1,438,203 small donors, more than doubling both the McCain 2008 campaign's number of small donors and the money raised from small donors. But Obama retained a very large lead over Romney in numbers of small donors (a 2,208,746 gap) and in the money raised from small donors (a $154 million gap). The Obama success in both numbers of small donors and funds raised from them was an important part of his 2012 fundraising. Reasons for the continued gap were again the greater emphasis placed on small donors by the Obama campaign and a more expansive use of technology.

Presidential candidates may also raise money from PACs (contribution limits of $5,000 in the primary and $5,000 in the general election). Contributions from PACs account for a small percentage of presidential candidates' overall receipts—in 2012, just 0.13 percent of total receipts.[39] As noted, party committees and presidential candidates can form joint fundraising committees; individuals in 2012 could give up to $75,800, and there was no aggregate limit on how much these joint committees could spend. Candidates may also contribute unlimited amounts to their own campaigns. In 2008, for example, Romney loaned $42.3 million to his campaign.[40] He later declared this a contribution rather than a loan.[41] At various points in the 2011–12 campaign there was speculation about Romney giving or loaning money to his campaign again.[42] Even though his campaign was reported to have a serious cash shortfall in the summer,[43] Romney did not contribute from his own funds to his campaign beyond the maxed-out contribution he and his wife gave the campaign and the joint Romney Victory Fund-RNC.[44] Bill Burton, who headed the pro-Obama Super PAC Priorities USA Action, cites Romney's decision not to infuse cash into his campaign in this period, when Priorities USA was attacking Romney on television, as "probably a mistake that led to the loss."[45] Others contend that if Romney had given millions to his own campaign it would have reinforced the narrative of his being rich and disconnected and trying to buy the election.[46]

Congressional candidates rely less on individual donations than do presidential candidates. In 2011–12, candidates for the Senate raised 63 percent of their receipts from individuals, with incumbents raising 74 percent, open-seat candidates raising 51 percent, and challengers raising 64 percent from individuals. Among House candidates in 2012, incumbents raised 52 percent from individuals, open-seat candidates 61 percent, and challengers 62 percent.[47] Incumbents rely less on individuals in proportional terms because they are much more likely to secure PAC contributions.

National party committees continue to rely heavily on individual contributions. The RNC has consistently raised the most from individual donors, hitting their peak in funds raised from individuals in 2008, with $403 million contributed. Both the RNC and the DNC raised substantially less from individuals in 2012 than they had in 2008. The likely reason is that both parties' presidential standard bearers declined public funding and therefore continued to raise money from individuals throughout the general election period. In 2004 both nominees accepted public funds and urged donors to give to the national party committees during the general election, as did Republican nominee John McCain in 2008. The party congressional campaign committees have seen a reversal in which party does best in securing individual contributions over the past four presidential election cycles. The National Republican Senatorial Committee (NRSC) and National Republican Congressional Committee (NRCC) raised substantially more money from individuals than the Democratic Senatorial Campaign Committee (DSCC) and Democratic Congressional Campaign Committee (DCCC) in 2000, and that was true for the NRCC again in 2004. In 2004 the DSCC pulled even with the NRSC in receipts from individuals and raised substantially more than the NRSC in 2008 and 2012. The same pattern held for the DCCC. The importance of individual donors to the Obama campaign and the DCCC and DSCC is examined in more detail in chapter 6.

With regard to the 2012 election cycle, the most controversial aspect of fundraising centered on Super PACs and section 501(c) organizations. Section 501(c) groups have existed for many years and include trade associations, section 501(c)(6), and labor unions, section 501(c)(5). But the *Citizens United* and *SpeechNow* court decisions and the heightened role of noncandidate spending sparked a surge in new groups seeking section 501(c)(4) status (social welfare organizations). This increase in applications became well known as a result of IRS delays in reviewing these applications and the perception that there was a bias against conservative applicants.[48] Groups granted section 501(c) status are required to report total contributions and expenditures but not individual donors or amounts given by any individual. Thus in 2010, American Crossroads reported to the FEC that it spent $25.8 million,[49] and Crossroads GPS, the associated 501(c)(4), reported that it spent $15.4 million on independent expenditures, plus an additional $1.3 million on electioneering communications reported to the IRS.[50]

Among the first Super PACs to organize was a group of prominent GOP political types headed by Karl Rove, Ed Gillespie, and Steven Law, who had long-standing connections to George W. Bush, the RNC, and Senator McConnell, respectively. They formed American Crossroads (a Super PAC) and Crossroads GPS, a section 501(c)(4) group, which expended $63 million in the 2010 cycle.[51] *New York Times* reporter Jim Rutenberg has written that Rove

> has had a major hand in helping to summon the old coalition of millionaires and billionaires who supported Mr. Bush and have huge financial stakes in regulatory and tax policy. . . . Their personal and corporate money—as well as that of other donors who have not been identified—has gone to a collection of outside groups Mr. Rove helped form with Mr. Gillespie, including American Crossroads and Crossroads GPS.[52]

Groups such as Crossroads were formed with the support of both parties and often as arms of existing interest groups long active in electoral
politics.

Section 501(c) groups were not new in 2012. They are named after section 501(c) of the Internal Revenue Code.[53] Charitable organizations that
may accept tax deductible contributions are 501(c)(3) groups and they
may not engage in partisan politics. But section 501(c)(4) groups, labeled
by the IRS as "social welfare organizations," may become involved in
elections so long as this is not their primary purpose. Trade associations
such as the U.S. Chamber of Commerce and labor unions are organized
under other parts of section 501(c).

Unlike Super PACs, section 501(c) groups are not required to disclose
their donors, and their expenditure reports are less frequent and may
come months after the election. They are often combined with Super
PACs as both types of groups seek to influence the outcomes of federal
elections by spending large sums of money in competitive races. These
groups have eclipsed other outside groups also named for a section of the
IRS code, section 527 organizations, which can spend unlimited amounts
but unlike Super PACs cannot expressly advocate for the election or
defeat of a candidate.

As noted, wealthy individuals had long been able to spend unlimited
amounts on independent expenditures, and between 1976 and 2004 that
level of activity had not generated much controversy. Tapping wealthy
individuals to help fund section 527 organizations in the 2004 election
was a precursor to right-leaning Super PACs' soliciting donations of millions of dollars from wealthy individuals in 2012. Some groups active in
2004, such as America Coming Together, Progress for America Voter
Fund, Swift Boat Veterans for Truth, the League of Conservation Voters,
POWs for Truth, and MoveOn.org, were fined by the FEC following the
2004 election for reporting and other violations.[54] At the time the fine
was seen by some observers as "the cost of doing business."[55] But others
view the fine as helping to dampen outside group fundraising in the 2008
cycle. After the 2008 election, Bob Bauer, the Obama campaign's general
counsel in 2008 and 2012, said, "There is no question. What the FEC did
in 2004 . . . did have an effect on donors to such groups in 2008."[56] The
Citizens United and *SpeechNow.org* rulings constituted a more fundamental change in the rules of the game for corporations and unions and
may have been seen as a sign that such activity by individuals and groups
was legitimate. The net effect of the court and FEC actions was to make

clear to donors that giving unlimited amounts to Super PACs and section 501(c) groups was legal. Harold Ickes, who helped raise money for Priorities USA, noted that because of these rulings it is "legitimate now" to give in large amounts.[57]

Just days after *Citizens United* v. *Federal Election Commission* was decided, President Obama called attention to the ruling in his 2010 State of the Union Address when he said,

> With all due deference to separation of powers, last week the Supreme Court reversed a century of law that I believe will open the floodgates for special interests—including foreign corporations—to spend without limit in our elections. I don't think American elections should be bankrolled by America's most powerful interests, or worse, by foreign entities. They should be decided by the American people. And I'd urge Democrats and Republicans to pass a bill that helps to correct some of these problems.[58]

Cameras caught U.S. Supreme Court associate justice Samuel Alito mouthing the words "not true," which only amplified the media attention to the exchange.[59] Would corporations use their new freedom to spend from their coffers on election campaign communications in 2012? How would unions respond? Would candidates and parties be overwhelmed by outside group spending?

Another school of thought on the enlarged role of outside groups in federal elections points not to the *Citizens United* and *SpeechNow* court decisions but rather to Congress's passage of BCRA, which banned parties from raising unlimited contributions and making unlimited party soft-money expenditures. For example, at the 2012 Harvard University postelection conference of campaign consultants, Charles R. Spies, general counsel and treasurer to the pro-Romney Super PAC Restore Our Future, stated that an enlarged role for large donors "is not about *Citizens United*. This is about . . . McCain-Feingold that . . . pushes money away from political parties, and pushes money away from candidates, and forces the money into the outside groups who have an advantage of being able to take more money. So this is not a *Citizens United* phenomenon."[60] What Spies's analysis omits is that BCRA's definition of electioneering limited the ways outside money could be used in federal elections; had that law remained in force, Super PACS and unlimited contributions to them would not be allowed.

As Jay Goodliffe and I explore in chapter 7, the impact *Citizens United v. Federal Election Commission* and *SpeechNow.org* v. *Federal Election Commission* had on the 2012 elections was substantial but more nuanced than the presumed surge in corporate money widely speculated about soon after the decision was handed down. As it turned out, publicly traded corporations were not substantial players in funding Super PACs. In the 2012 election cycle, most money raised by Super PACs (at least 93 percent of the $846.9 million) came from individuals.[61] And much of the money Super PACs raised came from a small group of individuals who made large contributions.

Spending in the 2012 Election

A recurrent theme in this book is the sharp rise in spending in 2012, with both sides—including the candidates, party committees, and outside groups—spending in excess of $1 billion on their presidential election efforts. Spending in the presidential contest has risen partially because candidates have now essentially abandoned the public financing system. The system had bipartisan participation from 1976 through 2004 for presidential general elections and until 2000 for most serious candidates seeking their party's nomination. But in 2008, Obama was the first nominee to bypass public funds in the general election,[62] and in 2012 both Romney and Obama bypassed the public grant in the general election, while only relatively unknown candidates such as former Louisiana governor Buddy Roemer and former New Mexico governor Gary Johnson chose to take public funds in the primaries.[63]

The result was that 2012 was the first campaign in more than three decades in which both nominees continued to devote substantial attention to fundraising through the general election period. A baseline of the number of fundraisers attended by major-party nominees before 2012 does not exist. But in 2012 the Associated Press tallied 182 fundraisers attended by Barack Obama or Mitt Romney between May 29th and election day. Romney was more active than Obama, attending 113 in this period compared with Obama's 69, and Romney was especially active in August, when he attended 30 fundraisers.[64] In chapter 3 John Green, Michael Kohler, and Ian Schwarber estimate that Obama attended 203 fundraisers in the nomination phase and Romney attended 163.[65]

Consistent with our system of separation of powers, candidates for Congress raise and spend money for their own campaigns, while candidates for president are simultaneously raising and spending money for their contests. Political parties at the federal (national) and state levels are also involved, as are interest groups and individuals making independent expenditures. Table 1-2 provides spending on federal elections for all of these participants for the 2000, 2004, 2008, and 2012 elections.

As we explore in this book, the 2011–12 election cycle saw a heightened role for interest groups operating as Super PACs and section 501(c) organizations and an expanded role for individuals, unions, and privately held corporations in making large contributions to these groups and in electioneering more broadly. Candidates for president are the most important players on each side, and, as we demonstrate, approached the funding of their campaigns in 2012 with different game plans. Party committees and Super PACS were able to receive even more substantial contributions because Super PAC contributions are unlimited. Accordingly, another recurrent theme of this book is the oversized role played by large donors in the 2012 election.

Super PACS are different from standard PACs because individuals giving to a Super PAC are not subject to the $5,000 a year contribution limit, as they are for a traditional PAC. As noted, corporations and unions also have no limits on how much of their general treasury funds they can give Super PACs. Both PACs and Super PACs are required to disclose donors and the amounts each donor contributed. Because some donors would rather not have their identity disclosed, several Super PACs have created an additional group, organized under section 501(c)(4) of the Internal Revenue Code as "social welfare organizations."

Team Sport

Politics in the United States involves two teams; each team includes the candidates and their campaign committees, the political party committees, and individuals and groups who mount their own independent campaigns. For Obama, the team consisted of the candidate's campaign, the DNC, the Super PAC Priorities USA Action, and interest group allies. For Romney the team included the candidate's campaign, the RNC, the Super PACs Restore Our Future and American Crossroads, and interest group allies. There are different rules for how these players raise and spend money, and these differences had consequences for the 2012 election. The idea that the financing and conducting of federal elections involves a team of the candidates plus those who spend in support of them or against

Table 1-2. *Total Expenditures in Federal Elections, 2000–12*
Millions of dollars

	2000	2004	2008	2012
Presidential candidates[a]	674	988	1,829	1,396
Congressional candidates[b]	978	1,099	1,297	1,766
National parties (federal)[c]	544	1,214	1,219	1,274
National parties (nonfederal)[d]	498	n.a.	n.a.	n.a.
State and local parties (federal)[e]	171	201	318	893
State parties (nonfederal)[f]	330	67	94	0
PACs[g]	320	532	767	1,120
Super PACs[h]	n.a.	n.a.	n.a.	809
Section 527 organizations[i]	101	442	258	155
Section 501(c) groups[j]	10	60	196	640
Issue advocacy[k]	248	n.a.	n.a.	n.a.
Individuals[l]	4	2	2	1
Total	3,876	4,605	5,981	8,056

Source: Data from Federal Election Commission, except as otherwise indicated.

a. Includes all presidential-election-related spending in prenomination, convention (including spending by host committees and the convention grant), and general election periods. Candidate transfers to party committees are deducted from the total to avoid double counting.

b. Includes all spending by congressional candidates. Candidate transfers to party committees are deducted from the total to avoid double counting.

c. Includes all spending by national party committees, including independent expenditures and coordinated expenditures on behalf of candidates. Contributions to candidates are deducted from the total to avoid double counting.

d. Transfers among party committees are deducted from total. Soft money made illegal by BCRA.

e. Includes all spending by state and local party committees, including money contributed to candidates, independent expenditures, and coordinated expenditures on behalf of candidates. The national party transfers were deducted from the Democratic and Republican state and local party disbursements.

f. Includes nonfederal (soft) share of state party expenses that must be paid with a mix of federal (hard) and some soft money during election cycle (Levin Funds).

g. Total includes independent expenditures and internal communication costs made by PACs. PAC contributions to federal candidates and super PAC independent expenditures (in 2012) are deducted from the total to avoid double counting.

h. Includes all spending of independent expenditure–only committees but does not include independent expenditures made by individuals or single candidates. Made possible by 2010 court decision.

i. In 2000 major transfers were removed. Estimate is much lower than the actual amount because 527 spending was only disclosed as of July 2000, due to the adoption of the new disclosure law. Data for 2004, 2008, and 2012 compiled from Center for Responsive Politics, "527s: Advocacy Group Spending" (www.opensecrets.org/527s/). Total includes spending by groups that were either thoroughly committed to federal elections or were heavily involved in federal elections but also doing substantial state and local work. Total includes electioneering communications made by 527 organizations.

j. 2000 total includes independent expenditures made by 501(c) groups. 2004 data from Campaign Finance Institute, "New CFI Analysis Shows Interest Groups Deploy 501(c) 'Advocacy' Organizations Alongside Their PACs and 527s to Increase Their Influence in Federal Elections: Study of 12 Leading Interest Groups Has Implications for Proposed 527 Political Organization Reforms" (www.cfinst.org/pr/prRelease.aspx?ReleaseID=71). Total includes groups spending at least $200,000 and consists of independent expenditures, electioneering communications, and other expenditures (including internal communication costs) made by 501(c) groups. 2008 data from Campaign Finance Institute, "Soft-Money Political Spending by 501(c) Nonprofits Tripled in 2008 Election." See www.cfinst.org/pr/prRelease.aspx?ReleaseID=221. Total includes groups spending at least $200,000 and consists of independent expenditures, electioneering communications, and other expenditures (including internal communication costs) made by 501(c) groups. 2012 data from Center for Responsive Politics, "Outside Spending" (www.opensecrets.org/outsidespending/). Total includes independent expenditures, electioneering communications, and other expenditures (including internal communication costs) made by 501(c) groups. We also have included estimates of spending by 501(c) groups given to us in interviews; see chapter 7.

k. Redefined by BCRA. Data from Campaign Media Analysis Group, compilation published in Kelly Patterson, "Spending in the 2004 Election," in *Financing the 2004 Election*, edited by David B. Magleby (Brookings, 2006), p. 71. This money was spent on broadcast ads in the top seventy-five media markets between March 8 and November 7, 2000. This figure may include some money reported by parties, PACs, 527s, or 501(c) groups elsewhere in the table.

l. Total includes independent expenditures made for or against candidates by individual donors.

their opponent is not new,[66] but the growth in Super PACs and section 501(c) groups has made it more important.

Considering the money that candidates spend in federal elections shows only part of the true picture. In some contests, spending by parties and interest groups can exceed the amounts spent by the candidates' campaigns. If campaign ads are a barometer of overall spending, then there is compelling evidence of the prominent role outside groups played in the 2012 presidential nomination. Michael Franz of the Wesleyan Media Project has found that "60 percent of all ads" in the 2012 GOP presidential nomination contest came from outside groups.[67] For example, Super PACs that supported Rick Santorum or Newt Gingrich "aired nearly double the number of ads of each of the candidates" they were supporting.[68]

In the 2012 Virginia U.S. Senate race, outside or independent spending by party committees and groups exceeded the two major-party general election candidates' spending by more than $15.5 million, and in the Indiana U.S. Senate race, independent and outside spending exceeded candidate spending by more than $14 million. Outside and party-independent expenditure money spent on behalf of former governor Tommy Thompson in the Wisconsin race exceeded what his campaign spent by more than $12 million. Outside-group and party independent expenditures exceeded candidate spending in several House contests as well.[69]

The different members of the team have presumed roles or specializations in the campaign, with some doing primarily negative television advertising (Super PACs), and others expected to make the positive case (candidates). Glen Bolger, a pollster in 2012 for Restore Our Future and American Crossroads, provides the conventional wisdom of campaign professionals when he says, "Making a positive spot around a candidate is much more difficult when you're on the outside of the campaign and it's much easier to do negative or definitional/contrast spots when you are on the outside."[70] The 2012 contest most cited for its lack of outside money was the Massachusetts U.S. Senate contest between Democrat Elizabeth Warren and Republican incumbent Scott Brown. In that race, both candidates agreed to give to charity half of the cost of any TV, radio, or online ad run by any third-party group supporting them or attacking their opponent. Scott Brown fulfilled the pledge when the American Petroleum Institute ran an ad in March 2012. But this was an exception, as most groups stayed out of the race.[71] One consequence of that as seen by Guy Cecil, the executive director of the DSCC, was that Scott Brown was forced to "carry all the negative,"[72] meaning outside groups were not doing the attacking, as often happens. As noted, in competitive 2012 Senate races the norm was substantial outside spending.

Other teammates are expected to pursue the ground game. In 2012 it was assumed that the Obama campaign would take care of the ground game for the Democrats in battleground states, and the Republican National Committee would do the same for Republicans. The ground game includes voter registration and mobilization. With early voting now possible in many states and with more and more people casting absentee ballots, the ground game requires not only knowing who the likely supporters of a candidate are but also tracking them to be sure they have returned their absentee ballots or voted early and monitoring turnout on election day. As Mike Lux of Progressive Strategies states, the 2008 and 2012 Obama campaigns "were absolutely unflinchingly devoted to voter mobilization in a way I've never seen a presidential campaign before or any other campaign for that matter."[73] In its commitment to voter mobilization, the Obama campaign took the lead in this critical component of the campaign in presidential battleground states, while the Republican National Committee mounted voter mobilization efforts within the GOP.[74] Congressional campaign committees or state parties managed voter mobilization in competitive congressional contests outside of presidential battleground states.[75] Interest groups also selectively invested in voter mobilization. For example, Montana, a presidential nonbattleground state, meant the Obama campaign did not do mobilization. The LCV filled the void by mounting a voter mobilization effort in support of John Tester, the state's incumbent Democratic U.S. Senate candidate.[76]

American elections are candidate centered,[77] and candidates are the focus of communications by party committees and outside groups such as Super PACs. Understandably, donors are more inclined to give to favored candidates than to parties or interest groups.[78] However, for those individuals who have the means to give more than the aggregate maximum allowed to candidates in 2011–12, contributing to party committees, PACs, and Super PACs was another way to influence the outcome of the election. Party committees are allowed to coordinate and communicate with candidates in ways that Super PACs are not, so contributions to candidates probably have a greater impact than contributions to Super PACs.

Although Super PACs do not enjoy the candidates' advantage of being able to purchase radio and television advertising at preferred rates, they can still play an important role in delivering messages, especially negative ones. In 2012 most Super PAC activity was focused on television ads.[79] In the presidential election it was common for candidates to have a Super PAC that supported them and attacked their opponents. In chapter 3, John Green and colleagues note that these candidate-connected Super PACs often ran more advertising than the candidate they were supporting. More than three-fifths of the Romney, Gingrich, and Santorum ads in the nomination phase of the campaign were run by their Super PACs; for Jon Huntsman the figure was 92 percent.[80] Moreover, the Super PACs were important in prolonging the GOP presidential contest.[81] As discussed in chapters 4 and 7, Super PACs were also important in the presidential general election, where they defined the candidates, often through negative advertising. This was especially the case with the Priorities USA ads on Mitt Romney's work for Bain and with Spanish language ads on immigration.[82] Although candidate-specific Super PACs were less visible in 2012 congressional contests, they are likely to become a staple of contested Senate contests and some House races in the future.

How the Two Teams Divided Up Spending in 2012

The team sport analogy applies to American politics both in how money is raised and in how it is spent. Taking the presidential campaigns and supporters of Barack Obama and Mitt Romney, for example, we summarize the expenditures for Team Obama and Team Romney in table 1-3.

When looked at as team efforts, overall expenditures on both the Obama and Romney teams surpassed the $1 billion mark. The difference lies in who on the team was doing the spending. Obama spent $255 million more than Romney out of money the campaign raised. Team Romney relied more on Super PACs and party committee or interest group independent expenditures, with his team besting Obama's team here by nearly $245 million. (For example, team Romney received $14 million more in independent expenditures from PACs, and $115 million more from Super PACs.) Obama's team outspent Romney's by more than $8 million in interest group internal communications, which are influential, often personal, contacts from groups a candidate might affiliate with such as unions, employers, and voluntary associations. The important point illustrated in table 1-3 is that Team Romney's spending was much more reliant on noncandidate expenditures than Team Obama's. As we demonstrate in this book, not all expenditures are of equal value or yield

Table 1-3. *Total Expenditures by the Two Presidential Election Teams in 2012*

	Team Obama	Team Romney
Candidate expenditures[a]	$755,753,668	$501,321,779
Contributions from other federal candidates[b]	$6,250	$101,722
Joint fundraising committee expenditures[c]	$116,589,192	$148,248,025
National party committee expenditures[d]	$143,631,224	$134,422,297
Super PAC independent expenditures	$136,303,062	$251,178,045
PAC independent expenditures	$10,462,338	$24,926,812
PAC internal communications	$9,614,987	$1,356,433
Section 527 organization expenditures[e]	$1,461,145	$2,327,544
Section 501(c) group expenditures[f]	$12,947,843	$127,316,180
Other independent expenditures[g]	$953,582	$2,106,839
Total	$1,187,723,291	$1,193,305,675

Source: Data compiled from Federal Election Commission and Center for Responsive Politics.

a. Candidate expenditures include candidate committee and convention grant expenditures. Candidate transfers to party committees are deducted from the total to avoid double counting.

b. Contributions from other federal candidates include in-kind contributions.

c. Transfers to affiliated committees and offsets to operating expenditures are deducted from the joint fundraising committee disbursement totals to avoid double counting.

d. National party committee expenditures include all expenditures of the DNC and RNC, including coordinated expenditures, independent expenditures, and other expenditures directly linked to the presidential campaigns. Operating expenditures were deducted from each organization's totals. Contributions to candidates are deducted from the total to avoid double counting.

e. Section 527 organization expenditures include electioneering communications and independent expenditures made by 527 organizations.

f. Section 501(c) group expenditures include independent expenditures, electioneering communications, and other expenditures (including internal communication costs) made by 501(c) groups.

g. Other independent expenditures include those from individuals or groups not otherwise registered as political committees who undertake independent expenditures as well as single candidate independent expenditure committees.

the same return. Generally speaking, candidate expenditures have the greatest value.

Congressional elections in 2012 were also a team sport. Table 1-4 shows the expenditures of candidates, party committees, and interest groups, including Super PACs.

In the presidential election, there was relative parity between the two sides with regard to spending; in the 2011–12 congressional elections the two teams were also at overall parity. Both teams spent in excess of $1.1 billion, with the Republicans' combined efforts coming in at about $81 million more than the combined Democratic spending. Note that we are combining House and Senate in table 1-4, and as we discuss in chapter 5, there were important differences in the patterns of fundraising in Senate and House races. But at this more macro level, Republican candidates raised about $97 million more than Democratic candidates. Repub-

Table 1-4. *Expenditures by the Democratic and Republican Congressional Election Teams in 2012*

	Democratic	Republican
Candidate expenditures[a]	$679,876,980	$776,582,914
Contributions from other federal candidates[b]	$5,883,690	$7,032,434
National party committee expenditures[c]	$192,512,403	$159,797,634
Super PAC independent expenditures	$121,294,632	$97,414,294
PAC independent expenditures	$33,197,175	$23,080,443
PAC internal communications expenditures	$7,722,657	$1,784,502
Section 527organization expenditures[d]	$40,306,920	$19,626,077
Section 501(c) group expenditures[e]	$33,191,291	$108,732,184
Other independent expenditures[f]	$102,311	$1,486,136
Total	$1,114,088,059	$1,195,536,618

Source: Data compiled from Federal Election Commission and Center for Responsive Politics.

a. Candidate transfers to party committees are deducted from the total to avoid double counting.

b. Contributions from other federal candidates include in-kind contributions.

c. National party committee expenditures include all expenditures of the DSCC, DCCC, NRSC, and NRCC including coordinated expenditures, and independent expenditures. Operating expenditures were deducted from each organization's totals. Contributions to candidates are deducted from the total to avoid double counting.

d. Section 527 organization expenditures include electioneering communications and independent expenditures made by 527 organizations.

e. Section 501(c) group expenditures include independent expenditures, electioneering communications, and other expenditures (including internal communication costs) made by 501(c) groups.

f. Other independent expenditures include those from individuals or groups not otherwise registered as political committees who undertake independent expenditures as well as single candidate independent expenditure committees.

licans also outperformed Democrats in total PAC receipts (by $39 million) and in spending by section 501(c) groups (by $76 million). Democrats bested Republicans in spending by national party committees (by $33 million), Super PACs (by $24 million), and other PAC-independent expenditures (by $10 million). Despite these differences in how the two teams raised money, the more striking finding here is the relative parity between the teams.

How the Money Was Spent

How campaigns spend the money they raise has changed over time. The advent of television is widely seen as one watershed in campaigns, and over time, television advertising has come to be seen as a major component of campaign budgets.[83] More recently the "ground game" of targeted voter communication, person-to-person persuasion, and mobilization has enjoyed resurgence in campaigns.[84] As with fundraising, the spending of money involves teammates and specialization. In some cases it is assumed that one participant will largely spend on television (Super

PACs), while another participant will focus on voter registration and mobilization (national party committees). The Obama campaigns of 2008 and 2012 were unusual in the extent to which they were heavily involved in both the ground and air games. Allied groups and the party committee played important reinforcing roles, but Obama's spending was more substantial on the ground than that of prior Democratic or Republican standard bearers.[85]

The Obama 2012 campaign was reported to have spent far more on large data analytics, on the Internet, and on social media than Romney did or than any campaign that preceded it. The widely shared consensus after the election was that Democrats had a substantial advantage in these areas in part because they had invested more in these tools in 2008 and 2012. According to the journalist Sasha Issenberg, Obama's data analytics department was ten times larger than Romney's, and Obama outspent Romney in online ads through mid-October by a factor of two, $52 million to $26 million.[86] Republicans, who had taken the lead in microtargeting and voter mobilization in 2004,[87] found themselves behind the Democrats in 2012 in the ground game of voter identification, persuasion, and mobilization. One indicator of the ground game is the number of field offices. Looking at the four battleground states from 2008 of Colorado, North Carolina, New Hampshire, and Ohio, Obama had more field offices in 2012 than in 2008, while Romney had more than McCain in Colorado and North Carolina but fewer than McCain in Ohio and New Hampshire (table 1-5). The widest gap in 2012 was in Ohio, where the Obama campaign staffed 131 field offices to Romney's 40. As RNC political director Rick Wiley stated, "[The old 72-Hour Task Force] works in a state like Pennsylvania where 96 percent of the population votes on election day, or Wisconsin where 70 percent vote on election day. [In] most of them now, that 72 hours is 72 days at this point. It really is."[88]

In 2012 television remained the principal way campaign money was spent.[89] Team Romney outspent Team Obama on television ads in the general election by $100 million ($469 million to $369 million).[90] Surprisingly, despite this spending gap, Team Obama ran more ads (632,391) than team Romney (590,795).[91] The reasons Romney spent more money for ads and had less to show for it included timing of his ad buys, his greater reliance on his Super PAC for advertising, and the programs on which he placed his ads. Both the Obama campaign and Priorities USA, Obama's Super PAC, purchased advertising time well in advance, whereas the Romney media team purchased ads one week at a time.[92] This most

Table 1-5. *Field Offices in Battleground States, 2008 and 2012 Presidential Campaigns*

	2008		2012	
State	McCain	Obama	Romney	Obama
Colorado	12	50	13	62
North Carolina	20	47	24	54
New Hampshire	14	19	9	22
Ohio	45	89	40	131

Sources: David B. Magleby, "Elections as Team Sports: Spending by Candidates, Political Parties, and Interest Groups in the 2008 Election Cycle," in *The Change Election: Money, Mobilization, and Persuasion in the 2008 Federal Elections*, edited by David B. Magleby (Temple University Press, 2011), p. 63; Andrea Levien, "Tracking Presidential Campaign Field Operations," *FairVote*, November 14, 2012 (www.fairvote.org/tracking-presidential-campaign-field-operations#.UgF JKNVnA6f).

likely drove up Romney's costs. Michael Franz, codirector of the Wesleyan Media Project, notes that "the price differential between week-to-week and long-term purchases can be significant."[93] Commenting on the Romney campaign's week-to-week ad-buying approach, the TV advertising expert Ken Goldstein describes the Romney campaign's media team as committing "malpractice": "The Romney campaign managed to pay more and get less systematically, market by market."[94]

Super PACs, unlike candidates, pay prevailing rates for ads and are not assured of lowest unit point rates. With about half of team Romney's TV ads paid for by Super PACs (50.3 percent), compared with 12 percent for team Obama,[95] Romney's team was at a substantial disadvantage in the rates it had to pay. Finally, the Obama campaign's data analytics unit matched data on the viewing habits of millions of viewers to its large database of voters who were deemed to be "persuadable." This led to an advertising strategy that used "60 channels during one week near the end of the campaign, compared with 18 for the Romney operation during the same period." Not only was the approach more targeted, but according to the Obama campaign, it was "able to get about 10 percent to 20 percent more efficient use of their money."[96]

Much of the spending by outside groups in the presidential race was negative in tone. Both the Obama campaign and Priorities USA attacked Romney on his ability to improve the nation's economy, and they did so soon after Romney was the presumptive nominee. The Obama campaign also made a strategic gamble by spending early rather than holding more money for the final weeks of the contest. As David Axelrod states,

One of the key decisions that we made . . . was to frontload our spending on television from May through August on the theory that that's when it would have the greatest impact. I don't think there is, in the modern age, an example of a television ad after Labor Day that was decisive in a presidential race. When you think of all the ads that we typically think of as having been impactful, most of them, or virtually all of them that I can think of, ran before the convention. And so we gambled on frontloading.[97]

Evidence that most of the money spent on television advertising was spent on negative or "contrast" ads, and much less was spent on positive ads, comes from the Wesleyan Media Project, which codes political ads; the project provides data that allows a comparison of the tone of ads in 2012 with prior cycles. In table 1-6 we compare the tone of ads from House and Senate candidates, party committees, coordinated expenditures, and group-funded ads in 2004, 2008, and 2012, with Super PACs included for 2012.

The overall tone of ads in congressional campaigns shifted over the period, from about one-third being attack ads in 2004 to half being attack ads in 2012. Ads classified as promoting a candidate have become less common since 2004, declining from 42 percent in 2004 to 25 percent in 2012. Outside groups have long been known to do more negative advertising than candidates. As more and more campaigning is done by outside groups, the trend of increased attack ads is likely to continue. Outside groups assume the positive messaging will be done by the candidate campaign but see negative or contrast advertising as open to them. There is also a widely shared view that attack ads can be effective.[98]

Interest groups have multiple ways they can spend money to influence elections beyond making contributions to candidates and party committees. Long before the creation of Super PACs, they could make independent expenditures with funds raised from limited and disclosed contributions. This mode of independent expenditures continues, and in 2012 the groups that made the largest independent expenditures included the Service Employees International Union (SEIU), the National Rifle Association (NRA), and the Affiliated Federal, State, County, and Municipal Employees (AFSCME). (See chapter 7.)

Another way interest groups spend money existed from 1996 through the 2002 election, when they could run so-called issue ad campaigns. These ads were often timed and targeted to help elect or defeat a federal

Table 1-6. *The Tone of Television Advertising in U.S. House and Senate Races, 2004, 2008, and 2012*[a]

Percent

	Contrast	*Promote*	*Attack*
2004			
Candidate	28.8	52.6	17.9
Party	14.5	11.6	73.4
Interest group	5.6	23.5	70.8
Coordinated	55.4	27.1	17.6
Overall	25.9	41.5	32.0
2008			
Candidate	26.4	47.8	25.5
Party	13.4	1.0	85.6
Interest group	1.5	28.1	70.1
Coordinated	43.4	21.8	34.8
Overall	21.1	33.5	45.2
2012			
Candidate	29.6	41.4	27.3
Party	8.2	0.4	89.4
Interest group	9.4	5.6	82.7
Coordinated	46.6	20.9	31.1
Overall	22.2	25.4	50.5

Source: Erika Franklin Fowler, Travis N. Ridout and Michael M. Franz. "Interest Group Advertising and Perceptions of Campaign Negativity," Working Paper, Wesleyan Media Project, electronic communication, August 12, 2013.

a. Percentages may not add to 100 owing to inclusions in totals of unclassified ads.

candidate, but such spending was not disclosed and contribution limits did not apply because the ads were interpreted to be about issues and not electioneering communications. By the 2004 cycle, BCRA definitions had taken effect, the intent of which was to more clearly differentiate ads about elections from ads about issues and to treat electioneering communications like other election expenditures. The law defined electioneering communication as ads that refer to a clearly identified federal candidate running within sixty days of a general and thirty days of a primary election and are targeted to a population of 50,000 or more people in a candidate's district or state. The definitions of electioneering communications were initially upheld by the Supreme Court, and a subsequent decision substituted a definition that effectively expanded issue advocacy again.[99]

As discussed in chapter 2, the regulatory environment has since changed owing to court decisions and FEC rules, such that in 2012 the focus shifted from conventional independent expenditures and section

527 groups to Super PACs. Although much of the attention directed to Super PACs and outside group activity in 2012 was centered on the presidential contest, several groups were important players in competitive congressional contests in 2012. The U.S. Chamber of Commerce, for example, started early; Rob Engstrom, senior vice president of the U.S. Chamber, states, "We began our first ad burst one year out from the election in three senate races and [in] . . . three congressional races that we thought would be reflective geographically [and] on issues of substance. We said at the time and we followed through that we would run the largest voter education initiative in our 100-year history."[100]

Interest groups, including Super PACs, used the 2010 midterms as a testing ground for 2012. For example, the American Crossroads Super PAC spent $21.6 million in 2010, and Crossroads GPS, the 501(c)(4) arm of Crossroads, spent at least another $15.4 million on congressional races in 2010.[101] Crossroads' strategy was to concentrate resources in particular contests. Speaking of Crossroads, Karl Rove stated, "We were running essentially eight and nine weeks of TV for congressional candidates in certain races, which is almost unheard of."[102]

Democrats had fewer and less well funded Super PACs in 2010. Having seen the role Super PACs and 501(c)s played in 2010, Democrats formed their own leadership-connected Super PACs and 501(c)s in 2011 for the 2012 cycle: the Majority PAC for the Senate (formed in 2010) and the House Majority PAC for the House (formed in 2011).[103] Other Republican groups that spent in congressional races in 2012 and linked to party leadership included the Congressional Leadership Fund, a Super PAC linked to Speaker John Boehner, and the closely affiliated Young Guns Action Fund (Super PAC) and Young Guns Action Network (501(c)(4)), tied to House Majority Leader Eric Cantor.[104] American Action Network was chaired by former Minnesota senator Norm Coleman.

Unions were also freed from long-standing constraints on expenditures by the recent court and FEC rulings. Before the 2010 and 2012 election cycles, unions were not allowed to communicate using general treasury funds with nonunion members. As Mike Podhorzer, the political director of the AFL-CIO, explained,

> Before the *Citizens United* and *SpeechNow* decisions unions were prohibited by the 1947 Taft-Hartley Act from talking to the general public about politics, which has really handcuffed us over the years. An incidental consequence of *Citizens United* was that we could

now talk to anybody we wanted to and so we formed Workers' Voice to do that very aggressively and to recruit workers who really supported our viewpoint but weren't in unions. . . . This expanded the universe of people we were interacting with in Ohio, Nevada, and Wisconsin [by] about a million people.[105]

Spending by outside groups in congressional primaries became more contentious in 2010 and 2012. Groups such as Club for Growth and Freedom Works have long fostered intraparty competition by spending for one candidate and against others largely within GOP nomination contests. In 2010 these groups were successful in defeating Utah Republican senator Robert Bennett at the state convention.[106] Another Republican, Lisa Murkowski of Alaska, was targeted for defeat by the Tea Party Express.[107] Murkowski lost in the GOP primary but won reelection as a write-in candidate in the general election. Outside money also helped Tea Party–supported Senate candidates, including Sharron Angle in Nevada and Christine O'Donnell in Delaware, secure the GOP nomination, both of whom were defeated in the general election.[108] In 2012 conservative groups helped defeat Indiana Republican senator Richard Lugar and helped Representative Richard Mourdock secure the nomination, and they were also supportive of Missouri representative Todd Aiken's bid for the Republican Senate nomination in 2012.[109] Both Aiken and Mourdock were defeated in the general election.

The success of outside groups in helping defeat incumbents and in playing a role in primaries will most likely reinforce the idea that incumbents in both houses will form their own Super PACs in the future. Charles R. Spies has set up fifteen Super PACs for congressional incumbents. On the utility of Super PACs for congressional candidates, Spies says,

They are far more valuable for primaries. If you've got an intraparty primary, it really changes the dynamics of a race because congressional primary spending of a few hundred thousand dollars is not unusual. If you're raising a million dollars you're doing really, really well. With that in mind, if you have a wealthy friend who wants to throw a couple of hundred thousand in, or somebody who wants to set up a group and raise a couple of hundred thousand dollars, that makes a huge, huge difference in a congressional primary. It really changes the playing field in terms of who can run and who has the ability to win.[110]

Recognizing the importance of spending by Super PACs in party nominations, groups such as American Crossroads recently announced the formation of a Conservative Victory Project PAC in response to two consecutive Senate election disappointments. They attributed Republican losses to the selection of unelectable nominees who were primarily associated with the Tea Party. This new Super PAC's purpose, therefore, is to support the most electable conservative in contested primaries and to work to prevent such disappointments in the future.[111] In response, the Tea Party–linked FreedomWorks group criticized the way American Crossroads spent its money, in 2012 especially, and threatened to form its own Super PAC to counter the Conservative Victory Project PAC.[112] It is also likely that one outcome of the proliferation of Super PACs and section 501(c) organizations in 2012 is that we will see more and more candidate-specific Super PACs spending money in future races. Included in this will be the further development of candidate-specific Super PACs for Senate candidates and some House candidates. As noted, we have already seen examples of this in 2012. Also in the wake of the 2012 election, former staff from the Obama campaign announced the creation of Organizing for Action, a section 501(c)(4) organization whose purpose was to help mobilize support for President Obama's agenda in his second term. The group made clear at its inception that its activities could include participation in future congressional elections.

An exception to this growing permissiveness by groups may be the IRS. In 2013 it was learned that the IRS, in the wake of a large influx of groups applying for tax-exempt section 501(c)(4) status, had subjected conservative and Tea Party–affiliated groups, and some progressive groups as well, to a protracted review process.[113] These "social welfare" groups had become an attractive way for donors to influence elections, even though not all of the money given to these groups could be spent on election-related activities. The advantage of the groups to donors is that there is donor anonymity, and gifts made to these groups are not subject to the gift tax. We describe these groups in detail in chapter 7.

Overview of the Book

After decades of relative stability in the regulatory environment of campaign finance, we have witnessed substantial change over the past few years. Anthony Corrado, an authority on this topic, examines in chapter 2 the most important changes to the law and administrative regulations and practices in this area leading up to the 2012 election. The *Citizens United* and *SpeechNow* cases are an important part of the more recent story of how the "rule book" on campaign finance has been rewritten, but they are only the latest chapters in what has been a series of cases and administrative rulings or nonrulings decided by the courts and the FEC that have substantially expanded what is permissible for party committees, groups, and individuals to spend in an effort to influence the outcome of a federal election.

Opponents of regulation in this policy area have mounted an aggressive litigation strategy over more than three decades,[114] which, when coupled with the structural limitations and frequent partisan deadlock on the FEC, has meant that defenders of FECA and BCRA have been quite consistently playing defense. Corrado not only reviews these developments but also gives us a sense of what the pending policy agenda is and is likely to be on such key elements of the law as disclosure, contribution limitations, and what constitutes permissible coordination between groups, parties, and candidates.

John Green, Michael Kohler, and Ian Schwarber look at the dynamics of the 2012 presidential nomination in chapter 3. The 2012 presidential nomination contest, waged solely within the GOP, had an early frontrunner in Mitt Romney, a late entrant in Texas governor Rick Perry, as well as former Minnesota governor Tim Pawlenty, Texas representative Ron Paul, and Minnesota representative Michele Bachmann. The contest also featured a set of candidates who had not been recent major players in national politics: former Speaker of the House Newt Gingrich, former Pennsylvania senator Rick Santorum, former CEO of Godfather's Pizza Herman Cain, and former Utah governor Jon Huntsman. Frequently mentioned nonentrants included Indiana governor Mitch Daniels, former Florida governor Jeb Bush, New Jersey governor Chris Christie, and former Alaska governor and 2008 vice presidential candidate Sarah Palin.

Some candidates dropped out soon after the Iowa caucuses and New Hampshire primary, such as Tim Pawlenty and Michele Bachman; others lingered a bit longer. Jon Huntsman dropped out a week after the New Hampshire primary, and Rick Perry quit the race just before the North Carolina primary on January 19, 2012. An important impact of Super PACs in 2012 was that they prolonged the primary season by allowing Gingrich and Santorum to continue their campaigns longer than they likely would have been able to do without the advertising funded by the Super PACs. Many of the attacks Obama later directed at Romney had been communicated during the primary phase by Republican candidates or by Super PACs aligned with these candidates.[115]

While much of the media spotlight was on the Republicans, Green reminds us of the preparations undertaken by the Obama campaign during this period and of the role Obama's Super PAC, Priorities USA, and other groups played in defining Romney in negative terms. Green also underscores the continued migration of presidential candidates away from public matching funds, which for decades had been the norm in presidential elections.

In chapter 4, Candice Nelson examines in greater detail how the money was raised and spent by the two sides and the implications of the different approaches to fundraising and campaigning. Among the major differences between the two teams in 2012 was the way the ground game was organized, the level of coordination and cooperation by interest groups on both sides, the ad-buying strategies, and the extent to which the two campaigns emphasized small and large donors.

Super PACs continued to be important to the general election, with Priorities USA and Restore Our Future together expending more than $228 million.[116] As noted, the share of the Romney team's overall effort that came from Restore Our Future was greater than the share of the Obama team's overall effort that came from Priorities USA. But, as Nelson shows, both sides benefited from the noncandidate campaign efforts. Nelson also examines the consequences of the first presidential general election in which both major-party standard bearers declined federal funds. One impact was the continued pressure on the candidates to attend fundraising events, many in nonbattleground states.

In chapter 5 Paul Herrnson, Kelly Patterson, and Stephanie Perry Curtis explore how congressional elections were financed in 2012. They find continuity with prior years in the role PACs play in financing House incumbents, in the role party committees play in independent expenditures in competitive contests, and in the low level of visibility for most House challengers. But they also find changes in the role Super PACs played, both those closely linked to current House and Senate leaders and those linked to broader-based party or ideological groups.

Elections following reapportionment and redistricting predictably have more open-seat contests and more incumbent versus incumbent races, and this was again the case in 2012.[117] Republicans benefited from the 2010 midterm election, where they picked up party control in eleven state legislatures, and in 2010 and 2011 had a net gain of six governorships.[118] Partisan control of the redistricting process appeared to help the GOP for the 2012 election and the remainder of the decade until the next reapportionment.[119]

In chapter 6, Diana Dwyre and Robin Kolodny examine the ways political parties, through their national committees, including congressional campaign committees, raised and spent money in the 2011–12 election cycle. As we demonstrate in this book, much of BCRA has been struck down by the Supreme Court, but the party ban on soft money remains in force. How have the parties adapted to a world without the unlimited contributions once allowed? They have adapted by increasing their hard money receipts, in part because BCRA raised the aggregate individual contribution limit for individuals, thus making room for the parties to expand their fundraising. The Democratic and Republican National Committees have also adapted by expanding joint fundraising activities with their presidential nominees.

In House and Senate elections, the DSCC, NRSC, the DCCC, and the NRCC—the "hill committees," as Dwyre and Kolodny label them—have also adapted by expanding their small and large donor fundraising, by pressing members for more contributions, and, in the case of the NRCC, by expanding PAC fundraising. While Super PACs compete with party committees for contributions, some Super PACs are extensions of congressional leadership and allies of the party committees in competitive races.

Given the importance of candidate-specific Super PACs in the 2012 presidential election, one uncertainty for congressional elections going forward is the role of candidate-specific Super PACs in congressional elections. The growth of Super PACs in the presidential campaign added to the fundraising competition for large donors to party committees. Would a donor who had maxed out to candidates and also maxed out to the RNC or DNC joint candidate-party effort give additional dollars within the aggregate limit to other party committees, or would they give to the presidential Super PACs? If candidate-specific congressional Super PACs become more common, will this diminish the money party committees can raise for their own independent expenditures?

In chapter 7, Jay Goodliffe and I examine how groups who were required to disclose their activities raised money and spent it. As we entered the 2011–12 election cycle, there was uncertainty about how Super PACs and section 501(c) organizations might impact the election. Would corporations, many of them sitting on large cash balances, use some of that money to fund campaign activity, for the first time in more than a century?[120] Or would corporations fear a backlash such as that experienced by Target in Minnesota in 2010, after the corporation made a campaign contribution to a Minnesota Republican gubernatorial candidate and gay marriage opponent? News of the contribution sparked protests and boycotts and is frequently cited as a reason for corporations to avoid making campaign contributions.[121] The limited disclosed activity of corporations in funding Super PACs suggests that corporations largely opted not to participate in this way in 2011–12.

The most anticipated change in the financing of 2012 was the advent of Super PACs, and this is a major theme of chapter 7. How did these organizations come up with the more than $828 million they raised in 2011–12, and how did they spend the $609 million they reported spending?[122] What role did corporations play in financing Super PACs? Did they change the campaign and influence the outcome? Observers often combined the spending of section 501(c) organizations with the spending of Super PACs. This was especially common in media coverage, where the spending by 501(c) organizations was sometimes referred to as "dark money."[123] Interest groups were also major players through traditional PACs, and some groups continued to make independent expenditures as they had done previously rather than form or give to a Super PAC for this purpose. We examine all the ways interest groups participated in 2012.

In chapter 8 Thomas Mann provides a summary of lessons learned from 2012 and other recent elections about the financing of federal elections. What are the possible ways the system could be improved, and what institutional steps would be necessary to accomplish them? Possible reforms range from deregulation to a constitutional amendment banning the kind of spending done by Super PAC and section 501(c) groups. Others favor more and more-timely disclosure. Still others focus on the supply side of reform, seeking to encourage more small donor activity.

When we place the 2012 election in the broader context of the 2004 and 2008 elections, we find that much has changed in campaign finance. The presidential public financing system has been largely discarded. Limits on contributions to candidates, party committees, and traditional PACs remain in place, but those wanting to give more and have it spent to benefit a particular candidate can now do so quite easily through the mechanism of Super PACs. If they want to avoid disclosure, they can do so through 501(c) organizations. Disclosure has long been one of the core elements of FECA, and its importance was reaffirmed by BCRA. The growth of section 501(c) organizations means disclosure was less a part of campaign finance in 2012 than in 2004 or 2008. Yet some parts of the two acts remain and appear to have accomplished their intended purposes. Individual contributions rose substantially in 2004, 2008, and 2012. Party committees, which some observers and academics said would be severely hobbled by BCRA,[124] have been able to substitute limited individual contributions for unlimited individual, corporate, and union soft-money contributions. In 2011–12, for example, the national and congressional party committees collectively raised $1.3 billion,[125] and as noted, small individual contributions have also surged, at least for Obama and some individual congressional candidates.

Given the pattern of increased spending over time, it is likely that we will see even more spending in the 2016 election cycle. It is also likely that the presidential candidates in future cycles will decline public funding and aggressively pursue fundraising, just as Obama and Romney did in 2012. Given an open seat for the presidency and a closely divided country, we can expect that even more money will be spent in 2015 and 2016 than was spent in 2011–12.

It is not as clear whether candidates will emphasize small donors as much as Obama did, but given the strategic advantages of a mixed strategy of large and small donors, it is likely that will be in the playbook for candidates who can appeal to small donors. Super PACs and section 501(c) groups now have established roles to play in our elections, including those with clear links to particular candidates, and it is likely that this spending will only increase in presidential elections. There are already signs that this will become more and more a part of contested congressional races, especially Senate contests. Super PACs linked to congressional leadership are also going to continue to be important.

Our Data and Methodology

Much of the data for this book comes from the Federal Election Commission, which provides ready access to data provided by those required to report to them, including the candidates, political party committees, and political committees. Candidate, party committee, and PAC data are provided to the FEC electronically for all participants except the Senate, which continues to submit data on paper, resulting in a delay for data entry. Those who report to the FEC are often amending and updating reports, which means the data set is frequently changing. We have used the most up-to-date data available from the FEC and have worked to ensure that the data reported across chapters are consistent and timely.

But not all money raised and spent in elections is reported to the FEC. Groups who report to the IRS and the Department of Labor do so with different reporting templates and timetables. Fortunately, groups such as the Center for Responsive Politics, the Sunlight Foundation, and ProPublica have been tracking many of these groups and were generous in sharing their data with us. As in the past, we also use sixty-eight on-the-record interviews with participants in the process, who often report how much they spent beyond what was reported to the FEC. We incorporate these data in our overall estimates. For a list of all interviews, see appendix A. All tables and figures in the book have source notes, and we generally cite in-text data in endnotes.

Notes

1. See appendix for list of interviews.

2. These figures are drawn from table 1-2 and then adjusted for inflation.

3. Super PACS 809, 501(c) 640, and Party IE 254.

4. *Citizens United* v. *Federal Election Commission,* 558 U.S. 310 (2010); *SpeechNow.org* v. *Federal Election Commission,* 599 F.3d 686 (D.C. Cir. 2010).

5. *Federal Election Commission* v. *Wisconsin Right to Life, Inc.,* 551 U.S. 449 (2007); *McConnell* v. *Federal Election Commission,* 540 U.S. 93 (2003).

6. James E. Campbell, "Symposium: Forecasting the 2012 American National Elections," *PS: Political Science & Politics* 45, no. 4 (2012): 610–54.

7. David B. Magleby, ed., *The Change Election: Money, Mobilization, and Persuasion in the 2008 Federal Elections* (Temple University Press, 2011).

8. Chris Cillizza, "Obama's Reelection Campaign Could Hit Billion-Dollar Mark," *Post Politics* (blog), *Washington Post,* December 12, 2010 (www.washingtonpost.com/wp-dyn/content/article/2010/12/12/AR2010121203181.html); Patricia Zengerle, "Analysis: Billion-Dollar Obama to Run Moneyed Campaign," *Reuters,* April 4, 2011 (www.reuters.com/article/2011/04/04/us-usa-election-obama-analysis-idUSTRE7330NY20110404).

9. Zengerle, "Analysis: Billion-Dollar Obama to Run Moneyed Campaign."

10. Navin Nayak, senior vice president for campaigns for League of Conservation Voters, telephone interview by David Magleby, March 4, 2013.

11. Ibid.

12. David Wasserman, "The House: The First Look at 2012," *Cook Political Report,* December 9, 2010 (http://cookpolitical.com/story/3026).

13. Some scholars report that seventeen Republican legislatures or governors controlled redistricting. This count excludes Texas as a Republican-controlled redistricting state because a federal court approved its redistricting map for the 2012 election. However, because the Supreme Court ordered that Texas use the legislature's redistricting district map, we have included Texas in this category, bringing the total to eighteen states. For the research using seventeen states, see Sundeep Iyer and Keesha Gaskins, "Redistricting and Congressional Control: A First Look," Brennan Center for Justice, 2012 (www.brennancenter.org/sites/default/files/legacy/publications/Redistricting_Congressional_Control.pdf)

14. Gary C. Jacobson, "How the Economy and Partisanship Shaped the 2012 Presidential and Congressional Elections," *Political Science Quarterly* 128, no. 1 (Spring 2013): 23.

15. Stuart Rothenberg, Nathan L. Gonzales, and Jessica Taylor, "House Ratings; November 2, 2012," *Rothenberg Political Report*, November 2, 2012 (http://rothenbergpoliticalreport.com/ratings/house/2012-house-ratings-november-2-2012).

16. 1972–2008 congressional data from *Financing the 2008 Election*, edited by David B. Magleby and Anthony Corrado (Brookings, 2011); 2010 and 2012 data from the Federal Election Commission (www.fec.gov) and the Center for Responsive Politics (www.opensecrets.org).

17. *McCutcheon v. Federal Election Commission*, 572 U.S. _____(2014).

18. Presidential candidate spending obtained from the Federal Election Commission, "Presidential Campaign Disbursements" (www.fec.gov/press/summaries/2012/ElectionCycle/24m_PresCand.shtml); congressional candidate spending obtained from the Federal Election Commission, "House and Senate Financial Activity" (www.fec.gov/press/summaries/2012/ElectionCycle/24m_CongCand.shtml). The $8 billion estimate of total spending in the 2012 federal elections is summarized in table 1-2.

19. Charles R. Spies, counsel and treasurer of Restore Our Future, interview by David Magleby, December 21, 2012.

20. Jennifer de Pinto and Sarah Dutton, "How Mitt Romney Became the Presumptive Nominee," *CBS News*, April 12, 2012 (www.cbsnews.com/8301-503544_162-57412775-503544/how-mitt-romney-became-the-presumptive-nominee/).

21. Robert Barnes, "Conservatives Make Their Mark," *Washington Post*, April 3, 2014.

22. Federal Election Commission, "Presidential Campaign Receipts" (www.fec.gov/press/summaries/2012/ElectionCycle/24m_PresCand.shtml); Federal Election Commission, "House and Senate Financial Activity" (www.fec.gov/press/summaries/2012/ElectionCycle/24m_CongCand.shtml); Federal Election Commission, "Presidential Campaign Receipts" (www.fec.gov/press/summaries/2000/ElectionCycle/24m_PresCand.shtml); Federal Election Commission, "FEC

Reports on Congressional Financial Activity for 2000," May 15, 2001 (www.fec.gov/press/press2001/051501congfinact/051501congfinact. html).

23. David B. Magleby, "Spending in the 2000 Elections," in *Financing the 2004 Election*, edited by David B. Magleby (Brookings, 2002), p. 10.

24. Paul Clark, Disclosure Business Architect, Federal Election Commission, e-mail communication with Stephanie Curtis, April 25, 2013.

25. Candice J. Nelson, "Spending in the 2000 Elections," in *Financing the 2000 Election*, edited by David B. Magleby (Brookings, 2002), p. 25.

26. Seth Gitell, "The Democratic Party Suicide Bill," *Atlantic*, July–August 2003, pp. 106–13.

27. Federal Election Commission, "2011–12 Election Cycle Data Summaries through 12/31/12" (www.fec.gov/press/summaries/2012/ElectionCycle/24m_Natl Party.shtml); Federal Election Commission, "Candidate and Committee Viewer" (www.fec.gov/finance/disclosure/candcmte_info.shtml).

28. Compiled from Federal Election Commission data.

29. Spencer Zwick, campaign finance director for Romney for President, Inc., interview by David Magleby and Jay Goodliffe, March 15, 2013.

30. David Magleby and Jay Goodliffe, 2008 and 2012 donor research.

31. Summary statistics from merged Federal Election Commission data.

32. Matt Waldrip, deputy national finance director for Romney for President, Inc., interview by David Magleby, March 12, 2013.

33. Number of small donors obtained from the Obama and Romney Campaigns. E-mail communication from Ann Marie Habershaw of the Obama campaign (May 16, 2013) and Matt Waldrip of the Romney campaign (March 26, 2013).

34. Magleby, "How the 2008 Elections Were Financed," in *The Change Election*, edited by Magleby, p. 29.

35. Email communication from Ann Marie Habershaw, chief operating officer, Democratic National Committee, Obama campaign, to David Magleby, May 13, 2013.

36. E-mail communication from Sal Purpura, director of treasury at John McCain 2008 and director of treasury at McCain-Palin Compliance Fund, March 17, 2009.

37. David B. Magleby, Jay Goodliffe, and Joseph Olson, "Donors to Obama and McCain in 2008: An Examination of New, Repeat, Large and Small Donors," paper presented at the 2011 Annual Meeting of the Midwest Political Science Association, Chicago, Ill., March 31–April 3, 2011,

38. E-mail communication from Ann Marie Habershaw of the Obama campaign to David Magleby, May 13, 2013.

39. Calculations made by author with data from Center for Responsive Politics, "Price of Amission," 2012 (www.opensecrets.org/bigpicture/ stats.php).

40. John C. Green and Diana Kingsbury, "Financing the 2008 Nomination Campaigns," in *Financing the 2008 Election*, edited by Magleby and Corrado, p. 103.

41. Michael Kranish, "Romney Will Eat Campaign Loans," *Boston Globe*, July 16, 2008 (www.boston.com/news/politics/politicalintelligence/2008/07/romney_will_eat.html).

42. Chris Cillizza and Aaron Blake, "Mitt Romney's Millions (and Why They Could Matter)," *The Fix* (blog), *Washington Post*, March 1, 2012 (www.washingtonpost.com/blogs/the-fix/post/mitt-romneys-millions-and-why-they-could-matter/2012/02/29/gIQAm0RJjR_blog.html?wprss=rss_politics).

43. Aaron Blake, "Why Is Mitt Romney Borrowing $20 Million?" *The Fix* (blog), *Washington Post*, September 19, 2012 (www.washingtonpost.com/blogs/the-fix/wp/2012/09/19/why-is-mitt-romney-borrowing-20-million/).

44. Dana Bash, "Romney's Donated $150,000 of Own Money to Presidential Bid," *Political Ticker* (blog), *CNN*, May 18, 2012 (http://politicalticker.blogs.cnn.com/2012/05/18/first-on-cnn-romneys-donated-150000-of-own-money-to-presidential-bid/); Michael Waldman, "Why Doesn't Mitt Romney Contribute to His Own Campaign?" *The Great Debate* (blog), *Reuters*, September 25, 2012 (http://blogs.reuters.com/great-debate/2012/09/25/why-doesnt-mitt-romney-contribute-to-his-own-campaign/).

45. Institute of Politics, John F. Kennedy School of Government, Harvard University, *Campaign for President: The Managers Look at 2012* (Lanham, Md.: Rowman and Littlefield, 2013), p. 149.

46. Jonathan Alter, *The Center Holds: Obama and His Enemies* (Simon and Schuster, 2013) p. 214.

47. FEC, "2011–12 Election Cycle Data Summaries through 12/31/12."

48. Jonathan Weisman, "I.R.S. Apologizes to Tea Party Groups over Audits of Applications for Tax Exemption," *New York Times,* May 10, 2013 (www.nytimes.com/2013/05/11/us/politics/irs-apologizes-to-conservative-groups-over-application-audits.html?pagewanted=all&_r=0).

49. Federal Election Commission, "Independent Expenditure–Only Committees," 2010 (www.fec.gov/press/press2011/ieoc_alpha.shtml).

50. Federal Election Commission, "Candidate and Committee Viewer" (www.fec.gov/finance/disclosure/candcmte_info.shtml); Center for Responsive Politics, "Crossroads GPS," 2010 (www.opensecrets.org/outsidespending/detail.php?cycle=2010&cmte=C90011719).

51. Federal Election Commission, "2009–2010 Election Cycle Data Summaries through 12/31/10," 2010 (www.fec.gov/press/summaries/2010/ElectionCycle/24m_IE_EC.shtml).

52. Jim Rutenberg, "Rove Returns, with Team, Planning G.O.P. Push," *New York Times*, September 25, 2010 (www.nytimes.com/2010/09/26/us/26rove.html?pagewanted=all&_r=0).

53. Internal Revenue Service, "Exemption Requirements: Section 501(c)(3) Organizations" (www.irs.gov/Charities-%26-Non-Profits/Charitable-Organizations/Exemption-Requirements-Section-501(c)(3)-Organizations).

54. Anthony Corrado, "The Regulatory Environment of the 2008 Elections," in *Financing the 2008 Election*, edited by Magleby and Corrado, p. 73.

55. Steve Rosenthal, president of the Organizing Group, interview by David Magleby, June 20, 2013.

56. Magleby, "A Change Election," in *The Change Election*, edited by Magleby, p. 12.

57. Harold Ickes, president of Priorities USA, telephone interview by David Magleby, December 12, 2012.

58. Barack Obama, "Text: Obama's State of the Union Address," *New York Times*, January 27, 2010 (www.nytimes.com/2010/01/28/us/politics/28obama. text.html?pagewanted=all); Barack Obama, State of the Union Address, January 27, 2010, White House Office of the Press Secretary (www.whitehouse.gov/the-press-office/remarks-president-state-union-address).

59. Martin Kady II, "Justice Alito Mouths 'Not True,'" *Politico Live* (blog), *Politico*, January 27, 2010 (www.politico.com/blogs/politicolive/0110/Justice_ Alitos_You_lie_moment.html).

60. Institute of Politics, *Campaign for President*, p. 156.

61. Compiled from Federal Election Commission data.

62. David B. Magleby, "Adaptation and Innovation in the Financing of the 2008 Elections," in *Financing the 2008 Election*, edited by Magleby and Corrado, p. 11.

63. Catalina Camia, "Obama, Romney Skip Taxpayer Money for Campaign," *USA TODAY*, April 27, 2012 (http://content.usatoday.com/communities/on politics/post/2012/04/mitt-romney-public-financing-presidential-campaign-/1#.U UzM-RxOR8E).

64. *Associated Press* staff reports; also Emily Chow, Ted Melnik, and Karen Yourish, "Presidential Campaign Stops: Who's Going Where," *Washington Post*, November 7, 2012 (http://wapo.st/2012-campaignvisits).

65. See Andy Kroll, "Obama Has Attended, on Average, One Fundraiser Every 60 Hours While Running for Reelection," *Mother Jones*, August 31, 2012 (www. motherjones.com/mojo/2012/08/obama-200-fundraisers-romney-record). Romney's total is estimated from Google searches of news articles about Romney fundraisers, collated by date, data from *Associated Press* staff reports; also see Chow, Melnik, and Yourish, "Presidential Campaign Stops."

66. David B. Magleby, "Electoral Politics as Team Sport," in *The State of the Parties*, edited by John C. Green and Daniel J. Coffey (Plymouth, U.K.: Rowman and Littlefield, 2011), pp. 81–100.

67. Michael M. Franz, "Interest Groups in Electoral Politics: 2012 in Context," *The Forum* 10, no. 4 (2012): 66.

68. Ibid., p. 67.

69. Senate races in 2012 in which outside spending by party committees and interest groups exceeded candidate spending include the following campaigns:

Thompson (R-WI), by $12,241,60; Timothy Michael Kaine (D-VA), by $10,011,811; Richard Mourdock (R-IN), by $7,169,250; Joseph Donnelly (D-IN), by $7,053,106; and George Allen (R-VA), by $5,513,735. In the House, candidates whose expenditures were exceeded by party committee independent expenditures and interest group outside spending include William L. Enyart (D-IL 12), by $3,177,991; Richard Michael Nolan (D-MN 8), by $3,039,998; Mark Critz (D-PA 12), by $2,929,992; and Charles Wilson (D-OH 6), by $2,734,466. Compiled by the author from Federal Election Commission data.

70. Glen Bolger, cofounder and partner at Public Opinion Strategies, interview by David Magleby, March 19, 2013.

71. Will Dooling, "In Massachusetts, Even the 'People's Pledge' Can't Keep Out the Outside Money," *Center for Media and Democracy's PR Watch*, October 17, 2012.

72. Guy Cecil, executive director of Democratic Senatorial Campaign Committee, interview by David Magleby, December 19, 2013.

73. Mike Lux, cofounder and president of Progressive Strategies, L.L.C., interview by David Magleby, January 14, 2013.

74. Rick Wiley, political director of the Republican National Committee, interview by David Magleby, February 11, 2013.

75. Cecil, interview.

76. Nayak, interview.

77. Martin P. Wattenberg, *The Rise of Candidate-Centered Politics: Presidential Elections of the 1980s* (Harvard University Press, 1991).

78. Clifford W. Brown Jr., Lynda W. Powell, and Clyde Wilcox, *Serious Money: Fundraising and Contributing in Presidential Nomination Campaigns* (Cambridge University Press, 1995)

79. Erika Fowler, "Presidential Ads 70 Percent Negative in 2012, Up from 9 Percent in 2008," Wesleyan Media Project (http://media project.wesleyan.edu/2012/05/02/jump-in-negativity).

80. Ibid.

81. Nick Ryan, who ran the Red White and Blue Fund, stated that "without the Super PAC that I ran for Senator Santorum, I don't think he would have been able to have the success or the funds necessary to be competitive" (Institute of Politics, *Campaign for President*, p. 141.).

82. Sean Sweeney, senior strategist at Priorities USA, interview by David Magleby, February 11, 2013.

83. Darrell M. West, *Air Wars: Television Advertising in Election Campaigns, 1952–2008*, 5th ed. (Washington: Congressional Quarterly, 2009).

84. David B. Magleby and J. Quin Monson, eds., *The Last Hurrah? Soft Money and Issue Advocacy in the 2002 Congressional Elections* (Brookings, 2004); David B. Magleby, Kelly D. Patterson, and J. Quin Monson, eds., *Electing Congress: New Rules for an Old Game* (Upper Saddle River, N.J.:

Prentice Hall, 2007); David B. Magleby, Kelly D. Patterson, and J. Quin Monson, eds. *Dancing without Partners: How Candidates, Parties, and Interest Groups Interact in the Presidential Campaign* (Lanham, Md.: Rowman and Littlefield, 2007); David B. Magleby and Kelly D. Patterson, eds., *The Battle for Congress: Iraq, Scandal, and Campaign Finance in the 2006 Elections* (Boulder, Colo.: Paradigm, 2008); Magleby, *The Change Election.* See also Rasmus Kleis Nielsen, *Ground Wars* (Princeton University Press, 2012).

85. Magleby, "A Change Election," p. 87.

86. Romney's data science team was less than one-tenth the size of Obama's analytics department. According to Sasha Issenberg, the Obama camp spent $52 million on online ads through mid-October to the Romney camp's $26 million. Issenberg, "A More Perfect Union: How President Obama's Campaign Used Big Data to Rally Voters," *MIT Technology Review*, December 19, 2012 (www. technologyreview.com/featuredstory/509026/how-obamas-team-used-big-data-to-rally-voters/).

87. Matt Bai, *The Argument: Billionaires, Bloggers, and the Battle to Remake Democratic Politics* (New York: Penguin Press, 2007) , pp. 24–28.

88. Wiley, interview.

89. Travis N. Ridout, Michael M. Franz, and Erika Franklin Fowler, "Why Are Interest Group Ads More Effective?" Working Paper, Wesleyan Media Project, presented at 2013 Annual Meeting of the American Political Science Association, Chicago, August 29–September 1, 2013.

90. Erika Franklin Fowler and Travis N. Ridout, "Negative, Angry, and Ubiquitous: Political Advertising in 2012," *The Forum* 10, no. 4 (2013): 54.

91. Ibid.

92. Sarah Bufkin, "Mitt Romney Ad Spending Spikes on Week-to-Week Purchases," *Huffington Post*, October 4, 2012 (www.huffingtonpost.com/2012/10/04/mitt-romney-ad-spending-week-to-week_n_1940951.html).

93. Quoted ibid.

94. Ken Goldstein, president of the Campaign Media Analysis Group, interview by David Magleby, February 11, 2013.

95. Personal correspondence from Erika Fowler to David Magleby, June 27, 2013.

96. T. W. Farnam, "Obama Campaign Took Unorthodox Approach to Ad Buying," *Post Politics* (blog), *Washington Post*, November 14, 2012 (www.washingtonpost.com/politics/the-influence-industry-obama-campaign-took-unorthodox-approach-to-ad-buying/2012/11/14/c3477e8c-2e87-11e2-beb2-4b4cf5087636_story.html).

97. Institute of Politics, *Campaign for President*, p. 135.

98. Richard R. Lau, Lee Sigelman, and Ivy Brown Rovner, "The Effects of Negative Political Campaigns: A Meta-Analytic Reassessment," *Journal of Politics* 69, no. (2007): 1176–1209.

99. *McConnell* v. *Federal Election Commission*; *Federal Election Commission* v. *Wisconsin Right to Life, Inc.*

100. Rob Engstrom, senior vice president of political affairs and federation relations and national political director, U.S. Chamber of Commerce, interview by David Magleby, December 14, 2012.

101. Compiled from Federal Election Commission data.

102. Karl Rove, cofounder and adviser to American Crossroads, interview by David Magleby, March 15, 2013.

103. FEC, "Independent Expenditure–Only Committees," 2010.

104. Maggie Haberman, "Cantor-Allied Young Guns Network Urges Non-Republicans to Vote in Lugar Race," *Politico, Burns and Haberman* (blog), April 27, 2012 (www.politico.com/blogs/burns-haberman/2012/04/cantorallied-young-guns-network-urges-nonrepublicans-121902.html).

105. Mike Podhorzer, political director at AFL-CIO, interview by David Magleby, December 18, 2012.

106. Michael Connolly, "Club for Growth PAC to Oppose Sen. Robert Bennett," *Club for Growth*, January 8, 2010 (www.clubforgrowth.org/perm/?postID =12355); Steve C. Wilson, "Freedom Works' Biggest Wins and Losses," *Post Politics* (blog), *Washington Post*, under (www.washingtonpost.com/politics/freedom-works-biggest-wins-and-losses/2012/12/22/19b02cc4-4855-11e2-b6f0-e851e741d 196_gallery.html#photo=1).

107. Center for Responsive Politics, "Tea Party Express/Our Country Deserves B Recipients, 2010," 2010 (www.opensecrets.org/outsidespending/recips.php? cmte=C00454074&cycle=2010).

108. Jonathan Weisman, "Tea Party Backs O'Donnell in Delaware," *Washington Wire* (blog), *Wall Street Journal*, August 30, 2010 (http://blogs.wsj.com/ washwire/2010/08/30/tea-party-endorses-odonnell-in-delaware/); Carl Cameron, "Tea Party–Backed O'Donnell Upsets Castle in Delaware GOP Race," *Fox News,* September 15, 2010 (www.foxnews.com/politics/2010/09/14/hours-polls-close-gloves-come-delaware/).

109. Monica Davey, "G.O.P. Voters Topple Lugar after 6 Terms," *New York Times*, May 9, 2012, p. 1; John Eligon and Michael Schwirtz, "Senate Candidate Provokes Ire with 'Legitimate Rape' Comment," *New York Times*, August 19, 2012 (www.nytimes.com/2012/08/20/us/politics/todd-akin-provokes-ire-with-legitimate-rape-comment.html).

110. Charles R. Spies, general counsel and treasurer to Restore Our Future, interview by David Magleby, August 14, 2012.

111. Jeff Zeleny, "Top Donors to Republicans Seek More Say in Senate Races," *New York Times*, February 2, 2013 (www.nytimes.com/2013/02/03/ us/politics/top-gop-donors-seek-greater-say-in-senate-races.html?pagewanted =all).

112. Nicholas Confessore, "Tea Party Group to Form Super PAC," *The Caucus* (blog), *New York Times*, September 23, 2011 (http://thecaucus.blogs.nytimes.com/2011/09/23/tea-party-group-to-form-a-super-pac/).

113. Jonathan Weisman, "Documents Show Liberals in I.R.S. Dragnet," *Politics* (blog), *New York Times*, June 24, 2013 (www.nytimes.com/2013/06/25/us/politics/documents-show-liberals-in-irs-dragnet.html?_r=0). John D. McKinnon, "IRS Halts Political Screening of Groups," *Wall Street Journal*, June 24, 2013 (http://online.wsj.com/article/SB1000142412788732368350457856581041 3786872.html).

114. James Bennet, "The New Price of American Politics," *Atlantic*, September 19, 2012 (www.theatlantic.com/magazine/archive/2012/10/the/309086/).

115. Jeremy W. Peters, "92 Percent of Ads in Florida Were Negative," *The Caucus: The Politics and Government Blog of the Times*, *New York Times*, January 31, 2012 (http://thecaucus.blogs.nytimes.com/2012/01/31/92-percent-of-ads-in-florida-were-negative/).

116. Federal Election Commission, "Independent Expenditure–Only Committee Financial Activity," 2012 (www.fec.gov/press/summaries/2012/ElectionCycle/PACYE.shtml).

117. Gary C. Jacobsen, "How the Economy and Partisanship Shaped the 2012 Presidential and Congressional Elections," *Political Science Quarterly* 128, no. 1 (2013): 22; for data on the 1990s, see David B. Magleby, "Outside Money in the 2002 Congressional Elections," in *The Last Hurrah?*, edited by Magleby and Monson, p. 20.

118. National Conference of State Legislatures, "2010 Legislature Party Control Switch," 2010 (www.ncsl.org/legislatures-elections/elections/2010-legislature-party-control-switch.aspx); "Election 2010: Governor Map," *New York Times*, 2010 (http://elections.nytimes.com/2010/results/governor).

119. Dylan Matthews, "How Redistricting Could Keep the House Red for a Decade," *WonkBlog*, *Washington Post*, November 8, 2012 (www.washingtonpost.com/blogs/wonkblog/wp/2012/11/08/how-redistricting-could-keep-the-house-red-for-a-decade/).

120. James A. Kahl, "Citizens United, Super PACs, and Corporate Spending on Political Campaigns: How Did We Get Here and Where are We Going?," *Federal Lawyer*, March 2012 (www.wcsr.com/resources/pdfs/federallawyer_citizens.pdf).

121. Brody Mullins and Ann Zimmerman, "Target Discovers Downside to Political Contributions," *Wall Street Journal*, August 7, 2010 (http://online.wsj.com/article/SB10001424052748703988304575413650676561696.html).

122. Center for Responsive Politics, "Super PACs" (www.opensecrets.org/pacs/superpacs.php).

123. Editorial Board, "A Campaign Awash in Cash," *Washington Post*, November 4, 2012 (www.washingtonpost.com/opinions/a-campaign-awash-in-

cash/2012/11/04/c422a6c8-2537-11e2-9313-3c7f59038d93_story.html); Juliet Lapidos, "Saving Wealthy Donors from Themselves," *Taking Note* (blog), *New York Times*, November 7, 2012 (http://takingnote.blogs.nytimes.com/2012/11/07/saving-wealthy-donors-from-themselves/).

124. Sidney Milkis, "Parties versus Interest Groups," in *Inside the Campaign Finance Battle: Court Testimony on the New Reforms*, edited by Anthony Corrado, Thomas E. Mann, and Trevor Potter (Brookings, 2003), pp. 40–48; Raymond LaRaja, "Will the BCRA Strengthen the Political System? Negative: BCRA Is Not Improving the Political System," *Journal of Policy Analysis and Management* 24, no. 3 (2005): 604–08.

125. FEC, "2012 Full Election Cycle Summary Data."

TWO

The Regulatory Environment of the 2012 Election

ANTHONY CORRADO

The financing of the 2012 election was like no other in the modern regulatory era, which began with the adoption of the 1972 Federal Election Campaign Act (FECA) after the Watergate scandal. Although much of the financial activity followed the patterns established in recent elections or mirrored the tactics adopted in prior campaigns, significant differences distinguished the 2012 election cycle from other recent presidential election cycles. These differences reflected the more permissive regulatory environment that emerged as a result of the Supreme Court's 2010 decision in *Citizens United* v. *Federal Election Commission* and subsequent legal and regulatory decisions.[1]

Between the 2008 and 2012 elections, federal campaign finance rules underwent the most significant changes since the comprehensive restructuring of the law in the 1970s. For the first time since the end of World War II, corporations and labor unions were allowed to spend monies from their treasuries in support of federal candidates.[2] A new variation of the federal PAC, which came to be known as the Super PAC, was sanctioned, and these committees were allowed to use unlimited contributions to expressly advocate the election of candidates, a practice that had previously been banned by FECA. The scope of disclosure laws was substantially narrowed, allowing extensive electioneering activities to be

Andrew Pepper-Anderson of Colby College assisted in the research for this chapter, which was supported by a Colby College Social Sciences Research Grant.

financed by monies that were hidden from public view. And nonprofit organizations were given greater leeway to participate in federal elections.

The new rules governing campaigning, which came into effect in 2012, fundamentally altered the regulatory structure established by FECA, ending some of the basic prohibitions that had served as pillars of federal campaign finance law. How and why these regulatory changes occurred is explained in this chapter. The new structure reshaped the regulatory environment and gave rise to a new sphere of unrestricted financial activity in federal campaigns. Multimillion-dollar contributions became a major source of funding, and undisclosed money flowed into the election process in amounts that dwarfed the secret slush funds uncovered in the Watergate investigations.

New Rules for Corporations and Labor Unions

Federal law imposes strict contribution limits and disclosure requirements on candidates and national party committees. These statutory provisions, which are based on FECA and subsequent rules adopted under the 2002 Bipartisan Campaign Reform Act (BCRA), did not change in advance of the 2012 election (see chapter 1). What did change were the rules applied to monies spent independently of candidates and party committees by political committees and other organizations.

As defined for purposes of tax law in section 527 of the Internal Revenue Code, political committees are organizations that are established for the principal purpose of influencing or attempting to influence the selection or election of individuals to public office at the federal, state, or local level.[3] These committees, which include candidate committees, party committees, and political action committees (PACs), are organized under section 527, the provision of the tax code that grants a tax exemption to such groups (that is, they are exempt from tax with the exception of any investment income). Most political committees involved in federal elections are required to register with the Federal Election Commission (FEC) and are subject to the rules established by federal campaign finance law. Some political organizations, however, are established to influence elections in general, do not specify any particular election in which they intend to be involved, and do not register with the FEC as federal committees. These organizations are commonly referred to as 527 organizations, to distinguish them from the committees that are governed by the

FEC. The legal changes that preceded the 2012 election permitted organizations other than political committees to make independent expenditures advocating the election of candidates. They also altered the rules governing PACs and 527 organizations, freeing these political spenders from many of the contribution restrictions imposed on any monies used to finance independent expenditures in federal races.

Most notably, the Supreme Court in *Citizens United* recognized the right of corporations and, by extension, labor unions to spend monies independently to advocate the election of candidates.[4] This decision struck down the prohibition on corporate and labor union expenditures in federal elections that had been in place since the 1947 Taft-Hartley Act. Furthermore, it allowed a variety of organizations that receive corporate or labor union money to spend these funds on federal electioneering activities in ways that were not permitted in previous elections.

Federal campaign finance rules regulate three different types of election spending: coordinated expenditures, independent expenditures, and electioneering communications. The FEC has established a multipronged test to define a coordinated expenditure, which includes coordination, conduct, and content. For example, an expenditure may be deemed coordinated if (a) it advocates the election of a candidate or pays for the distribution or republication of materials prepared by a campaign; and it is made either (b) in consultation with, in concert with, or at the suggestion of a candidate, a member of a campaign staff, or a candidate's agent; or (c) after substantial discussions with a candidate.[5] In general, any spending that is coordinated with a candidate or party committee is considered an in-kind contribution and is subject to the applicable contribution limits and source prohibitions. This restriction on coordinated activity applies to all political spenders, with the exception of party committees. Owing to the unique relationship between parties and their candidates, parties are allowed to spend a specified amount in coordination with their candidates based on a formula established by FECA.[6]

Independent expenditures and electioneering communications are regulated because they are forms of direct support for a candidate, either by expressly advocating a candidate's election or by serving as the functional equivalent of express advocacy. An independent expenditure is any expenditure that is not coordinated with a candidate (or party) and expressly advocates the election or defeat of a candidate (that is, uses such terms as "vote for," "elect," or "Jones for Congress"). Those who make independent expenditures must disclose any disbursements of $250 or more, as well as the sources of their funding, to the FEC.[7] An "electioneering communication" is a broadcast advertisement featuring a federal candidate that is aired within thirty days of a primary or sixty days of a general election. This category of election spending was established by BCRA in an effort to regulate the monies used to finance some "issue advertisements" that did not expressly urge a vote for a candidate. The act prohibited the use of corporate or labor union treasury funds to pay for electioneering communications, thereby extending the prohibition on the use of corporate and labor union funds to ads that were viewed as the functional equivalent of express advocacy. However, these communications could be financed with unlimited individual or PAC contributions. The act requires that any organization that spends $10,000 or more in a calendar year on such advertisements must disclose its expenditures to the FEC, as well as any donation of $1,000 or more and the identity of the donor.

The Supreme Court's controversial 5-4 decision in *Citizens United* changed the law on independent spending and electioneering communications. Before this decision, only individuals, PACs, and parties were allowed to make independent expenditures, and only donations from individuals or political committees could be used for electioneering communications. The court's ruling allowed independent spending by both for-profit and nonprofit corporations, as well as unions, and approved the use of corporate and labor funds to pay for electioneering communications.[8] The ruling essentially permitted any organization that is allowed to engage in political activity to spend money independently in support of candidates. It also sanctioned the use of contributions from any source allowed to make donations in federal elections.[9]

At issue in *Citizens United* was the question of whether corporations had the same right as individuals, parties, and political committees to make independent expenditures directly advocating a federal candidate. The court's majority held that the First Amendment did not permit restrictions on speech based on the identity of the speaker. The government may not privilege some viewpoints or speakers (for example, individuals) over others (for example, corporations), since this "deprives the public of the right and privilege to determine for itself what speech and which speakers are worthy of consideration."[10] Instead, First Amendment protections extend to the political speech of all, including corporations and other associations of individuals (including, presumably, labor unions, which received treatment equal to corporations under federal campaign finance laws). Corporations and other associations therefore should not be treated differently simply because they are not "natural persons."[11]

Following the doctrine first advanced in the landmark *Buckley* v. *Valeo* case, the majority further held that there is no justification for prohibiting independent corporate spending, since independent expenditures do not pose a risk of corruption or the appearance of corruption, which is the only governmental interest recognized by the court as a basis for restricting spending.[12] In rendering this judgment, the court adhered to a narrow conception of corruption understood as a quid pro quo transaction between a candidate and a donor and rejected the broader conception of corruption, which includes the use of money to gain undue influence or access to an elected official, that had been advanced by the court in the 2003 *McConnell v. Federal Election Commission* decision that had upheld the constitutionality of BCRA.[13]

Accordingly, the court struck down the ban on corporate expenditures in federal elections and recognized the right of corporations to make independent expenditures. It also overturned the ruling in *McConnell*, which had upheld the prohibition on the use of corporate and labor funds for electioneering communications. The court did, however, uphold the disclosure requirements by a vote of 8-1, noting that disclosure rules "impose no ceiling on campaign-related activities" and "do not prevent anyone from speaking." It further stated that "disclosure permits citizens and shareholders to react to the speech of corporate entities in a proper way. . . . [It] enables the electorate to make informed decisions and give proper weight to different speakers and messages."[14]

The court's decision was quickly tested in a lawsuit filed in March 2010 against Montana's ban on corporate independent expenditures, which was first adopted in 1912. Two corporations, Western Tradition Partnership and Champion Painting, and an incorporated organization, Montana Shooting Sports Association, challenged Montana's prohibition against corporate expenditures, arguing that it was unconstitutional under *Citizens United*. The state sought to distinguish its law from federal law by arguing that the statute had been adopted in response to the state's history of corporate influence in elections and therefore did serve the governmental interest in safeguarding against corruption. The Montana Supreme Court upheld the statute, accepting the corruption interest and stating that the state's political environment is "especially vulnerable to continued efforts of corporate control to the detriment of democracy and the republican form of government." The court also noted that the statute helped protect the integrity of Montana's judicial system, since state judges are elected in nonpartisan elections.[15]

The case, *American Tradition Partnership* v. *Bullock*, was appealed to the Supreme Court. The court agreed to review the case, giving hope to opponents of the *Citizens United* decision that it might serve as an opportunity for reconsidering or at least modifying that ruling. On June 25, 2012, however, the U.S. Supreme Court summarily reversed the Montana Supreme Court's ruling without hearing the case, noting that it was inconsistent with its ruling in *Citizens United* and that the arguments presented in support of the statute had already been rejected.[16] With this, the court made clear that its opinion applied to state statutes and that the majority of justices still supported the decision.

The *Citizens United* decision mandated a significant change in the law with respect to the role of corporate and labor union monies in federal elections. However, it is important to note that before the decision, organizations that were not registered as federal political committees with the FEC could already use corporate and labor funds to pay for election-related activities or communications, so long as they were not used to finance express advocacy or electioneering communications and so long as they did not coordinate their efforts with candidate or party committees. This included section 527 committees and nonprofit organizations, particularly social welfare organizations organized under section 501(c)(4) of the tax code and business associations organized under section 501(c)(6), which spent substantial sums of money on election-related activity in both the 2004 and 2008 elections.[17]

Before *Citizens United*, 527s and nonprofit organizations could spend unlimited funds, including corporate and labor money, on issue advertisements or broadcast communications that did not qualify as electioneering communications (that is, ads that featured a candidate but were aired outside of the thirty- and sixty-day windows that triggered regulation). As a result of the Supreme Court's 2007 ruling in *Federal Election Commission* v. *Wisconsin Right to Life*, they could also pay for advertisements close to an election that feature candidates if the ads could reasonably be interpreted as something other than an appeal to vote for or against a specific candidate.[18] In addition, they could finance direct mail, telephone programs, and Internet-based communications that featured candidates, as well as nonpartisan voter registration and turnout efforts. In short, these organizations could spend money on activities that indirectly supported candidates without being subject to campaign finance regulations.

The major effect of *Citizens United* was thus to enhance the utility of corporate and labor money by permitting these funds to be used to directly advocate the election of candidates. Critics of the decision, including President Obama, predicted that the ruling would unleash a flood of corporate spending in elections. Yet few for-profit corporations took advantage of this option in the 2010 or 2012 elections. To the extent that corporations did become more involved in federal elections, they demonstrated a preference for making contributions to organizations that supported their views or shared their interests. In this way, the group that received corporate donations, rather than the corporate donor, was responsible for the spending.

Corporations, labor unions, and other entities that wanted to make contributions to be used for independent expenditures or electioneering communications had a number of options available to them. They could contribute to a 527 committee, a social welfare organization, or a trade association. Or they could give to a new form of federal political committee—the Super PAC.

The Rise of Super PACs

The decision in *Citizens United* made it easier for the courts to resolve another case, *SpeechNow.org* v. *Federal Election Commission*, which was initially filed in 2008.[19] The *SpeechNow* decision significantly altered the regulatory structure established by FECA and thus the strategic calculus of groups seeking to participate in federal elections. Before this decision, groups that wanted to solicit unlimited contributions had to rely on an organizational alternative that did not qualify as a federal PAC, such as a section 527 committee or a 501(c)(4) organization. But these 527 committees could not use the monies they received to finance independent expenditures and could only use contributions from individuals to finance electioneering communications, and the section 501(c)(4) groups could not have election activity as their primary purpose. Since most nonprofit organizations are incorporated entities, they typically focused their efforts on issue advertising and other non-express-advocacy activities. But this all changed after the legal ruling in *SpeechNow*, which made such efforts to circumvent contribution limits unnecessary.

The SpeechNow Decision

SpeechNow was established by David Keating, the executive director of the conservative group Club for Growth, as an unincorporated, tax-exempt political committee under section 527 of the tax code. Speech-Now's declared purpose was solely to make independent expenditures in support of federal candidates from monies received from individual donors. It did not plan to make direct contributions to candidates. On this basis, the organization challenged the legality of several provisions of the law as applied to their proposed activities, including the contribution limit imposed on individual donations and the requirement that only limited contributions could be used to make unlimited expenditures. The organization also challenged the political committee registration requirement, arguing that it did not need to register with the FEC as a PAC and thus be subject to the same contribution limits and disclosure requirements as other PACs.

To this end, SpeechNow submitted an advisory opinion request to the FEC in November 2007, asking whether its intended activity—to raise funds from individuals to pay for independent expenditures expressly advocating candidates—would require it to register as a political committee subject to FECA contribution restrictions.[20] The FEC General Counsel's Office prepared a draft opinion for commission discussion stating that SpeechNow would be subject to contribution limits and would be required to register as a PAC once it had raised or spent more than $1,000 in a calendar year for the purpose of influencing federal elections.[21] But at the time the draft was considered, the commission had only two members, and four were needed for a quorum to take action. Consequently, the commission could not issue an opinion on the question and notified SpeechNow of that fact at the end of January 2008.[22]

Two weeks after receiving the FEC's response, SpeechNow filed a lawsuit in federal district court challenging the constitutionality of the contribution limits and disclosure requirements imposed on PACs by FECA, arguing that these restrictions were not justified in the case of a political committee that only intended to make independent expenditures.[23] SpeechNow contended that a group of individuals should have the same right as an individual to make independent expenditures from unlimited monies and that limits on contributions unconstitutionally restricted their donors' freedom of speech by limiting the amount an individual could give to SpeechNow, which in effect limited the amount the organization could spend. The group also argued that independent expenditures do not pose a risk of corruption since there is no interaction with a candidate; a limit on donations to a group acting independently of a candidate was thus an unjustified infringement on First Amendment rights since it did not serve to prevent corruption or the appearance of corruption, the only government interest recognized by the courts as a rationale for restricting political speech.[24] The committee further claimed that the disclosure requirements of the federal law were unconstitutionally burdensome because a PAC must report all contributions and expenditures of $200 or more, not just the amounts spent on independent expenditures.

The district court did not accept SpeechNow's constitutional arguments. In the view of the court, limits on contributions to committees solely making independent expenditures did not restrict the amount a committee could spend; they simply restricted the source and amount of contributions, which served the government's interest of preventing corruption or the appearance of corruption. Citing *McConnell*, the court noted that the Supreme Court had "affirmed Congress's power to enact prophylactic measures aimed at the 'more subtle but equally dispiriting forms of corruption,' such as the sale of access that can occur even when contributions are made to entities that are legally independent of candidates' own campaign organizations."[25] The court also argued that the ruling in *McConnell* made clear that Congress had an interest in preventing the circumvention of otherwise valid contribution limits and that limits on the monies used to finance independent expenditures served this purpose.[26]

SpeechNow's appeal happened to be heard by the U.S. Court of Appeals for the District of Columbia a week after the *Citizens United* opinion was issued. The appellate court rendered its decision two months later. Even though the *SpeechNow* case involved different issues from those in *Citizens United*, the case is often linked to *Citizens United* because the appellate court relied on the high court's opinion in that case in offering its analysis, which it described as "straight-forward."[27] The appellate court accepted the Supreme Court's view that the government's interest in preventing corruption should be limited to quid pro quo transactions and that independent expenditures do not pose a risk of corruption. The court declared, "In light of the [Supreme] Court's holding as a matter of law that independent expenditures do not corrupt or create the appearance of *quid pro quo* corruption, contributions to groups that make only independent expenditures also cannot corrupt or create the appearance of corruption. The Court has effectively held that there is no corrupting 'quid' for which a candidate might in exchange offer a corrupt 'quo.'"[28] The court thus concluded that there is no justification for limiting contributions to groups that only make independent expenditures.

The court did, however, uphold the disclosure and reporting requirements that would be applicable to SpeechNow as a federally registered PAC, noting that these requirements "impose no ceiling on campaign related activities" and "do not prevent anyone from speaking."[29] The court acknowledged that SpeechNow would have additional reporting requirements to those applied to an organization that was not registered as a PAC with the FEC but decided the additional burden would be "minimal," especially given the "relative simplicity" with which an independent expenditure–only committee would operate.[30] The court also held that disclosure "deters and helps expose violations of other campaign finance restrictions" and that "the public has an interest in knowing who is speaking about a candidate and who is funding that speech, no matter whether the contributions were made toward administrative expenses or independent expenditures."[31] Accordingly, disclosure promoted valuable governmental interests, which justified the need for SpeechNow to register as a federal political committee and report to the FEC.

FEC Implementation

Congress made no effort to revise the statutory language of FECA to incorporate the changes required by the *SpeechNow* decision. Implementation of the decision was therefore left to the FEC, but the agency did not promulgate new rules to clarify the effect of the case.

The commission did consider initiating a rulemaking process in January and June 2011 but disagreed on the content of a notice of proposed rulemaking and produced a deadlocked 3-3 vote on both occasions.[32] The division was along partisan lines, with the commissioners originally proposed for the FEC by Republican leaders (hereafter the *Republican commissioners*) on one side and those originally proposed by Democratic leaders (hereafter *Democratic commissioners*) on the other.[33] The sticking point was the unwillingness of the Republican commissioners to expand the rulemaking and accommodate the Democratic commissioners' desire to include a request for public comments on disclosure rules and expenditures by U.S.-based corporations owned in whole or part by foreign nationals. In December 2011 two Democratic commissioners relented and joined the three Republicans in approving a proposal for rulemaking limited to questions focused on the repeal of the corporate spending restrictions invalidated by *Citizens United*, such as the definition of permissible corporate and labor union independent expenditures and electioneering communications.[34] But no regulations governing the activity of independent expenditure–only committees were promulgated before the 2012 elections. Consequently, the rules under which these committees operated were not based on formal regulations; instead, they emerged from the case-by-case advisory opinion process used by the FEC to provide guidance in response to specific queries concerning the application of the law in particular circumstances.[35]

The commission began determining the rules for independent expenditure–only political committees in two advisory opinions issued in July 2010, one in response to a query presented by Club for Growth, which had a PAC that made contributions to candidates, and the second in response to Commonsense Ten, a pro-Democratic PAC that registered with the FEC in June 2010 to make independent expenditures in support of federal candidates.[36] Both organizations wanted to solicit unlimited contributions to pay for independent expenditures. Both also stated that they would not make contributions to candidates and would comply with any relevant disclosure requirements. The major difference between these requests was that Club for Growth was seeking to create a committee that would solicit unlimited contributions solely from individuals, whereas Commonsense Ten was planning to solicit unlimited contributions from individuals, political committees, corporations, and labor organizations that would be deposited into the account it had already established for limited contributions.

The FEC decided that these organizations could proceed with their plans to establish independent expenditure–only committees. These committees could accept unlimited contributions, not only from individuals but also from corporations, labor unions, and political committees. They could not, however, accept contributions from entities that were prohibited from making any contributions in connection with federal elections, which included national banks, federal contractors, foreign nationals, and corporations organized by an act of Congress.[37] The committees would be subject to public disclosure rules and would have to report all contributions and expenditures of $200 or more to the FEC on a regular basis in accordance with the reporting timetables applicable to PACs. The FEC thus gave official recognition to the independent expenditure–only PAC, which quickly came to be known in common parlance as the Super PAC, to distinguish it from a traditional PAC organized principally to make donations to candidates from monies subject to FECA contribution limits.

The FEC's approval of Super PACs begged the question of whether a group had to establish a separate committee devoted to independent expenditures to accept unlimited donations or whether an existing PAC could simply establish a separate bank account for this purpose. This question was presented to the agency in August 2010 in an advisory opinion request submitted by National Defense PAC (NDPAC), a federal PAC that raised money and made contributions to candidates who were military veterans and shared the committee's values.[38] The NDPAC intended to make contributions and independent expenditures in support of candidates. The committee asked the agency if it was permissible to maintain separate bank accounts, one for limited monies that would be used to make contributions to candidates and another for unlimited funds that would be used for independent expenditures, with administrative costs and other expenses allocated between the two accounts. Because both activities were allowed, NDPAC felt "there was no basis to prohibit them from being conducted at the same time by the same committee, provided that they are separately accounted for."[39]

The FEC failed to issue an advisory opinion in response to NDPAC's request, because they could not arrive at an opinion that garnered the necessary four votes.[40] Consequently, Rear Admiral (Ret.) James Carey, the founder and treasurer of NDPAC, went to court to seek approval of the PAC's plan. The District Court for the District of Columbia granted a preliminary injunction to NDPAC that prohibited the FEC from enforcing contribution limits on the funds maintained in the separate account for independent expenditures while the case, *Carey* v. *Federal Election Commission*, was being litigated. In doing so, the court noted that the FEC had not adequately explained in its argument why separate accounts would not satisfy the same objective as separate PACs. The court further stated that NDPAC's proposal would comply with a previous ruling, *EMILY's List* v. *Federal Election Commission*, which had allowed that organization to solicit limited monies for candidate contributions and unlimited monies for other expenditures in connection with federal elections.[41]

Before the case was fully argued in court, the FEC agreed to a stipulated order and consent judgment that allowed NDPAC to maintain separate accounts for limited and unlimited contributions and to pay administrative expenses from both accounts based on the percentage of its financial activity that came from each account (for example, the amount spent on contributions as compared with the amount spent on independent expenditures). In October 2011 the FEC announced that it would allow other nonconnected PACs (that is, PACs that are not affiliated with a corporation or labor union) to establish a separate bank account for contributions to be used for independent expenditures.[42] In this way, the FEC sanctioned a hybrid form of a PAC that allowed some traditional PACs to adopt the organizational characteristics of a Super PAC.[43] In short, the FEC decided that a nonconnected PAC could function as both a traditional PAC and a Super PAC. All that a PAC had to do was maintain separate accounts for monies raised for contributions and monies received for independent expenditures; pay administrative expenses based on the share of financial activity represented by each account; and report the receipts and expenditures in both accounts in accordance with federal PAC disclosure requirements. Hybrid PACs and Super PACs in general are discussed in chapter 7.

The FEC did, however, refuse to extend this option to leadership PACs or other committees affiliated with federal candidates. A leadership PAC is a PAC established by an elected official that can make contributions to other candidates and fund that official's noncampaign expenses, including travel, administrative costs, and consultants. In 2012 there were 456 leadership PACs that made contributions to candidates, including some connected with freshman members.[44] In October 2011 the Constitutional Conservatives Fund, a leadership PAC sponsored and established by Senator Mike Lee of Utah, sought permission to receive unlimited contributions to finance independent expenditures. The PAC made clear that these expenditures would expressly advocate the election or defeat of federal candidates other than Senator Lee, that it would not be coordinated with candidates, and that candidates who benefited from these expenditures would not be involved in fundraising for the PAC's independent expenditure account.

Nonetheless, the FEC told the PAC that it could not solicit unlimited contributions, citing BCRA's ban on soft-money fundraising. In an advisory opinion approved by a 6-0 vote, the commission stated that a leadership PAC by definition is "directly or indirectly established, financed, maintained, or controlled" by a federal officeholder or candidate. Therefore, any fundraising done by the PAC was restricted to funds that were subject to federal contribution limits and source prohibitions, since

BCRA's soft-money ban, which was upheld by the Supreme Court in *McConnell* and "remains valid," covers federal candidates, officeholders, their agents, and any entities they directly or indirectly establish or maintain, or that act on their behalf. That the PAC would use the funds solely to finance independent expenditures for candidates other than Senator Lee did not matter in regard to this prohibition. Accordingly, the PAC was restricted to receiving contributions of no more than $5,000 per donor and was prohibited from accepting corporate and labor union funds.[45]

Ironically, the FEC action that received by far the most public attention during this formative period of Super PAC development was the decision that had the narrowest implications for the future, since it applied to the relatively unique situation of a media personality discussing his Super PAC on his television program. The comedian Stephen Colbert wanted to establish a Super PAC, largely as a vehicle for satirizing the state of campaign finance regulation. Colbert, who was represented by the former FEC chair Trevor Potter, asked the commission whether he could promote his Super PAC on his popular nightly television program, *The Colbert Report*. The key substantive issue in this advisory opinion request was the question of whether any mention or discussion of the Super PAC on the show would constitute in-kind contributions by the program's distributor, Viacom. Colbert also asked whether any such in-kind contributions would be covered by the "press exemption" and thus be exempt from FEC disclosure requirements.[46]

The FEC determined that Colbert could establish a Super PAC and decided that any costs of airtime or production associated with the coverage of the Super PAC or discussion of its activities on Colbert's program would fall under the press exemption and would not have to be reported to the FEC as in-kind contributions. Any costs incurred by Viacom in providing services to the PAC in other settings—for example, producing independent advertisements to be distributed outside of the show or as paid advertisements on other shows or networks—would be considered in-kind contributions that had to be reported. Viacom would also be required to report any costs incurred to administer the Super PAC, if these costs were not paid from committee receipts.[47] With these answers to his queries, Colbert established a Super PAC named Americans for a Better Tomorrow, Tomorrow. He regularly discussed the PAC on his show to highlight issues in campaign finance, particularly the inefficacy of contribution limits and disclosure requirements.[48]

Debating the Ground Rules

Super PACs began to form quickly once the FEC issued its initial guidance and established a procedure for registering such committees. By the time of the 2010 election, eighty-three Super PACs had registered with the FEC and reported having raised $85 million and spent more than $65 million on independent expenditures supporting or opposing federal candidates.[49] The top spender was American Crossroads, a conservative Super PAC organized with the assistance of the Republican strategist and former George W. Bush White House chief of staff Karl Rove, which financed $21 million of independent expenditures. American Crossroads also established an associated 501(c)(4) nonprofit organization, Crossroads GPS, which reported an additional $17 million in spending.[50] Other top-spending Super PACs included America's Families First Action Fund, a liberal organization that supported Democrats in House races, which reported $6 million of independent expenditures; Club for Growth Action, $5 million; National Education Association Advocacy Fund, $4.2 million; and Commonsense Ten, $3.3 million.[51]

By late spring 2011, hundreds of Super PACs were being established. These included another variant, candidate-specific Super PACs, which were created to support particular candidates and essentially act as parallel, albeit independent, campaign committees for those candidates. In most instances, these committees were established by a former staff member, political adviser, or associate of the candidate supported by the group (see chapter 7). By the end of the year, at least one candidate-specific Super PAC had been created for each of the major presidential contenders. These committees provided donors with a means of giving unlimited contributions to help their preferred candidate. They thereby eviscerated the functional meaningfulness of the contribution limits imposed on candidate campaign committees. A donor who gave the maximum to a presidential candidate could continue to help simply by contributing to the Super PAC focused on electing that candidate.

The most important restriction imposed on Super PACs was the prohibition against coordinating their activities with candidates or party committees. Under FEC regulations, these committees had to operate independently of the candidates or parties. Any coordinated election activities would be considered in-kind contributions and would violate the proviso that allowed a political committee to qualify as a Super PAC. Although these regulations prohibit certain interactions between candidates and independent political committees, they do not prohibit all inter-action: they do not require an independent committee to be wholly independent of a candidate. This aspect of the FEC's coordination rules has been a matter of controversy for years, so it is not surprising that the scope of permissible interaction between Super PACs and candidates became an issue that led to a number of requests for FEC rulings.

In July 2011, Majority PAC (the new name of the committee established as Commonsense Ten) and House Majority PAC, two Super PACs formed to support Democratic Senate and House candidates, asked the commission if federal officeholders, candidates, and national party officials could solicit contributions on their behalf or at least participate in their fundraising efforts.[52] In rendering its judgment, the commission again relied on the BCRA ban on soft-money fundraising, which it noted was "not disturbed by either *Citizens United* or *SpeechNow*."[53] The opinion also cited the FEC regulations adopted in April 2010 to implement BCRA's fundraising prohibition, which allow federal candidates or officeholders to attend, speak at, or be featured guests at nonfederal fundraising events at which funds outside the amount limitations and source prohibitions of FECA are solicited. The regulations explicitly state that federal candidates and officeholders may appear at such events, so long as they solicit only funds that comply with federal limits.[54] But the regulations did not explicitly cover federal fundraising events where a committee was raising money that would directly benefit federal candidates or officeholders, including, most likely, a candidate participating at an event. The FEC treated this as a distinction without a difference and unanimously affirmed that a federal officeholder, candidate, or national party official could speak at, attend, or be a featured guest at Super PAC fundraisers and events, so long as the federal official did not solicit contributions of more than $5,000, in accordance with BCRA's ban on soft-money fundraising by federal candidates and party leaders.

The FEC's decision revealed how porous the line between an "independent" committee and a candidate could be for practical purposes. Candidates or other campaign officials, as well as elected officials, were allowed to attend Super PAC fundraisers, meet with donors or prospective donors, give stump speeches, and even have their pictures taken with donors. So long as the candidate or party leader left the "asking" to someone else, such participation was permissible under federal law. Super PACs were thus allowed to essentially conduct fundraisers in the same manner as candidate or party committees, with only a slight variation.

If a candidate could appear at a Super PAC fundraiser, would a joint fundraising effort be permissible? Candidates often engage in joint fundraising efforts with party committees that are designed to raise money for both a candidate's campaign committee and national and state party committees. Could a Super PAC participate in joint fundraising efforts with a candidate or other committees? The American Future Fund (AFF), a 501(c)(4) organization, asked the FEC if it and its PAC, American Future Fund Political Action (AFFPA), could participate in joint fundraising efforts that would involve other organizations, including candidate committees and AFFPA's separate independent expenditure account.[55]

The FEC prepared two draft advisory opinions, both indicating that any joint fundraising effort that includes a candidate as a participant may not also include a Super PAC or 501(c) organization that is raising unlimited funds. Joint fundraising efforts involving AFF, AFFPA, and its Super PAC account would be allowed, but involvement of a federal candidate's campaign committee would not. Because a joint fundraising committee is an organization that is directly or indirectly established by a candidate, or acts on behalf of a candidate, a committee involving a candidate's campaign is subject to the fundraising restrictions imposed by BCRA, which means that only funds subject to federal contribution limits and prohibitions may be solicited or received. Under these draft opinions, joint fundraising efforts that include solicitations for unlimited contributions or corporate and labor contributions could not include a candidate. Joint fundraising efforts conducted by PACs, Super PACs, and other entities not registered with the FEC, however, would be permitted.[56] Before the FEC reached a decision on an opinion, AFF withdrew the portions of its request that proposed candidate involvement in its joint fundraising efforts. On the remaining questions concerning joint fundraising efforts involving Super PACs, the FEC deadlocked, and no advisory opinion was issued to resolve the question.

American Crossroads' request for permission to work with elected officials on issue advertisements proved to be even more controversial. In October 2011 American Crossroads sought permission to air broadcast ads featuring incumbent members of Congress who were up for reelection in 2012 and who would be discussing policy issues in the ads. The committee was explicit in noting that the planned ads would be "fully coordinated" with these members of Congress, would echo candidates' campaign themes or be "thematically similar" to the candidates' own campaign ads, and would be designed to "improve the public's percep-tion" of these candidates. However, the ads would not meet the "content standard" of FEC coordination rules because they would not include express advocacy, would not be aired close to an election during the "electioneering communications" period, and would not include previ-ously distributed campaign material.[57] Basically, American Crossroads asked whether a Super PAC could work with members of Congress on issue ads without violating FEC coordination rules and requiring the pay-ments for these ads to be treated as coordinated expenditures. They fur-ther inquired whether the payments for these ads would be treated as in-kind contributions to these candidates and if the production of such ads would limit Crossroads' ability to make independent expenditures in sup-port of the featured elected officials in the future.

The FEC failed to answer these questions. The commissioners proved to be deeply divided on the issue of whether a Super PAC could coordi-nate with candidates on issue advertisements and on the question of whether such ads would constitute a contribution. The result was a 3-3 deadlock, with the commissioners again dividing along partisan lines on the question of how the regulations and provisions of FECA should be applied in the case. The Democrats felt that the ads should be considered a contribution and therefore be prohibited because American Crossroads stated that the ads were intended to "improve the public's perception of the featured member of Congress in advance of the 2012 campaign sea-son."[58] The Republican members argued that the group's intent was not relevant and that the Democratic members were clinging to an interpre-tation of the coordination rules that had been rejected when the revised rules were adopted in 2010.[59] As a result, no opinion was issued, and Crossroads did not make the proposed ads.

Similarly, in February 2012, the commissioners disagreed on another matter involving advertising and the activities of American Crossroads. In this instance, the issue was the Super PAC's use of campaign materials taken from a publicly available website. But instead of arising from an advi-sory opinion request, the issue came before the FEC as an enforcement mat-ter generated by a complaint filed by the Ohio Democratic Party. The Ohio Democrats alleged that American Crossroads had made an excessive in-kind contribution to the 2010 Portman for Senate Committee by including several snippets of committee film footage in its ads supporting Rob Port-man for election to the Senate. The footage had been obtained from two YouTube videos, one posted by the Portman for Senate Committee that showed the candidate and his family on the campaign trail, and the other posted by "robportman" entitled "Portman's Statewide Jobs Tour."[60] American Crossroads included brief snippets from these videos as part of the content of an ad supporting Portman, which they aired at a cost of more than $450,000.[61]

As in the case of the Crossroads advisory opinion request on issue ads, three commissioners argued that the use of these campaign materials should be considered a "contribution" because "republication" of campaign materials is considered an in-kind contribution to a campaign.[62] Because Super PACs are prohibited from making contributions to candidates, these three commissioners felt there was reason to believe that a violation of the law had occurred and an enforcement proceeding was warranted. The three Republican commissioners disagreed, arguing that FEC precedents allowed the use of photographs and other brief snippets of material drawn from a candidate's website that was "open to the world," without counting such material as a campaign donation. Furthermore, there was no evidence that American Crossroads had coordinated its ads with the Portman campaign or republished campaign materials; it had not repeated verbatim the Portman campaign's message but rather had created one of its own.[63] These commissioners contended that there was no indication that a violation had occurred. Since four votes are needed for a finding that might lead to an enforcement action, no further action was taken on the matter.

As these latter controversies indicate, the FEC was deeply divided along partisan lines on a number of the issues concerning Super PAC activity. The agency thus failed to issue clear guidance on some of the particular activities Super PACs might undertake. The agency did give form and sanction to this new type of federal committee, and it drew some clear lines by prohibiting leadership Super PACs and the solicitation of contributions to Super PACs by federal officeholders, candidates, and national party officials. But a number of the central issues regarding Super PACs were not resolved. Most important, the specific circumstances in which a political organization would have to register as a Super PAC, the level of independence these committees must maintain in their interactions with candidates, particularly with respect to non-express-advocacy activities, and the use of candidate campaign materials retrieved from public websites arguably remain unsettled.

In 2012, Super PACs capitalized on the lenient rules applied to their activities. The most active committees raised most of their funding from six- and seven-figure contributions that greatly exceeded the maximum amounts established for contributions to candidates and party committees (see chapter 7).[64] Some committees, particularly candidate-specific committees and those established to act as partisan operations to abet party efforts in congressional races, invited elected officials to their fundraising events. These committees did not pursue the types of interactions on which the FEC did not issue guidance, such as coordinated efforts on issue ads or other non-election-related activities. But that does not mean that Super PACs may not do so in the future.

Because the FEC deadlocked on some key questions, these queries are likely to be presented to the commission again, perhaps after a change in commission members. Or political actors may decide to undertake actions without seeking FEC opinion (as was the case in the formation of candidate-specific committees). Advisory opinions from the FEC offer a form of safe-harbor guidance for actions taken in specific circumstances; they do not have the force of regulations or statutory law. How Super PACs will adjust to the regulatory uncertainty in future elections remains to be seen. One response would be to accept the FEC's failure to issue an advisory opinion as an indication that a proposed action was not approved and therefore not permitted. Another interpretation would be that the FEC did not find a proposed action in violation of the rules and thus it was permissible. The willingness of a group or organization to test the limits of the law may therefore dictate the future path of Super PAC activities. Given the divisions within the commission over the interpretation of the law, it is likely that the rules will continue to be tested and challenged by political actors in the years ahead.

The Diminishing Scope of Disclosure

Super PACs offered donors an easy way to give unlimited amounts in support of a candidate. These donors also had the option of giving to a 527 committee or 501(c) organization, since these groups also operate outside the constraints of federal contribution limits. Although an analysis of the reasons why donors chose one alternative over another is beyond the scope of this chapter, the diverse disclosure requirements applied to different types of organizations were certainly one factor that influenced donor behavior.

Like candidates, parties, and PACs, Super PACs are required to report their contributions and expenditures to the FEC. Section 527 committees are also required to disclose their contributions and expenditures. These committees, which are political committees that are not registered with the FEC, report their finances to the IRS in accordance with the law adopted in 2000 that first imposed disclosure requirements on these organizations. Any 527 with gross annual receipts of $25,000 must report all contributions of $200 or more and any expenditures of $500 or more.[65]

Tax-exempt 501(c) organizations are not required to publicly disclose all of their finances because political activity is not their principal purpose. These organizations are allowed to spend a portion of their funds on political activity, with the exception of 501(c)(3) charitable organizations. Charitable organizations are prohibited under tax law from intervening in candidate elections.[66] This prohibition is a trade-off for the tax benefit given to charities: they are not only tax-exempt, but donations made to these organizations are generally tax-deductible for the donor. Consequently, 501(c)(3)s are typically not involved in financing candidate-related election activities.

Section 501(c)(4) social welfare organizations, as well as labor unions organized under 501(c)(5) and trade associations under 501(c)(6), are allowed to raise and spend money on election activities, so long as this is not the organization's primary purpose. How much an organization may spend on political activity is a matter of great debate. Section 501(c)(4) of Title 26 of the U.S. Code states that these organizations are "not organized for profit but *operated exclusively* for the promotion of social welfare."[67] But the regulations adopted by the IRS in implementing the statute note that "an organization is operated exclusively for the promotion of social welfare if it is *primarily engaged* in promoting in some way the common good and general welfare of the people of the community."[68] The courts have interpreted the statute to mean that an organization may not engage in more than an insubstantial amount of political activity.[69] However, what constitutes an insubstantial amount has never been clearly defined by the IRS. Generally, practitioners assume that an organization must limit its spending on activities that fall outside its principal purpose to a minor share of its budget. How much an organization might spend on political activity thus varies widely and can range from less than 10 percent of total spending to more than 40 percent, depending on the budgetary choices made by an organization and the aggressiveness of its approach with respect to the law.

Since 501(c)s do not have to publicly disclose all the monies they raise and spend on political activity, it is not surprising that these organizations became a popular alternative to Super PACs. Donors who wanted to give large sums yet remain anonymous could do so by giving to a tax-exempt group. A number of groups and political operatives that formed Super PACs thus established affiliated 501(c)(4)s to offer donors this option. These committees did, however, have to disclose to the FEC the monies they spent on independent expenditures and electioneering communications. In *Citizens United*, the court strongly affirmed this requirement and expected that these contributions and expenditures would be disclosed to the public. But this expectation was not fully realized owing to action taken by the FEC that substantially weakened the disclosure rules.

FEC Actions on Disclosure

In 2007 the FEC adopted revised disclosure regulations for electioneering communications. Before these new rules were instituted, those who made electioneering communications had to disclose their donors in one of two ways: They could either report all donors who gave $1,000 or more in a calendar year or, if a separate bank account was established for electioneering communications, they were required to report only those persons who gave $1,000 or more to that separate account. The revised regulations significantly narrowed the requirements for donor disclosure by requiring that only those who made a contribution specifically "for the purpose of furthering electioneering communications" had to be reported.[70] The commission adopted this standard based on the rules for independent expenditures, which required spenders who were not federal political committees to disclose donors who made a contribution "for the purposes of furthering an independent expenditure."[71]

In justifying this revision, the commission highlighted the changed circumstances created by the Supreme Court's decision in *Wisconsin Right to Life*. This decision allowed corporations and labor unions, as well as other organizations, to finance communications before an election that were not considered the functional equivalent of express advocacy and thus did not qualify as electioneering communications. Because corporations and labor unions receive funds through a variety of means, the Court's decision raised the regulatory issue of how to separate and track the sources of the monies used to finance electioneering communications for purposes of disclosure. The commission resolved this issue by restricting disclosure to those donors who had specifically given money for electioneering communications. As the commission explained,

> In the Commission's judgment, requiring disclosure of funds received only from those persons who donated specifically for the purpose of furthering ECs [electioneering communications] appropriately provides the public with information about those persons who actually support the message conveyed by the ECs without imposing on corporations and labor organizations the significant burden of disclosing the identities of the vast numbers of customers, investors, or members, who have provided funds for purposes entirely unrelated to the making of ECs.[72]

The FEC might have resolved this difficulty by requiring these organizations to establish a separate, disclosed account for electioneering communications. But instead, it chose to restrict disclosure in a way that made it possible for groups that made electioneering communications to report the amounts they spent but not the sources of their funding.

Furthermore, at least three of the six commissioners indicated that disclosure of a donor would be required only if a donor gave money for a specific electioneering communication, not just for the general purpose of furthering such communications. The three Republican commissioners expressed this understanding of the law in 2010 in response to a complaint filed by the Democratic Congressional Campaign Committee (DCCC) against the conservative 501(c)(4) Freedom's Watch. The DCCC sought an enforcement action against the group, alleging that Freedom's Watch had violated the law by financing electioneering communications in the 2008 election without disclosing its sources of funding, specifically casino mogul Sheldon Adelson, who was the group's principal financier.[73] The FEC did not find reason to believe that a violation had occurred and dismissed the complaint. In dismissing the complaint, the Republican commissioners issued a statement explaining their reasoning in which they noted that disclosure would be required if a donor gave to finance a specific expenditure that had to be reported.[74] In short, if a donor gave to finance a particular ad or communication, then that donation would have to be disclosed. A contribution made for general purposes such as paying for ads by the group generally or without specifically designating how it should be spent would not need to be disclosed.

Not surprisingly, advocates of BCRA opposed the FEC's revised regulations. Representative Chris Van Hollen, a leading advocate of campaign finance regulation, filed suit in April 2011 against the FEC, contending that the agency's interpretation of the disclosure requirement was contrary to the clear intent of the law.[75] The district court agreed and invalidated the regulation limiting the disclosure of donors for electioneering communications. In the view of the court, BCRA required those who make electioneering communications to disclose all contributors, and there were no terms limiting disclosure to those who give for the purpose of furthering a specific communication.

The FEC did not appeal the district court decision, but two nonprofit groups that had intervened in the case, Hispanic Leadership Fund and the Center for Individual Freedom, did. In September 2012, the D.C. Circuit Court reversed the lower court decision and reinstated the FEC's disclosure regulation.[76] The court also remanded part of the case to the lower court to consider Van Hollen's argument that the FEC had acted in an arbitrary and capricious manner in adopting the revised rules.[77] This aspect of the litigation was not decided before the 2012 election. Thus the narrower disclosure rules remained in effect.

The consequences of the FEC's regulatory decision relating to disclosure were apparent in the 2010 elections. The new rules significantly undermined the efficacy of disclosure requirements. In 2010 close to half of the $298 million in spending disclosed by organized groups did not include information about their sources of funding.[78] An analysis of FEC reports conducted by Public Citizen, a public interest group, revealed that of the 308 groups, excluding party committees, that reported spending money in the 2010 federal elections, only 166 (53.9 percent) provided any information about the sources of the funding. Moreover, of the fifty-three groups that reported expenditures on electioneering communications, only eighteen (34 percent) disclosed the donors who provided the money for these expenditures. This represented a significant difference from 2006, when thirty of the thirty-one groups that reported electioneering communications disclosed their sources of funding, or 2004, when forty-six of the forty-seven groups that reported such communications disclosed their donors.[79] In short, organizations quickly began to adapt their disclosure practices to less restrictive disclosure rules, thereby establishing the approach that most nonprofit organizations would follow in 2012.

Conclusion

The regulatory developments that occurred between the 2008 and 2012 elections exposed the diminished efficacy of what remained of the Watergate reforms that defined the modern campaign finance system. The hallmark of these reforms—the presidential public funding system—has become irrelevant as a means of financing presidential campaigns. The contribution limits imposed on candidates have become increasingly meaningless as a tool for limiting the influence of wealthy donors, since these donors have a variety of means available to give unlimited sums in support of candidates, most notably, by making contributions to Super PACs, which can essentially function as surrogate campaign organizations for candidates. The rise of Super PACs has effectively ended the contribution limits imposed on PACs, although any contributions these committees make to candidates must still come from limited monies. The spending restrictions on corporations and labor unions have been struck down, but the ban on corporate and labor contributions to candidates and parties remains in place.

The rules on disclosure still ensure transparency for the financial activity of candidates, parties, and PACs, but the finances of other organizations have become more opaque. In particular, 501(c) organizations find it increasingly easy to avoid public disclosure of their sources of funding. In previous presidential election cycles, the disclosure rules failed to cover the financial activity of 501(c) organizations that spent funds on election-related activity that did not qualify as candidate advocacy or electioneering communications. In advance of the 2012 election cycle, BCRA's extension of disclosure to electioneering communications had been rolled back by the FEC, despite the Supreme Court's support of this requirement.[80] Groups that spend money in this way can easily avoid disclosing their donors, since contributions given to further specific communications are rare. Donors typically do not specify particular purposes for their contributions, and ads are typically developed and broadcast well after contributions are received. Consequently, most of the money raised to finance electioneering communications is now undisclosed, and the same rationale used to keep these donors anonymous—that their contributions are not made to explicitly further a particular communication—can also be applied to the monies raised to pay for independent expenditures.

The transparency of campaign money has also been diminished by practices that are becoming more commonplace. Many of the organizations that are free to spend money directly to support candidates are established under generic names such as American Action Network, American Future Fund, Americans for Job Security, and Americans for Prosperity, which give voters little information about the interests that support their activities. Those that are required to disclose, such as Super

PACs and 527s, can obscure the sources of at least some of their financial support by accepting contributions from other organizations, such as 501(c)(4)s or trade associations, so that the donor in the first instance remains hidden from public view. This is particularly true in the case of Super PACs with affiliated nonprofit organizations. With this structure, the nonprofit organization can raise money from donors who are not disclosed, and then make unlimited donations to the Super PAC, which needs only to report the contribution as a donation from the nonprofit. For example, in 2012, the nonprofit FreedomWorks gave $2.6 million to FreedomWorks for America, its affiliated Super PAC.[81] The original sources of this large sum remained hidden from the public.

The changes that took place in advance of the 2012 election thus gave form to the post–*Citizens United* regulatory environment by reinforcing and solidifying two distinct, yet thinly separated, spheres of financial activity, one in which contributions are limited, the other in which they are not. Candidates and parties operate in the limited sphere. Super PACs, tax-exempt organizations, and other nonparty independent political groups operate in the unlimited sphere. Within this unlimited sphere, groups can establish complex organizational structures that facilitate the solicitation of disclosed and undisclosed contributions. They may accept contributions in amounts and from sources that are prohibited for candidates and parties, and they may spend these funds to directly advocate the election of a candidate or indirectly support the election of a candidate. They may also work closely with other independent groups, since there are no restrictions on coordination among groups, allowing them to mount coordinated campaigns in support of candidates or shared interests.

The rules have thus developed in a way that offers major advantages to nonparty organizations. As a result, these groups, rather than the parties, are responsible for a rapidly growing share of the financial activity that takes place in elections, and the amounts of undisclosed funding are increasing at a significant pace. This pattern is likely to continue so long as these groups have a strong incentive to participate in electoral politics. For the rules now permit financial practices that were supposed to end with the adoption of FECA in 1974 and BCRA in 2002. The law has entered a new stage in its evolution, one that raises the question of whether an effective system of financial regulation capable of limiting the influence of wealthy interests and ensuring full transparency is possible, given the current state of the law.

Notes

1. *Citizens United* v. *Federal Election Commission*, 130 S. Ct. 876 (2010).

2. Congress prohibited any expenditures by corporations or labor unions in connection with federal elections under the provisions of the 1947 Taft-Hartley Act (61 Stat. 136 [1947]). For background, see Robert E. Mutch, *Campaigns, Congress, and Courts: The Making of Federal Campaign Finance Law* (New York: Praeger, 1988), pp. 154–59.

3. 26 U.S.C. sec. 527(e)2.

4. *Citizens United* v. *Federal Election Commission*.

5. Federal Election Commission, *Coordinated Communications and Independent Expenditures*, June 2007 (updated January 2013) (www.fec.gov/pages/brochures/indexp.shtml#CC). See also *Code of Federal Regulations* 11, sec. 109.21.

6. In 2012 a national party could spend $21.7 million in coordination with its presidential nominee, up to $2.5 million in a Senate race (depending on a state's voting-age population), and $45,600 in a House race ($91,200 in a state with only one representative). See Federal Election Commission, "2012 Coordinated Expenditure Limits" (www.fec.gov/info/charts_441ad_2012.shtml).

7. 2 U.S.C. sec. 434(c)(1).

8. For background and detailed discussion of the case, see Anthony Corrado, "The Regulatory Environment of the 2008 Elections," in *Financing the 2008 Election*, edited by David B. Magleby and Anthony Corrado (Brookings, 2011), pp. 57–64.

9. Charitable organizations established under section 501(c)(3) of the tax code are not allowed to support candidates. Contributions from foreign nationals who do not have permanent residence in the United States (that is, do not have a green card) are not permitted in federal, state, or local elections. National banks, federal contractors, and corporations organized by an act of Congress are also prohibited from making contributions in federal elections.

10. *Citizens United*, 898.

11. Ibid., 899.

12. *Buckley* v. *Valeo*, 424 U.S. 1 (1976); *Citizens United*, 909.

13. *McConnell* v. *Federal Election Commission*, 540 U.S. 93 (2003).

14. *Citizens United*, 914, 916.

15. *Western Tradition Partnership* v. *Attorney General of Montana*, 211 MT 238, p. 222–23.

16. *American Tradition Partnership* v. *Bullock*, 132 S. Ct. 2490 (2012).

17. For a discussion of the role of 527 committees in recent elections, see Allan J. Cigler, "Interest Groups and the Financing of the 2004 Elections," in *Financing the 2004 Election*, edited by David B. Magleby, Anthony Corrado, and Kelly D. Patterson (Brookings, 2006), pp. 222–34; and Allan Cigler, "Interest Groups and

the Financing of the 2008 Elections," in *Financing the 2008 Election*, edited by Magleby and Corrado, pp. 269–80.

18. *Federal Election Commission* v. *Wisconsin Right to Life*, 551 U.S. 449 (2007). For a discussion of this case, see Corrado, "The Regulatory Environment of the 2008 Elections," pp. 54–57.

19. *SpeechNow.org* v. *Federal Election Commission*, 599 F.3d 686 (D.C. Cir. 2010).

20. Federal Election Commission, Advisory Opinion Request 2007-32.

21. This is the financial threshold specified in federal law that triggers the need to register as a political committee with the FEC.

22. Federal Election Commission, "Ongoing Litigation: *SpeechNow.org* v. *Federal Election Commission*" (www.fec.gov/law/litigation/speechnow.shtml# dc_dc_docs).

23. This litigation began with the filing of two separate complaints, one by SpeechNow and another, *Keating* v. *Federal Election Commission*, filed by David Keating, who declared his intention to contribute more than $5,000 to Speech-Now. The cases were combined and heard as one case by the court.

24. *Buckley* v. *Valeo*, 26–29.

25. Memorandum Order, *SpeechNow.org* v. *Federal Election Commission*, case no. 08-9248, July 1, 2008, p. 18 (www.fec.gov/law/litigation/speechnow_ order_deny_pi.pdf); *McConnell* v. *Federal Election Commission*, 153.

26. Ibid., p. 19.

27. *SpeechNow.org* v. *Federal Election Commission*, p. 693.

28. Ibid., p. 695.

29. Ibid., p. 697.

30. Ibid., p. 698.

31. Ibid., p. 699.

32. The FEC deadlocked on two 3-3 votes on draft notices of proposed rule-making at its January 20, 2011, meeting. Two draft notices of proposed rule-making were considered at its June 15, 2011, meeting, one failing on a 2-4 vote, the other on a 3-3 vote.

33. The Federal Election Commission is a nonpartisan agency whose members are nominated by the president and subject to Senate approval. But soon after its establishment, Democrats and Republicans began an informal practice of ensuring that the membership consisted of three members of each party. For background, see Brooks Jackson, *Broken Promise: Why the Federal Election Commission Failed* (New York: Priority Press, 1990), pp. 23–37, and Project FEC Task Force, *No Bark, No Bite, No Point: The Case for Closing the Federal Election Commission and Establishing a New System for Enforcing the Nation's Campaign Finance Laws* (Washington:: Democracy 21 Education Fund, April 2002) (www.democracy21.org/uploads/%7BB4BE5C24-65EA-4910-974C-759644EC 0901%7D.pdf).

34. Federal Election Commission, "Independent Expenditures and Election-eering Communications by Corporations and Labor Organizations," *Federal Register* 248 (December 27, 2011), 80803.

35. For background on the issues associated with the emergence of Super PACs, see Richard Briffault, "Super PACs," *Minnesota Law Review* 96, no. 5 (2012), pp. 1629–78, and R. Sam Garrett, *Super PACs in Federal Elections: Overview and Issues for Congress*, Congressional Research Service Report, R42042, April 4, 2013.

36. Federal Election Commission, Advisory Opinions 2010-09 and 2010-11.

37. FEC, Advisory Opinion 2010-11. See also 2 U.S.C. secs. 441b(a), 441c, and 441e.

38. Federal Election Commission, Advisory Opinion Request 2010-20.

39. Ibid., p. 4.

40. Memorandum Opinion on Motion for Preliminary Injunction, *Carey* v. *Federal Election Commission*, Civil Action No. 11-259-RM (D. D.C.), p. 6.

41. *EMILY's List* v. *Federal Election Commission*, 581 F.3d 1 (D.C. Cir. 2009); Memorandum Opinion, *Carey*, pp. 8–14.

42. Federal Election Commission, "FEC Statement on *Carey* v. *Federal Election Commission*: Reporting Guidance for Political Committees That Maintain a Non-Contribution Account," press release, October 5, 2011.

43. Alex Knott, "FEC Relaxes Donation Rules for Hybrid PACs," *Roll Call*, October 5, 2011 (www.rollcall.com/news/fec_relaxes_donation_rules_hybrid_pacs-209249-1.html); R. Sam Garrett, "Super PACs in Federal Elections: Overview and Issues for Congress," Congressional Research Service (April 4, 2013), p. 23.

44. The number of leadership PACs is based on the summary prepared by the Center for Responsive Politics (www.opensecrets.org/pacs/industry.php?txt=Q03 &cycle=2012).

45. Federal Election Commission, Advisory Opinion 2011-21, pp. 3–4.

46. Federal Election Commission, Advisory Opinion Request 2011-11.

47. Federal Election Commission, Advisory Opinion 2011-11.

48. R. Sam Garrett, "Seriously Funny: Understanding Campaign Finance Policy through the Colbert Super PAC," *Saint Louis University Law Journal* 56, no. 3 (2012): 711–23.

49. Briffault, "Super PACs," pp. 1656–57.

50. Based on data compiled by the Center for Responsive Politics, "2010 Outside Spending, by Group," 2010 (www.opensecrets.org/outsidespending/summ.php?cycle=2010&chrt=V&disp=O&type=A).

51. Ibid.

52. Federal Election Commission, Advisory Opinion 2011-12.

53. Ibid., p. 4.

54. See Federal Election Commission, "Final Rules for 11 CFR 300.64: Participation by Federal Candidates and Officeholders at Nonfederal Fundraising Events," *Federal Register* 75 (May 5, 2010), p. 24375.

55. Federal Election Commission, Advisory Opinion Request 2012-25.

56. See, for example, Federal Election Commission, Advisory Opinion 2012-25, Draft A, Agenda Document 412-69, September 28, 2012 (http://saos.nictusa.com/saos/searchao;jsessionid=88720FA3FAF4E791A46AC9312E6D2A0D?SUBMIT=continue&PAGE_NO=-1).

57. Federal Election Commission, Advisory Opinion Request 2011-23, pp. 1 and 3.

58. FEC, Advisory Opinion 2011-23 (American Crossroads), Statement of Chair Cynthia L. Bauerly and Commissioner Ellen L. Weintraub, December 1, 2011, p. 1 (www.fec.gov/members/former_members/bauerly/statements/AO_2011-23_American_Crossroads_CLB_ELW_Statement.pdf). See also T. W. Farnam, "FEC Fails to Make Ruling on 'Super PAC' Advertising Issue," *Washington Post*, December 1, 2011.

59. FEC, Advisory Opinion 2011-23 (American Crossroads), Statement of Vice Chair Caroline C. Hunter and Commissioners Donald F. McGahn and Matthew S. Petersen, December 1, 2011 (www.fec.gov/members/statements/AO_2011-23_Crossroads_Statement.pdf).

60. Federal Election Commission, Matter under Review 6357, Statement of Reasons, Chair Caroline C. Hunter and Commissioners Donald F. McGahn and Matthew S. Petersen, February 22, 2012 (http://eqs.nictusa.com/eqsdocsMUR/12044312281.pdf), p. 2.

61. Kenneth P. Doyle, "FEC Deadlocks 3-3 on Ruling Whether Super PAC's Ads Copied Campaign Ads," *Bureau of National Affairs Money & Politics Report*, February 28, 2012.

62. Ibid.

63. FEC, Matter under Review 6357, pp. 3–5.

64. Anthony Corrado, "The Money Race: A New Era of Unlimited Funding?," in *Campaigning for President 2012*, edited by Dennis W. Johnson (New York: Routledge, 2013), p. 74.

65. Public Law 106-230, 114 Stat. 477. See Anthony Corrado, "Money and Politics: A History of Federal Campaign Finance Law," *The New Campaign Finance Sourcebook*, edited by Anthony Corrado and others (Brookings, 2005), pp. 34–35.

66. See 26 U.S.C. secs. 01(c)(3) and 501(h).

67. Ibid., 501(c)(4), emphasis added.

68. *Code of Federal Regulations* 26, sec. 1.501(c)(4)-1(a)(2)(i) (2013), emphasis added.

69. See *Better Business Bureau* v. *United States*, 326 U.S. 279 (1945), and *Easter House* v. *United States*, 12 Ct. Cl. 476 (1987).

70. *Code of Federal Regulations* 11, sec. 104.20(c)(9) (2013).

71. Federal Election Commission, "Explanation and Justification for Final Rules on Electioneering Communications," *Federal Register* 72 (December 26, 2007), 72899, p. 72911.

72. Ibid.

73. Federal Election Commission, Matter under Review 6002, Re: Complaint against Freedom's Watch, Inc. (http://eqs.nictusa.com/eqsdocsMUR/10044 272034.pdf).

74. Ibid., In the Matter of Freedom's Watch, Inc., Statement of Reasons of Chairman Matthew S. Petersen and Commissioners Caroline C. Hunter and Donald F. McGahn, August 13, 2010 (http://eqs.nictusa.com/eqsdocsMUR/10044 274536.pdf).

75. *Van Hollen* v. *Federal Election Commission*, No. 11-cv-00766 (D.D.C.).

76. *Van Hollen* v. *Federal Election Commission*, No. 12-5118 (D.C. Cir.). See also Federal Election Commission, "Ongoing Litigation: *Van Hollen* v. *Federal Election Commission*" (www.fec.gov/law/litigation/van_hollen.shtml).

77. *Center for Individual Freedom and Hispanic Leadership Fund* v. *Van Hollen*, No. 12-5117 (D.C. Cir).

78. Megan R. Wilson, "Who's Buying This Election? Close to Half the Money Fueling Outside Ads Comes from Undisclosed Donors," Center for Responsive Politics, *OpenSecrets*, November 2, 2010 (www.opensecrets.org/news/2010/11/whos-buying-this-election.html).

79. Public Citizen, *Disclosure Eclipse*, November 18, 2010 (www.citizen.org/documents/Eclipsed-Disclosure11182010.pdf).

80. *McConnell*, 197.

81. This figure is based on the contributions reported in FreedomWorks for America's FEC disclosure filings as reported by the Center for Responsive Politics. See Center for Responsive Politics, "FreedomWorks: Donor Detail" (www.open secrets.org/outsidespending/donor_detail.php?cycle=2012&id=FreedomWorks& type=O&super=S).

THREE

Financing the 2012 Presidential Nomination Campaigns

JOHN C. GREEN, MICHAEL E. KOHLER,
AND IAN P. SCHWARBER

Although the 2012 election set new federal campaign finance records (see chapter 1), spending for the presidential nominations was less than it had been in 2008. The principal reason for this decline was the uncontested Democratic nomination. However, President Obama spent markedly more in real terms than President George W. Bush did during his uncontested nomination in 2004 ($441 million for Obama and $311 million for Bush, in 2012 dollars). Republican candidate spending in 2012 was also down from 2008 in real terms, although the eventual 2012 GOP nominee, Mitt Romney, spent $47 million more than his 2008 counterpart, John McCain.[1]

Overall expenditures in the 2012 presidential nomination campaign were influenced by two novel features: an almost complete absence of public funds (and associated restraints on spending) and the presence of new Super PACs aligned with the major candidates (a new source of spending). This new and expanded funding linked with the candidates did not fully make up for the decline in 2012 candidate nomination spending.[2] But this pattern of private cash and Super PACs is likely to intensify in 2016, when both parties will have open presidential contests.

Rules, Rivals, and Resources

Federal campaign finance laws, the structure of competition, and the availability of resources all had a bearing on presidential nomination finance in 2012. On the first count, federal court rulings in 2010, beginning with *Citizens United* v. *Federal Election Commission*, allowed for unlimited donations to Super PACs. On the second count, only the Republicans had a competitive primary season, ultimately generating a financial advantage for President Obama. And on the third count, close supporters of the major candidates in both parties organized Super PACs.

Rules

Presidential campaign finance is governed by federal statutes, interpreted by the federal courts, and implemented by the Federal Election Commission (see chapter 2). The result is two sets of rules in presidential campaigns: contingent regulations that apply to candidates who voluntarily accept public financing and mandatory regulations that apply to all federal candidates.[3]

In 2012 contingent finance regulations had little direct impact because both major candidates refused public financing. This refusal was the culmination of a sixteen-year trend of increasing nonparticipation by presidential candidates in the public finance system.[4] But the complete absence of public financing for the major candidates was itself a factor in 2012, eliminating restraints on spending associated with the system. This lack of restraint allowed both major party nominees, especially President Obama, to deploy a more comprehensive finance strategy.

A key element of mandatory finance regulations is limits on contributions to candidates (see chapter 2). In 2012, for example, the maximum individual donation to a candidate was $2,500 per election, for a total of $5,000 in a given primary and general election. These limits help define a threefold division in the election calendar for purposes of nomination finances: a primary season, a bridge period, and a general election campaign.

The primary season includes the calendar year preceding the nomination contests and concludes when active competition ceases. The 2012 primary season officially began January 1, 2011, and ended in the spring of 2012. Traditionally, observers have identified an "invisible primary," the competition to raise funds, in the calendar year before the actual contests begin. In 2012 winning the invisible primary was not as critical to the outcome as it had been in 2008 and 2004.[5]

The bridge period, less precisely defined, takes place between the end of the competitive primary season and the official nominations at the national conventions. In 2012 this period was roughly from June 1 to September 1, 2012.[6] Together, the primary season and bridge period can be referred to as the nomination campaign. As its name implies, the general election campaign begins after the national conventions and lasts until election day.

During the nomination campaign (primary season and bridge periods), candidates operate under primary election contribution limits, and during the general election campaign, they operate under general election contribution limits. Although candidates may raise general election contributions during the nomination campaign, these funds cannot be spent until after the national conventions.[7] In 2012 this feature of the law created cash-flow problems for the Romney campaign during the bridge period.

In addition, individual primary and general election contributions can be raised along with party contributions via joint fundraising committees between a candidate and party organizations and then transferred to the candidate's campaign committee. In 2012 Obama established a joint fundraising committee a year earlier than such committees had been established in 2004 or 2008. Romney followed the more typical pattern of establishing a joint fundraising committee in the spring of 2012. Even when Romney's campaign faced a cash-flow problem in the 2012 bridge period, he did not loan his campaign personal funds. Federal campaign finance law allows candidates to spend unlimited amounts of personal funds on their own campaigns. In 2008 Romney spent heavily on his own behalf, but self-financing did not play a major role in 2012.

Spending outside of the candidate committees can occur throughout the nomination campaign and is increasingly part of a team effort to support presidential candidates.[8] The regulation of such outside money had been evolving toward independent expenditures, and in 2010, federal court decisions dramatically advanced this trend (see chapter 2).

First, in *Citizens United* v. *Federal Election Commission,* the U.S. Supreme Court ruled that placing limits on independent expenditures drawn from corporate, association, or labor union general treasury funds was in violation of the First Amendment. Then, in *Speechnow.org* v. *Federal Election Commission,* the U.S. Court of Appeals for the District of Columbia Circuit ruled that individuals can make unlimited (but fully reported) contributions to political action committees for the sole purpose of independent expenditures, and it cited *Citizens United* in support of the ruling (see chapter 2).

These court decisions allowed for the creation of independent expenditure–only political action committees popularly known as Super PACs. In practical terms, a Super PAC may raise donations in unlimited amounts (and thus in excess of limits on contributions to candidates) for the purpose of making independent expenditures in campaigns. In June 2011 the Federal Election Commission (FEC) issued an advisory opinion that federal officeholders and candidates, as well as national party officers, could "attend, speak at, and be featured guests at fundraisers" for Super PACs as long as they did not solicit funds.[9] This advisory opinion facilitated a linkage between Super PACs and presidential candidates. Such Super PACs had a major impact in the 2012 nomination campaign.

Rivals

In addition to campaign finance regulations, nomination finance is influenced by the structure of competition among rival candidates. This structure has two basic elements: the number of candidates running and the schedule of the nomination contests.

As with many recent incumbent presidents, Barack Obama did not face a primary challenge in 2012, which meant that his campaign could concentrate on preparing for the general election. Meanwhile, a large number of GOP candidates vied for the opportunity to challenge Obama in the general election. This field was slower to develop, less stable, and less successful financially than it had been in 2008. A number of potentially strong candidates chose not to enter the race, while others ran less effective campaigns than anticipated. Eventually, the Republican race became a contest between frontrunner Mitt Romney and two main rivals, Rick Santorum and Newt Gingrich.

In the lead-up to 2012, the Democratic and Republican National Committees attempted to change the schedule of nomination contests to reduce frontloading, that is, the scheduling of contests toward the beginning of the season.[10] The original plan was to begin the contests later than in recent years, with four early contests occurring in February (Iowa, New Hampshire, South Carolina, and Nevada) and other state contests to be held in March or thereafter.[11] Although this bipartisan plan was not followed, the nomination contests were nonetheless more evenly spread over the calendar than in 2008. This new schedule proved to be a hurdle for the frontrunner, Mitt Romney, and an opportunity for his principal rivals.

Resources

The campaign finance laws and the structure of competition set the basic parameters for candidates' finances, with each candidate calculating how best to raise and spend the funds necessary to be successful. In this regard, two general fundraising approaches have been common: a high-dollar insider strategy and a small-donor outsider strategy.

A high-dollar fundraising strategy relies on national prominence and strong connections with established fundraising networks. One common tactic is to form a leadership PAC to finance pre-election-cycle activities and secure allies by contributing to their campaigns. Another tactic is to recruit a cadre of high-dollar fundraisers, known as bundlers. If successful, such a strategy reinforces candidate prominence, secures a resource advantage in the initial contests, and provides financial resilience if the candidate encounters setbacks. The goal is a decisive victory that settles the nomination, at which point the strategy can be applied to financing bridge period activities and preparing for the general election campaign. Republican George W. Bush in 2000 and 2004 and Democrat Hillary Clinton in 2008 used this approach, as did Mitt Romney, Rick Perry, and Jon Huntsman Jr. in 2012.[12]

A small-donor strategy depends on novelty and clear issue positions to raise money from beyond established financial networks. One common tactic is to solicit smaller, multiple donations via social media, e-mail, telephone calls, and direct mail. If successful, such a strategy establishes credibility, undermines better-financed opponents, and produces sufficient funds to compete in the initial contests. The goal is to secure early victories, which will translate into success by the end of the primary season, at which point the strategy can be applied to financing the bridge period activities and preparing for the general election campaign. Republican John McCain in 2000, Democrat Howard Dean in 2004, and Ron Paul in 2008 used this approach, as did Ron Paul, Herman Cain, and Michele Bachmann in 2012.[13]

As he had in 2008, Obama used a mixed fundraising strategy, using elements of high-dollar and small-donor fundraising.[14] Like John McCain in 2008, Republicans Rick Santorum and Newt Gingrich also followed a mixed strategy.[15]

Super PACs linked with presidential candidates were prominent in the 2012 nomination campaign. In each case, operatives close to the candidate organized independent expenditure–only PACs, offering donors a credible, if indirect, connection to the candidate. In this regard, Super PACs fit well with high-dollar fundraising efforts, such as those employed by Romney and Obama.

Super PACs also provided expanded opportunities for wealthy individuals to serve as patrons by making very large contributions in support of a presidential candidate. Such patrons have long been a staple of presidential nomination campaigns, but typically by means of personal independent expenditures or activities of tax-exempt organizations.[16] Although there is some overlap between these types of donors and other kinds of fundraising, patrons may have different motivations. As Spencer Zwick noted,

> I actually think they tend to be two different types of people. Take Sheldon Adelson, for instance. He wrote and writes very large checks to Super PACs. Sheldon has never been someone who goes out to raise a bunch of money. He doesn't pick up the phone and call his associates and ask them to give necessarily. He sits down and writes a check. So it's not—it wasn't like a cannibalization of our raisers. There are certainly some who said, "Oh great. With this avenue, I can just write a large check. I feel like I'm having an impact."[17]

Like other forms of outside money in presidential campaigns, donations from patrons can allow otherwise underfunded candidates to be competitive. In 2012 the Santorum and Gingrich campaigns were beneficiaries of patrons via Super PACs (and Sheldon Adelson was the chief patron for the Super PAC linked with Gingrich).

Campaign Receipts and Disbursements in 2012

Table 3-1 lists total adjusted receipts and disbursements for all presidential candidates for the nomination campaign (January 1, 2011–August 31, 2012). For the major-party nominees, Obama and Romney, these totals are also divided into the primary season and bridge period. In addition, the table includes receipts and expenditures for the largest joint fundraising committees for Obama and Romney, similarly divided by the calendar.

A combined total of $899 million was raised by all presidential candidate committees in the 2012 nomination period. This figure was 31 percent less than the $1.3 billion raised during the same period in the 2008 cycle.

Table 3-1. *Receipts and Disbursements, 2012 Presidential Nomination Campaigns*[a]

Millions of dollars

Candidate	Receipts[b]	Disbursements[c]
Democratic Party		
Obama for America	441.3	354.8
Primary	261.5	154.0
Bridge	179.8	200.8
Obama Victory Fund 2012	84.2	62.0
Primary	33.0	31.2
Bridge	51.2	30.8
Swing State Victory Fund	3.2	0.2
Primary	3.0	0.1
Bridge	0.2	0.1
Republican Party		
Romney for President Inc.	283.6	233.1
Primary	123.6	106.6
Bridge	160.0	126.6
Romney Victory Inc.	104.5	68.8
Primary	71.0	13.8
Bridge	33.5	55.0
Paul	41.1	40.0
Bachmann	25.9	25.6
Gingrich	25.0	24.9
Santorum	23.6	23.4
Perry	20.6	20.2
Cain	16.9	16.9
Huntsman	9.2	9.2
Pawlenty	6.0	6.0
Roemer	0.8	0.7
Karger	0.6	0.6
Libertarian Party		
Johnson	2.8	2.8
Green Party		
Stein	1.2	1.1
Independent Party		
Terry	0.5	0.5
Constitution Party		
Goode	0.2	0.2

Source: Based on disclosure filings reported to the Federal Election Commission (www.fec.gov/finance/disclosure/cand cmte_info.shtml).

a. Primary season data are from January 2011 through May 2012 except for Romney Victory Inc., which is from January 2011 through June 2012. Bridge period data are from June 2012 through August 2012 except for Romney Victory Inc., which is from July 2012 through September 2012.

b. Transfers to affiliated committees and total contribution refunds are deducted from the joint fundraising committee receipt totals to avoid double counting.

c. Transfers to affiliated committees and offsets to operating expenditures are deducted from the joint fundraising committee disbursement totals to avoid double counting.

A total of $760 million was spent by all 2012 presidential candidates, 36 percent less than the $1.2 billion spent in 2008.[18] However, candidate funds raised and spent in 2012 were greater than in 2004 ($810 million and $705 million, respectively).[19]

Obama Campaign Committee

One reason for the decline in fundraising and expenditures in 2012 was that President Obama did not face a contested nomination. Overall, the main Obama campaign committee (Obama for America) raised $441.3 million during the nomination campaign (the primary season and bridge period), an 8.7 percent decline from the 2008 figure of $483 million. And he spent $354.8 million in 2012, a 12 percent decline from the $400 million in 2008. (In addition, the absence of other Democratic opponents meant that $390 million less was raised and $329 million less was spent in 2012 than in 2008.)[20]

During the 2012 primary season, Obama raised $261 million and spent $154 million, down 14 and 42 percent, respectively, from the 2008 figures of $305 and $267 million. In the bridge period, Obama raised another $180 million, up 2 percent from the $176 million in 2008, and spent $201 million, a 51 percent increase over the $133 million in 2008.

It is instructive to compare Obama's 2012 finances with the 2004 finances of George W. Bush, an incumbent who also faced no primary opposition. In 2012 dollars, Obama raised 42 percent more than Bush ($441 million versus $311 million) and spent 33 percent more ($355 million versus $267 million) during the nomination campaign. In percentage terms, this differential was smaller in the primary season (37 percent more for Obama) than in the bridge period (50 percent more). A major difference was that Obama did not accept any public financing in 2012, whereas Bush did accept public funds for the 2004 general election.[21]

General election contributions in 2012 accounted for $41.3 million of Obama's nomination campaign receipts (9.4 percent of total receipts): $25.7 million in the primary season (9.8 percent) and $15.6 million in the bridge period (8.6 percent). The 2012 total figure is lower than the $49 million Obama raised in the comparable 2008 time frame. And as in 2008, Obama was able to take advantage of the efficiency of raising primary and general election funds at the same time, something the Romney campaign decided not to do.[22]

Obama Joint Fundraising Committees

The Obama campaign's high-dollar fundraising effort included joint fundraising committees to a larger extent than in previous nomination campaigns. High-dollar donors are important to funding the joint candidate-party "victory committee" because most donors to joint fundraising committees have already maxed out in donations to the candidate.

Obama Victory Fund 2012, a joint fundraising committee with the Democratic National Committee (DNC), provided $32.3 million of Obama for America's individual donations (7.3 percent of the total receipts): $11.3 million in the primary season (4.3 percent of the season's funds) and $21 million in the bridge period (11.6 percent of the period's funds). (To avoid double counting, these funds are included under Obama for America in table 3-1.)

As table 3-1 reports, Obama Victory Fund 2012 raised $84.2 million in addition to donations to Obama for America: $33.0 million in the primary campaign and $51.2 million during the bridge period. A total of $62.0 million was disbursed to other Democratic party organizations, about evenly divided between the primary season ($31.2 million) and the bridge period ($30.8 million).

Obama Victory Fund 2012 was established in April 2011, a year earlier than joint fundraising committees in previous presidential cycles. In June 2008, for example, Obama had established a similar joint fundraising committee, also called Obama Victory Fund, just months before the general election. During the bridge period, this fund transferred $28 million in contributions to the Obama campaign, raised an additional $37 million, and spent $35 million for partisan purposes. A second joint fundraising committee, Democratic White House Victory Fund, also established in June 2008, raised another $9.8 million for the DNC during the bridge period.

In 2012 another Obama joint fundraising committee, Swing State Victory Fund, raised funds for Democratic state parties during the nomination campaign. Established in December 2011, this committee raised $3.2 million during the nomination campaign, mostly during the primary season, but nearly all of its disbursements occurred in the general election. This effort was described as "a new phase in the Obama campaign's effort to further tap into support from its base of elite donors, many of whom have already given the legal individual maximum to Obama and the Democratic National Committee."[23] In August 2008 a similar joint effort with Democratic state parties, Committee for Change, raised some $745,000 during the bridge period. In both 2012 and 2008, these funds were spent in the most competitive swing states.[24]

Romney Campaign Committee

The eventual 2012 Republican nominee, former Massachusetts governor Mitt Romney, raised $284 million and spent $233 million during the nomination campaign through his main campaign committee, Romney for President Inc. These amounts were greater than those raised for the 2008 GOP nominee, John McCain—27 percent more than the $223 million McCain raised and 23 percent more than the $189 million he spent.

Romney raised $124 million in the primary season, almost twice as much as McCain's $65 million, and he spent $107 million, about 75 percent more than McCain's $60 million.[25] Although McCain had the nomination secured in February 2008 and thus had a longer bridge period for fundraising, during the bridge period Romney raised $160 million versus McCain's $149 million, and he spent $126 million to McCain's $122 million.

General election donations accounted for $43.4 million of Romney's 2012 nomination receipts: $2.5 million during the primary season (2 percent) and $40.9 million in the bridge period (25.5 percent). According to Spencer Zwick of the Romney campaign, this pattern was part of the Romney finance plan:

> All through the primary we did not take general election funds for this simple reason: Why spend time in raising money that you can't spend? That was the first part of it. The second part of it, I actually think we would have raised less for the primary, and here's why. When the maximum contribution you can take is $2,500, then you want to get people that can go out and raise money. Then you say, "Okay, for you to become a Romney Star or Romney Stripe, which were our donor programs, you needed to raise $250,000 or $500,000, respectively." . . . My view was once Mitt becomes a nominee, we'll be able to go get that $2,500 for the general elections, but let's not give people the easy way out.[26]

In 2008 McCain stopped raising campaign funds once he accepted public funding for the general election campaign.

Romney Joint Fundraising Committee

In 2012 Romney's high-dollar fundraising efforts also included a joint fundraising committee. This effort was also greater than in previous campaigns—and at a level comparable to Obama (see table 3-1). Romney Victory Inc., a 2012 joint fundraising committee with the Republican National Committee (RNC), provided $5.6 million of the individual donations to Romney for President Inc.: $2.5 million in the primary season and $3.1 million in the bridge period (about 2 percent in both cases). (To avoid double counting, these funds are included under Romney for President, Inc. in table 3-1.)

As table 3-1 reports, Romney Victory Inc. raised $104.5 million in addition to donations for Romney for President, Inc. This fundraising was tilted toward the primary season ($71 million). The joint fundraising committee disbursed $68.8 million to other Republican organizations, tilted toward the bridge period ($55 million).

Romney Victory Inc. was established in April 2012, at roughly the same point in the election cycle as some of McCain's joint fundraising committees in 2008.[27] However, $22.8 million was transferred from joint fundraising committees to the 2008 McCain campaign committee during the nomination campaign—more than four times as much as was transferred to Romney in 2012. The difference between 2012 and 2008 reflects McCain's acceptance of public financing in the general election. But because the Romney campaign was not planning to accept general election funds, it adopted a different approach. According to Spencer Zwick, "Our fundraising was done through Romney's [Victory Inc.] because we took over the party and controlled the entire fundraising operation for Romney's Victory. It wasn't that the party didn't have a fundraising arm in the Romney campaign; it was all done through Romney's Victory."[28]

Net Financial Advantage

Overall, Obama enjoyed a financial advantage over Romney throughout the 2012 nomination campaign, raising 80 percent more ($160 million) and spending 62 percent more ($104 million). In the primary season, Obama's fundraising edge was greater than his spending advantage over Romney ($122 million versus $18 million), but in the bridge period, Obama's fundraising edge was less than his spending edge over Romney ($37 million versus $86 million).

At the start of the general election campaign, Obama had $88.7 million in cash on hand, and Romney had $50.4 million. For Obama, this figure was about the same as in 2008 ($84 million), but for Romney, the figure was almost twice the amount of McCain's in 2008 ($28 million).[29]

These patterns reflect strategic decisions made by the Obama and Romney campaigns. During the primary season, Romney financed a competitive primary race, while Obama built up his war chest as he awaited the result of the GOP nomination contest. Then during the bridge period, Romney focused on replenishing his empty war chest, while Obama engaged in extensive campaign spending. These patterns also illustrate the traditional advantages of an incumbent president who has no primary opposition. Such an advantage may well be larger in the absence of public financing.

Other Candidate Committees

In 2012 other GOP presidential candidates raised a total of $169.7 million and spent $167.5 million. These figures are down about 45 percent from the $306 million raised and $301 million spent by unsuccessful GOP candidates in 2008.[30]

Although Texas representative Ron Paul raised about the same amount in both 2008 and 2012 ($41 million), the other second-tier candidates were less successful than their counterparts in 2008. For example, former House Speaker Newt Gingrich ($25 million), former Pennsylvania senator Rick Santorum ($24 million), and Texas governor Rick Perry ($21 million) each raised markedly less than New York City mayor Rudy Giuliani ($62 million) or Romney ($112 million) raised in 2008.

Santorum, Gingrich, and Perry each raised more in 2012 than former Arkansas governor Mike Huckabee had raised in 2008 ($19 million). Other 2012 candidates were less successful than Huckabee had been, including businessman Herman Cain ($17 million), Minnesota representative Michele Bachmann ($11 million), former Utah governor Jon Huntsman Jr. ($9 million), and former Minnesota governor Tim Pawlenty ($6 million). Taken together, these figures reveal the fundraising weaknesses of the rest of the Republican field in 2012. For the sake of completeness, it is worth noting that minor-party candidate fundraising during the 2012 nomination campaign was $4.7 million, up 47 percent from $3.2 million in 2008.

Table 3-2. *Individual Contributions to Major-Party Nomination Campaigns*[a]

Millions of dollars

Candidate	Amount of individual donations			
	200 or less	*201–999*	*1,000–2,499*	*2,500–5,000*
Democrat				
Obama	147.0	142.9	67.1	69.8
Primary	99.3	71.9	33.3	40.6
Bridge	47.7	71.0	33.8	29.2
Republicans				
Romney	39.5	41.3	39.6	102.3
Primary	13.4	14.3	19.6	70.8
Bridge	26.1	2.7	20.0	31.5
Paul	13.7	13.6	8.0	4.5
Gingrich	9.9	6.2	3.1	3.0
Santorum	9.8	6.1	3.0	2.7
Perry	1.0	1.1	2.4	15.1
Cain	8.3	3.8	2.0	1.8
Bachmann	4.3	1.9	0.6	0.4
Huntsman	0.5	0.5	0.9	1.8

Source: "May Was the Presidential Candidates' Best Money Month So Far in 2012, with Obama Still Doing (Slightly) Better Than Romney," table 3, Campaign Finance Institute (www.cfinst.org/Press/Releases_tags/12-06-22/May_Was_the_Presidential_Candidates%e2%80%99_Best_Money_Month_So_Far_in_2012_with_Obama_Still_Doing_Slightly_Better_Than_Romney.aspx); "Obama's Long-Term Small-Donor Strategy Begins to Show Dividends against Romney in August," table 3, Campaign Finance Institute (www.cfinst.org/Press/PReleases/12-09-24/Obama%e2%80%99s_Long-Term_Small-Donor_Strategy_Begins_to_Show_Dividends_against_Romney_in_August.aspx).

a. All figures include donations to the Obama and Romney committees made through their joint fundraising committees. Primary season: January 1, 2011–May 31, 2012; bridge period: June 1–August 31, 2012.

Sources of Candidate Funds in 2012

Where did the candidates' funds come from in 2012? With few exceptions, individual donors accounted for the vast majority of funds. Table 3-2 reports the source and size of total contributions from individual donors to the major candidates. All the itemized donations from each individual are combined into a single figure, so multiple donations from a single person are taken into account. For Obama and Romney, the figures are again divided into the primary season and the bridge period.

Obama Campaign

The figures in table 3-2 reveal the large scale and scope of Obama fundraising in 2012. On one hand, Obama raised $147 million from donors who gave less than $200 in aggregate (34.4 percent of his total) and \$142.9 million from donors who gave between \$200 and \$999 in aggregate (33.5 percent). On the other hand, he also raised \$67.1 million from donors who gave \$1,000 to \$2,499 in aggregate (15.7 percent) and \$69.8 million from donors who gave \$2,500 or more in aggregate, including the maximum donation of \$5,000 for the primary and the general elections (16.3 percent).

Obama donors who gave \$200 or less were more common in the primary season than in the bridge period (40 and 26 percent, respectively), but donors who gave more than \$2,500 made up about the same proportion (16 percent).

Obama raised less money in the smallest category of donors in 2012 than in 2008 (\$147 million versus \$236 million), and these funds accounted for a smaller percentage of his individual contributions (34 percent and 46 percent, respectively). But when the two lowest categories are combined, Obama's percentage in 2012 was a little larger than in 2008. This pattern may reflect the effect of multiple and repeated small donations that put individual donors above the \$200 threshold.[31]

Obama also raised less in the highest contribution category in 2012 than in 2008 (\$69.8 million versus \$84.6 million), but the category's share of total funds was about the same. Obama received very little money from PACs, and less in 2012 than in 2008, when he raised \$25.9 million in the bridge period (or about 5 percent of total receipts).[32]

As in 2008, the sources of Obama's 2012 funds reflect his mix of high-dollar and small-donor strategies. In terms of high-dollar fundraising, the Obama campaign reported some 638 bundlers who raised \$50,000 or more for the nomination campaign in 2012, a figure slightly larger than the 605 reported in 2008.[33] Although about two-thirds of the bundlers were new in 2012, the occupational profile was similar to 2008 but with less support from the financial industry.[34] Obama also attended 203 fundraising events between April 2011 and the middle of August 2012—a modern record for a sitting president—compared with 123 in 2008.[35]

Obama also aggressively pursued small donations in 2012. In fact, much of Obama's fundraising edge over Romney resulted from such funds.[36] As in 2008, the campaign invested heavily in expertise, technology, and data. It hired dozens of "engineers, developers, data scientists, and other specialists," built a new state-of-the-art software platform, and created a single comprehensive database for the campaign.[37] These operations focused on sophisticated data collection, analysis, and experimentation, with a strong emphasis on innovation. "If we just run that same campaign, we stand a good chance of losing," said Obama campaign manager James Messina in 2011. "We've got to run a new campaign."[38]

In this regard, the Obama effort was described as less "viral" and more "granulated" in 2012 compared with 2008.[39] It deployed more extensive multichannel appeals through social media, e-mail, telephone, and direct-mail marketing to solicit potential donations. This expanded effort was managed effectively by innovative website design, including improvements to the MyBO tool, the hub of the website. An example is Quick Donate, a program that stored credit card information so that past donors could make one-click contributions on tablets and smartphones. These efforts facilitated microgiving (small and repeated donations) as well as microbundling (directing small donations to the campaign). All told, this innovative effort produced 4.3 million donations totaling $250 million over the entire 2012 campaign.[40]

Romney Campaign

In contrast to Obama's mixed strategy, Romney pursued a high-dollar fundraising strategy. As table 3-2 shows, Romney raised $102 million from donors of $2,500 or more in aggregate, accounting for 46 percent of his individual receipts—almost three times the proportion of such donors for the Obama campaign, which resulted in $32 million more in receipts. Romney raised $39.5 million from donors who gave $200 or less, for 18 percent of receipts from individuals—about half of the proportion of such donors for the Obama campaign (and $107.5 million less than Obama).

This pattern was even more lopsided during the primary season, when 60 percent of Romney's individual funds came from the largest level of donations ($70.8 million) and just 11 percent from the smallest category ($13.4 million). However, the size of donations became more balanced in the bridge period, with 39 percent in the highest category ($31.5 million) and 33 percent in the lowest category ($26.1 million). Romney raised $900,000 in PAC donations in 2012, about twice what he had raised in 2008.

In 2012 Romney and his wife Ann made personal donations for a total of $150,000 to his own campaign committee and the joint RNC-Romney committee. This pattern was a dramatic contrast with 2008, when Romney loaned $44.6 million to his own committee during the nomination campaign. These loans were eventually converted into personal contributions by Romney, making the 2008 effort one of the largest self-financed major-party nomination bids ever.[41] At the beginning of the 2012 election cycle, Romney did not rule out using his personal fortune in this fashion.[42]

Romney prepared for this insider strategy in a traditional fashion, building on and learning from his 2008 presidential nomination bid. He renamed his leadership PAC Free & Strong America and raised $7.5 million in the 2010 election cycle (compared with $3 million for the previously named Commonwealth PAC in the 2006 cycle).

In 2008 the Romney campaign reported 345 bundlers, but in 2012 the campaign did not release such a list. In the summer of 2012, *USA Today* identified 1,200 individuals who served as fundraisers for the Romney campaign, many associated with finance and banking.[43] While this estimate may overstate the number of bundlers, it seems likely that the number was larger than in 2008 and perhaps larger than for Obama in 2012.[44] Similarly, the Romney campaign did not release a list of Romney fundraising events, but a rough count from news sources suggests at least 163 such events during the nomination campaign, compared with 137 in 2008.[45]

According to Spencer Zwick, the Romney campaign made a strategic decision to raise maximum primary donations. "One of the strategic objectives, especially early on, was to try and get to as many maxed-out donors as possible and to build that early."[46] One goal of this process was to expand the base of large donors who then had an "investment" in the Romney campaign:

> In the finance world, following an investment means that they will go find like-minded people who are in their circle of influence who can do the same. And if you're somebody that invests $2,500, in my opinion and in our researchers' opinion, you have friends that can also do $2,500. . . . So by starting with rich friends, associates, people that we knew, we said, "First things first. Everyone write a maxed-out contribution." Once they've done that, basically, we have them—you know, once we have them in the door, they marketed their own campaign level to others.[47]

This message was communicated to regular donors solicited through other venues, such as Super PACs.

In relative terms, Romney's insider strategy was successful. During the primary season, Romney raised as much from donors who gave $2,500 or more as all his opponents combined, including Obama. In this category of donors, Romney also raised three times as much as McCain had in 2008 and more than twice his own 2008 performance.

Romney made less effort to cultivate small donations and to launch a digital effort until later in the campaign, in part, according to Spencer Zwick, because of the cost. "I think it requires an early investment. Somebody told me, 'Well, if you had an additional $50 million to spend on digital in the last two months on the campaign, would it make a difference?' In my opinion, I don't think we would have raised more money." Such fundraising is most effective, said Zwick, when the candidate becomes a "cause," and "Mitt Romney never became a cause until after the gavel went down in Tampa and he was the nominee. Then people from all over the country started throwing in small-dollar checks."[48]

Other Republican Candidates

Two other Republican candidates, Perry and Huntsman, also pursued high-dollar fundraising strategies. Perry raised 77 percent of his funds from donors who gave $2,500 or more. Huntsman raised 49 percent of his funds in this donor category, and, taking a page from the 2008 Romney campaign, he lent his campaign $5.1 million. Perry raised 5 percent of his funds from donors who gave $200 or less, and Huntsman raised 14 percent.

Several Republican candidates opted for small-donor strategies. By far the most successful of these was Ron Paul, who raised 34 percent of his funds from donors who gave $200 or less ($13.7 million) and nearly as much from donors in the $200 to $999 range ($13.6 million). Like Obama, Paul had an extensive online fundraising effort.[49] And like Obama, he did not do as well in 2012 among the smallest category of donors as he did in 2008, but he had comparable figures when the two categories of smaller donors are combined. This pattern may also reflect the effect of individuals who chose to make multiple small contributions.

Michele Bachmann and Herman Cain also depended heavily on small donations, accounting for 59 and 52 percent of their individual funds, respectively. Bachmann also transferred $2 million from her congressional campaign committee, and Cain lent his campaign $675,000. Rick Santorum and Newt Gingrich relied heavily on small donations as well, raising about $10 million each, accounting for about 45 percent of their total receipts.

Many of these candidates might have benefited in the short run from accepting federal matching funds in the primary season. But it is debatable whether such candidates would have been more successful in the long run, given the state-by-state and aggregate spending limitations imposed in return for public funds. In any event, most of these candidates were ideologically opposed to public financing.

One of the original Republican candidates who accepted matching funds ($333,751) was former New Mexico governor Gary Johnson, who became the 2012 Libertarian Party presidential nominee. Another of the original Republican candidates, former Louisiana representative Buddy Roemer, also accepted matching funds ($285,470); he eventually sought the nominations of Americans Elect and the Reform Party but received neither.

Outside Money in 2012

The 2012 presidential nomination campaign broke numerous records for spending outside of the candidate committees. Table 3-3 reports four measures of outside money, for and against the candidates: independent expenditures by Super PACs; independent expenditures by other groups; partisan communication costs by other groups; and electioneering communication costs reported by 527 committees. Here, again, the figures for the Obama and Romney campaigns are separated into the primary season and the bridge period. Given the limitations of reporting requirements, these figures may understate the level of outside money.

These data indicate that outside spending during the nomination campaign totaled at least $230 million in 2012 (30 percent of total candidate spending). This spending was almost three times the $85 million spent in 2008 (7 percent of total candidate spending).[50] These figures do not include undisclosed expenditures by section 501(c) tax-exempt groups, which could possibly double the level of outside spending (see chapter 2).

The largest source of outside money listed in table 3-3 was independent expenditures from Super PACs: $159 million, which represented 69 percent of all outside spending during the nomination campaign. A total of $110 million and 69 percent of these independent expenditures were self-reported as being against candidates, while $48 million was spent in support of candidates—a two-to-one advantage of opposition to a candidate. And the largest portion of this spending was against Obama during the bridge period ($39.8 million, 25 percent of Super PAC independent expenditures).

A total of $70 million was spent against Republican candidates: $19 million against Romney in the bridge period (11 percent of the total),

Table 3-3. *Outside Money Spent in 2012 Presidential Nomination Campaigns*[a]
Millions of dollars

Party and candidate	Super PAC independent expenditures		Other group independent expenditures		Partisan communication costs		Electioneering communication costs	
	For	Against	For	Against	For	Against	For	Against
Democratic: Obama	2.1	40.2	0.9	55.6	1.6	0.6	<100K	3.6
Primary	0.1	0.4	0.5	2.2	0.4	0.4	<100K	3.6
Bridge	2.0	39.8	0.4	53.4	1.2	0.2	0	0
Republican: Romney	14.4	30.4	0.7	6.4	<100K	0.1	0.2	0
Primary	7.1	11.5	0.5	3.6	<100K	<100K	0.2	0
Bridge	7.3	18.9	0.2	2.8	<100K	0.1	0	0
Other Republicans	31.8	39.6	0.7	0.2	0	0	0.7	0
Bachmann	<100K	0	0	<100K	0	0	0.7	0
Cain	0.4	<100K	<100K	<100K	0	0	0	0
Gingrich	13.6	18.8	<100K	<100K	0	0	0	0
Huntsman	2.8	0	<100K	<100K	0	0	0	0
Paul	4.0	<100K	<100K	0.1	0	0	0	0
Perry	4.1	<100K	0	<100K	0	0	0	0
Santorum	6.9	20.8	0.7	0.1	0	0	0	0

Source: Compiled from Federal Election Commission data.

a. Expenditures reported as for or against a candidate are self-reported by the groups who made the expenditures. Primary season: January 1, 2011–May 31, 2012; bridge period: June 1–August 31, 2012.

and during the primary season, $11.5 million against Romney (7 percent), $21 million against Santorum and $19 million against Gingrich (for a total of 24 percent). Looked at another way, Romney's allies spent almost $80 million against opponents during the nomination campaign, while his opponents' supporters spent about $30 million against Romney—more than a two-to-one ratio of negative spending between Romney allies and supporters of rival candidates.

Spending for the candidates was concentrated in the GOP primary, with candidate backers spending $14 million for Gingrich (8 percent of Super PAC spending); $7 million for Romney (4 percent); $7 million for Santorum (4 percent); $4 million each for Paul and Perry (2.5 percent); and $3 million for Huntsman (1 percent). In the bridge period, Romney's allies spent another $7 million for him (4 percent); Obama's supporters spent $2 million on his behalf (1 percent).

Independent expenditures by groups other than Super PACs were also large, totaling $64.5 million, or 28 percent of all outside spending. The largest portion of this spending was against Obama during the bridge period: $53.4 million, or 86 percent of all such spending. In contrast, just $6 million, or 9 percent of such spending, was directed against Romney, divided roughly between the primary season and the bridge period.

Independent expenditures during the nomination campaign totaled $223 million in 2012, a more than fourfold increase over 2008. Super PACs accounted for most of this increase, but independent expenditures by other groups also increased by $13 million (25 percent). This aggregate figure is more than twice the level of independent expenditures in the 2004 nomination campaign ($28.5 million).[51]

In addition, $2.3 million was spent in partisan communication costs, about 1 percent of all outside spending. All these funds were deployed in the bridge period, with $1.6 million (69 percent) spent for Obama. Unlike independent expenditures, partisan communication costs fell dramatically from the $19 million spent in 2008, when $12 million (68 percent) was spent for Hillary Clinton during the primary season. The 2012 figure is also smaller than the $8 million spent in 2004.[52]

In the 2012 nomination campaigns, electioneering communication costs were $4.5 million (2 percent of all outside spending). Here, too, the largest expenditure, $3.6 million (82 percent), was against Obama during the primary season. These figures were also dramatically lower in 2012 than in 2008, when electioneering communications equaled $13 million. The great bulk of this 2008 spending (67 percent) was deployed in favor of Democratic candidates Clinton, John Edwards, and Obama in the primary season. The 2012 figure was also much lower than the $36.5 million spent in 2004, when nearly nine of every ten dollars were spent against George W. Bush.[53]

Candidate-Linked Super PACs

Some Super PACs were closely linked to presidential candidates. Table 3-4 takes a closer look at the largest of these organizations. Each Super PAC's nomination campaign receipts are reported, along with the percentage of all individual donations over $5,000 (equal to the $5,000 maximum allowed for individual candidate donations in 2012). Next, the table reports each Super PAC's nomination campaign expenditures. To put these figures in context, this number is then expressed as a percentage of expenditures from the candidates' own committees.

During the nomination campaign, candidate-linked Super PACs raised $157.3 million and spent $127.4 million, about 17 percent of total candidate receipts and expenditures. A key feature of Super PACs is their ability to accept donations in unlimited amounts. Most of the individual donations to these Super PACs were greater than $5,000, and many of the donations were very large. As one might expect, the large donations accounted for most of these Super PACs' receipts—an average of 82 percent of funds raised were from donations of $50,000 or more (excluding the 9-9-9 PAC, linked with Herman Cain, which reported no donations over $5,000). Federal Election Commission records show that thirteen individuals made donations of more than $1 million.

Another feature of Super PACs is their ability to make unlimited independent expenditures in favor of a candidate or against a candidate's rivals. These Super PACs averaged 28 percent of each candidate's own campaign expenditures, but there was wide variation in this regard, ranging from 73 percent of Winning Our Future (linked with Gingrich) to a low of 3 percent for the Revolution PAC (linked with Paul).

By far the largest of these Super PACs was Restore Our Future (linked with Romney). It raised $89.6 million during the nomination campaign (57 percent of the presidential candidate-linked Super PAC receipts) and spent $69.4 million (55 percent of these expenditures). Donations of more than $5,000 accounted for 99 percent of all donations and gifts of $50,000 or more accounted for 87 percent (with the latter a bit higher in the bridge period). Restore Our Future's expenditures equaled 42 percent

Table 3-4. Candidate-Linked Super PAC Finances in 2012 Presidential Nomination Campaigns[a]

		Receipts			Expenditures		
Party and PAC	Candidate	Millions of dollars	Percent greater than $5,000	Percent greater than $50,000	Millions of dollars	Percent candidate expenditures
Democratic						
Priorities USA Action	Obama	25.5	97	91	21.2	8
	Primary	10.6	98	89	5.8	5
	Bridge	14.9	97	92	15.4	10
Republican						
Restore Our Future	Romney	89.6	99	87	69.4	42
	Primary	56.5	99	85	48.9	54
	Bridge	33.1	99	91	20.5	27
Revolution PAC	Paul	1.2	61	37	1.2	3
Winning Our Future	Gingrich	23.7	100	99	18.3	73
Red White and Blue Fund	Santorum	8.2	98	87	8.2	35
9-9-9 Fund	Cain	0.6	0	0	0.6	4
Our Destiny PAC	Huntsman	3.1	99	88	3.1	34
Make Us Great Again	Perry	5.4	99	87	5.4	27

Source: Compiled from Federal Election Commission data.
a. Primary season: January 2011–May 2012. Bridge period: June 2012–August 2012.

of Romney's campaign committee spending. The bulk of this spending, 48.9 million (70 percent of the total) occurred in the primary season, and 30 percent in the bridge period. These figures reflected Romney's high-dollar fundraising strategy and the priority of securing the nomination.

Restore Our Future was established and managed by former Romney aides.[54] Officially organized in October 2010, it announced its plans shortly after Romney entered the race in June 2011. Restore Our Future was the first Super PAC to be explicitly linked to a presidential candidate; its announcement stated, "This is an independent effort focused on getting Romney elected president."[55] Charles Spies of Restore Our Future later told reporters, "Mitt Romney has appeared at Restore Our Future events to deliver his message of belief in America, prosperity by free enterprise, and undoing the failed policies of President Obama. . . . At no time has Mitt Romney solicited funds for Restore Our Future."[56] One of the major donors to Restore Our Future was Edward W. Conard, a former director of Bain Capital and a $1 million contributor.[57]

The second largest Super PAC was Priorities USA Action (linked with Obama). During the nomination campaign, it raised $25.5 million and spent $21.2 million (about 16 percent of these candidate-linked Super PAC receipts and expenditures). Donations greater than $5,000 accounted for 97 percent of its receipts, and donations $50,000 or more made up 91 percent of all receipts. Its spending equaled 8 percent of Obama's own expenditures during the nomination campaign. Unlike Restore Our Future, the bulk of Priorities USA Action's activity occurred during the bridge period, during which it spent $15.4 million (73 percent of its funds), largely against Romney. Because Obama ran unchallenged for renomination, he and his Super PAC could focus on the opposing party only, an advantage Romney did not have.

Established in April 2011 by two former Obama aides and other prominent Democratic operatives, Priorities USA Action mirrored Obama's mixed fundraising strategy.[58] Initially, its fundraising was less successful than the Super PACs that were opposed to Obama, perhaps because of the President's criticism of Super PACs in general. But in February 2012, the Obama campaign announced that it would support Priorities USA Action's fundraising efforts, with campaign and administration officials attending PAC events, but not directly soliciting contributions.[59] One major donor was the comedian Bill Maher, who made a $1 million contribution in March 2012.[60]

Romney's chief Republican rivals were associated with the third and fourth largest of these Super PACs. The third largest, Winning Our Future (linked with Gingrich),[61] was established by a former Gingrich aide in December 2011. The fund was roughly the same size as Priorities USA, raising $23.7 million. But unlike Priorities USA, Winning Our Future spent most of the $18.3 million it raised during the primary season. All donations were greater than $5,000, and 99 percent of its receipts were from donations of $50,000 or more. Two donors, casino magnate Sheldon Adelson and his wife Miriam, each contributed $7.5 million. These donations alone accounted for almost two-thirds of the funds Winning Our Future raised. The Super PAC's spending equaled 73 percent of Gingrich's own campaign expenditures.

The fourth largest of these Super PACs was the Red White and Blue Fund (linked with Santorum).[62] Established by a former Santorum aide in October 2011, it raised and spent $8.2 million during the nomination campaign (5 and 6 percent of these candidate-linked Super PACs' receipts and expenditures, respectively). In this case, 46 percent of the donations received were larger than $5,000, and 87 percent of all receipts came from donations of $50,000 or more. This Super PAC also had two major donors: investor Foster Friess gave a total of $2.1 million, and energy executive William Dorn gave $2.2 million. These two donors accounted for more than half of this Super PAC's funds. The Red White and Blue Fund's spending equaled 35 percent of Santorum's own campaign spending.

Other Republican candidates were also linked with Super PACs. Make Us Great Again was established by a former aide to Rick Perry in July 2011.[63] It raised and spent $5.4 million (between 3 and 4 percent of these candidate-linked Super PAC receipts and expenditures). Here, 81 percent of the donations were greater than $5,000, and 87 percent of its receipts came from donations of $50,000 or more. Its spending was 27 percent of Perry's own campaign expenditures. Texas businessman George "Brint" Ryan was one of the major donors to this Super PAC ($250,000).

A former campaign aide to Huntsman established Our Destiny PAC in August 2011.[64] This Super PAC raised and spent $3.1 million; eighty-one percent of its donations were larger than $5,000, and 88 percent of all receipts came from donations of $50,000 or more. The largest donor was the candidate's father, Jon Huntsman Sr., who gave a total of $2.2 million, or seven of ten dollars that Our Destiny raised. This PAC's spending equaled 34 percent of Huntsman's own expenditures.

The Super PACs linked with the remaining GOP candidates were smaller and less focused on high-dollar donations; they also spent less. A former aide to Ron Paul helped establish the Revolution PAC in July 2011. It raised and spent $1.2 million, but only 4 percent of its donations were larger than $5,000 and only 37 percent of its receipts were from donations of $50,000 or more. Its spending represented just 3 percent of the candidate's own expenditures. Business associates of Herman Cain established the 9-9-9 Fund in October 2010. This PAC raised and spent $600,000; only 2 percent of its donations were greater than $5,000 and none of its donations were $50,000 or more. Its spending equaled just 4 percent of Cain's own expenditures.[65]

The Dynamics of the Republican Primary Season in 2012

The 2012 Republican presidential field developed slowly and was not complete until the summer of 2011. A number of potentially strong candidates decided not to seek the GOP nomination, including 2008 vice presidential nominee Sarah Palin, former Arkansas governor Mike Huckabee (the second-place candidate in 2008); Governors Mitch Daniels (Indiana), Haley Barbour (Mississippi), and Chris Christie (New Jersey); and U.S. Senator John Thune (South Dakota).[66]

Former Massachusetts governor Mitt Romney was generally regarded as the early frontrunner, based on his performance in the 2008 primaries and his extensive preparation for another presidential bid.[67] However, he did not form a presidential exploratory committee until April 2011 and did not formally enter the race until June 2. A central question of the campaign was who the "anti-Romney" candidate would be.

A number of possible candidates were already auditioning for this role, including former Speaker of the House Newt Gingrich (who entered the race on May 11); Texas representative and 2008 presidential candidate Ron Paul (May 13); businessman Herman Cain (May 21); and former Minnesota governor Tim Pawlenty (May 23). And more soon followed: former Pennsylvania senator Rick Santorum (June 6), former Utah governor Jon Huntsman Jr. (June 21), Minnesota representative Michele Bachmann (June 27), and Texas governor Rick Perry (August 13).

These candidates represented ideological differences within the Republican Party. Pragmatic conservatism was represented by Huntsman, who had served as Obama's ambassador to the People's Republic of China, and Pawlenty, who had been considered for vice president in 2008.

Broad-based conservatism was represented by Gingrich, Santorum, and Perry. Paul spoke for libertarian Republicans, while Cain and Bachmann were Tea Party favorites and social conservatives. It was not entirely clear where Romney fit into this spectrum.

Romney led in initial polls, benefiting from the misfortunes of two rivals. After a poor debate performance on June 13, Pawlenty withdrew from the race (and later endorsed Romney). And during the same month, top staffers resigned from the Gingrich campaign, essentially "firing" their candidate. Contrary to expectations, Gingrich stayed in the race.

Frontrunner Romney soon faced a series of challenges. The first came in mid-August when Michele Bachmann finished first in the Iowa straw poll. Romney finished seventh, a far cry from his first-place finish in 2007. On the same day, Rick Perry entered the presidential race and quickly surged to the front in the polls. But Perry's poor debate performances soon undermined his prospects. Then Herman Cain stepped into the lead in a number of polls in October and November. However, allegations of sexual misconduct caused Cain to withdraw from the race on December 3. Cain endorsed Gingrich, who then moved into first place in the polls, a place he held until the end of the year.

These early shifts in the contest revealed Romney's problems with key elements of the Republican base. But at the same time, Romney was running away with the invisible primary. As figure 3-1 shows, he held a large and growing lead in funds raised throughout 2011. By the end of 2011, Romney's campaign committee had raised $57 million, more than all of his opponents combined. This success was especially dramatic when compared with the candidates who would be competitive in the primaries and caucuses, Gingrich and Santorum. By the end of 2011, both candidates combined had raised about $15 million, or one-quarter of Romney's funds. This differential would have been even larger except for a surge in Gingrich's receipts in the fourth quarter, when he raised $9.8 million, in tandem with his improved poll standing.

A similar pattern held for Super PAC fundraising. Restore Our Future (Romney) raised $17.9 million in 2011, more than all Republican candidate-linked Super PACs combined. Winning Our Future (Gingrich) raised $2 million, and the Red White and Blue Fund (Santorum) raised $729,000. Thus Romney's allied Super PACs raised six times as much as the Super PACs of his principal opponents.

Most of the Republican contenders made a strong effort in the Iowa caucuses on January 3, 2012, and a total of $16.5 million was spent on

Figure 3-1. *GOP Cumulative Receipts, 2012 Presidential Primaries*

Millions of dollars

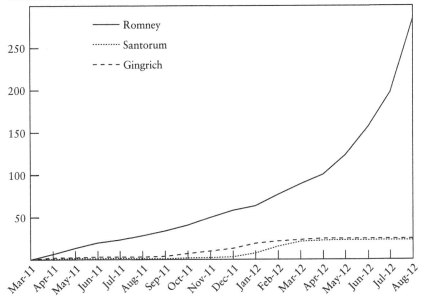

Source: Federal Election Commission, "Candidate and Committee Viewer" (www.fec.gov/finance/disclosure/candcmte
_info.shtml).

advertising in the state, 18 percent higher than the $14 million spent in 2008.[68] The Romney campaign was ambivalent about campaigning in Iowa, given Romney's loss to Mike Huckabee in 2008.[69] But in mid-November, the campaign decided to contest Iowa and ran a more sophisticated campaign than it had four years earlier.[70] Romney also benefited from $4 million of independent expenditures by Restore Our Future against Gingrich.[71]

The result was largely a two-candidate affair, with Romney and Santorum essentially tied in the winner's circle. On caucus night, Romney appeared to win by eight ballots. Severely underfunded, Santorum owed his success to his extensive retail campaigning in the Hawkeye State—a pattern reminiscent of Huckabee's success in 2008. Despite having won the Iowa straw poll earlier, Bachmann finished last on caucus night and withdrew from the race.[72]

Romney took his (modest) momentum to the New Hampshire primary, where Huntsman was his main opponent. Huntsman had skipped

Iowa in favor of New Hampshire, as John McCain had done in 2000 and 2008. He visited the state repeatedly, spent heavily, and benefited from independent expenditures from the Our Destiny PAC. Romney won the primary, which in 2008 he had lost to John McCain. Huntsman finished third and withdrew from the race. A total of $5.4 million was spent on advertising in this first primary.[73]

Having succeeded in Iowa and New Hampshire, Romney was expected to clinch the nomination by winning South Carolina, a conservative state with a history of backing Republican frontrunners. But instead, Gingrich defied recent history by winning handily. This outcome had many causes. The Palmetto State was less hospitable to Romney than past GOP frontrunners for religious and ideological reasons, and Romney had done poorly there in 2008.[74] Gingrich benefited from the endorsement of Sarah Palin; Perry's withdrawal from the race (and endorsement of Gingrich); and being from the neighboring state of Georgia. But a major factor was financial: Winning Our Future, a Super PAC linked with Gingrich, made $3 million in independent expenditures against Romney. The Gingrich and Romney teams, including their Super PACs, spent about the same amount in South Carolina, with a total of $12.4 million expended on advertising in the state.[75]

The contest then moved to Florida, where Romney and his allies made use of their ample resources. A total of $21.2 million was spent on advertising in the Sunshine State.[76] Restore Our Future spent $10.7 million in independent expenditures, including $9.9 million against Gingrich. Analysts calculated that Gingrich was outspent four-to-one in television advertising.[77] Romney won in Florida, another state he had lost to McCain in 2008, receiving close to a majority of the vote. After Florida, Gingrich was no longer the main challenger in the Republican contest; both his fundraising and that of Winning Our Future began to decline.

A strong showing in the Nevada caucus seemed to reestablish Romney's frontrunner status, but then on February 7, Santorum won three "beauty contests" in Colorado, Missouri, and Minnesota, where no delegates were awarded. These symbolic victories attracted considerable attention and pushed Santorum to the front of the polls, boosted his campaign fundraising, and brought new contributions to the Red White and Blue Fund. Thereafter Romney participated in a broader range of contests. For example, he won a narrow victory over Ron Paul in the Maine caucuses, and he won the Conservative Political Action Conference (CPAC) straw poll held in Washington, D.C.[78]

A major confrontation between Romney and Santorum followed in the Michigan primary. Because Romney was born in the Wolverine State, the contest took on added significance. Romney hoped to replicate his 2008 victory, and Santorum looked for his first substantial primary win. At least $6.5 million was spent in the state, including $2.7 million in independent expenditures by Restore Our Future and $1.7 million by the Red White and Blue Fund.[79] Romney won Michigan by a narrow margin, and on the same day, he also won the Arizona primary.

The campaigns moved on to the ten primaries and caucuses on Super Tuesday, March 6. At least $11.5 million in advertising was spent on these contests, $9.5 million of which came from Super PACs.[80] Ohio was the center of the campaign, where Romney outspent Santorum and Gingrich four to one on television. Restore Our Future paid for some $3 million of independent expenditures in the Buckeye State and $5.5 million in many of the other states. Overall, the Red White and Blue Fund spent just $250,000, and Winning Our Future spent $3.3 million, mostly to help Gingrich hold his home state of Georgia. Romney won by a slim victory in Ohio, and he also won Massachusetts, Alaska, Idaho, Vermont, and in Virginia, where Gingrich and Santorum had failed to qualify for the ballot. Santorum won Tennessee and Oklahoma as well as North Dakota, where no delegates were assigned; Gingrich won Georgia.

After Super Tuesday, Romney pressed his remaining financial advantage, while his rivals exhausted their funds and went into debt. Although Santorum won four contests in March, he suspended his campaign on April 10. But by then, the Romney campaign was having financial problems of its own, with cash on hand down to about $10 million.[81] Gingrich suspended his effort on May 2, but taking no chances, Romney continued to raise and spend funds in the remaining contests, securing a majority of the GOP delegates late in May.

Super PACs played a critical role during the primary season. Figure 3-2 illustrates this impact by plotting the cash-on-hand and Super PAC independent expenditures for Romney and his main rivals. (Santorum and Gingrich are combined for ease of presentation.) Romney's success in the invisible primary enabled him to build up large cash reserves until the end of 2011; his rivals trailed far behind. The frontrunner's cash on hand declined sharply once the primary season began, and although his rivals saw a modest increase in available funds, they still lagged far behind.

Super PAC spending filled gaps in candidate campaign finances during the first quarter of 2012. For Romney, these expenditures contributed to

Figure 3-2. GOP *Cash on Hand and Independent Expenditures,*
2012 Presidential Primaries[a]

Millions of dollars

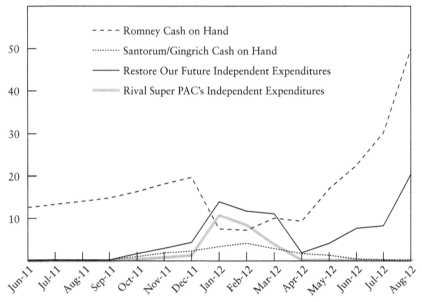

Source: FEC, Candidate and Committee Viewer (www.fec.gov/finance/disclosure/candcmte_info.shtml).
a. Rival Super PAC independent expenditures are the combined totals of the Red White and Blue Fund (Santorum) and Winning Our Future (Gingrich) Super PACs.

his successes in Iowa, New Hampshire, Florida, Michigan, and Ohio. For Gingrich, such spending made possible his success in South Carolina; Santorum's Super PAC kept him competitive. Charles Spies of Restore Our Future described the role of Super PACs in this way:

> It's a tool that levels the playing field. You can see in the presidential race, I think most people would say that Restore our Future's advertisements were critical for Governor Romney winning the Republican primary but the corollary to that is the money that went in the PACs, supporting Santorum and Gingrich probably kept them alive for a few months longer than they might otherwise have been. Although, overall, Super PACs may have had somewhat of a neutralizing effect—if you don't have one you're basically defenseless.[82]

Without Super PACs, the nomination race would likely have ended quickly, one way or another. In this sense, Super PACs accomplished their main purpose.[83]

The Obama Campaign during the Republican Primary Season

What did the Obama campaign and its allies do during the Republican primaries? As reported in table 3-1, the campaign itself spent $154 million between April 2011, when the President announced he was seeking reelection, and the end of May 2012. Of course, they also spent time raising funds, with an extensive schedule of fundraising events and the aggressive pursuit of small donations. But just as importantly, the campaign assembled a strong voter mobilization operation. It was part grass roots (local campaign offices), part net roots (social media and online activities), and part group roots (allied organizations, such as members of the America Votes Coalition).

This organization recruited and deployed thousands of volunteers, tapping into an array of social and community networks. Improving on the 2008 experience and anticipating a difficult election in 2012, the Obama campaign sought to rekindle enthusiasm for Obama and to arouse the Democratic base. One Ohio volunteer said, "You know, hope and change were fine, but now we have to roll up our sleeves and get the job done."[84] And an Ohio campaign worker described this operation as "campaigning with a purpose."[85] One Romney campaign official used similar language when describing the effects of the Obama organization: "It was a bit of a surprise. I mean, we had read all the articles, which included the huge number of offices they had, in different states, and our political people thought that that was more for show than anything else—*it turned out it actually had a purpose to produce* (emphasis added)."[86]

In this regard, Obama had both a time and financial advantage over Romney: A Romney campaign official said "There's no time to invest. I mean the Obama campaign, by its own estimates, spent $100 million investing [in the] get-out-the-vote campaign. The Romney campaign invested $80 some million on winning the primary."[87]

According to Obama campaign senior strategist David Axelrod, the campaign anticipated that the GOP "would have a big primary, and we had the time to put things in motion," and "that would ultimately redound to our benefit in terms of organization."[88]

Priorities USA Action was active during the Republican primary season as well, making some $2.1 million in independent expenditures against Republican candidates in close contests. For example, during the Michigan primary, the Super PAC spent $198,422 on ads focused on Romney's opposition to the auto bailout.[89] Sean Sweeney of Priorities USA Action described the decision: "So we saw they were not in the area in Michigan, we went on the air, and we got a great read, because there wasn't a lot of spending in Michigan, so we locked in a terrific rate."[90] As the GOP contest moved to a conclusion in May, Priorities USA Action spent $3.9 million and Restore Our Future spent $4 million in independent expenditures, heralding the beginning of the bridge period activities.

The Bridge Period

The 2012 bridge period resembled the 2004 campaign in that both featured a well-prepared incumbent president (George W. Bush and Obama) and a challenger who was recovering from a primary battle (John Kerry and Romney). But unlike 2004, Obama and Romney did not face the spending restraints of the public financing system.[91] In June 2012, Obama had $97.5 million in cash on hand, while Romney had $22.5, an almost five-to-one advantage. As table 3-1 shows, Obama spent $200 million in June, July, and August, while Romney spent $126 million.

In June, the Obama campaign and its allies began a sustained attack on Romney with a $12 million ad buy in ten battleground states. By mid-July, Obama had spent $100 million on advertising, three-quarters of which was critical of Romney, and he achieved a four-to-one spending advantage over Romney in television ads. By mid-August, the Obama campaign had spent $207 million in advertising, compared with Romney's $67 million. David Axelrod described the Obama campaign's bridge period strategy this way: "We had an imperative to define the race and to define Mitt Romney before the conventions, and it was better to take money out of September and October and put it into May, June, and July."[92]

Romney's cash shortage was especially problematic in June and July. Much of his cash on hand was made up of general election contributions, which could not be spent until after the Republican National Convention. As Spencer Zwick of the Romney campaign said, "We were short on cash that we could spend. We were raising money. We were raising more money every month than Barack Obama, but again we were raising money into a general election account and to Romney Victory for the party, but we couldn't spend it until the gavel went down in Tampa."[93]

But Romney's high-dollar fundraising strategy was also part of the difficulty, as Zwick noted: "The problem is that we had maxed out too many people in the primary."[94] Romney could have made a large personal loan or contribution to fund his campaign at this critical juncture, as he did in 2008, but this action would have highlighted his wealth, which was already a negative campaign theme. Eventually, the campaign was able to address this situation by obtaining $20 million in bank loans, secured by the funds already raised for the general election but which could not be spent until after the convention.[95]

Like Bob Dole in 1996 and John Kerry in 2004, the Romney campaign lacked the finances to respond to opposition attacks at a crucial moment during the bridge period.[96] According to Neil Newhouse of the Romney campaign,

> [The Obama campaign] spent money in April, May, and June and even after our primaries were over, defining Romney based on their terms. We were on the air then, but we didn't have the financial resources because we still were using primary money, that money we'd all be using in a primary election to advertise in four states. I mean it was a lopsided media war for the first two or three months of the campaign simply because we didn't have the money to compete.[97]

The Obama campaign strategy carried risks—if it had failed to define Romney, it might have lacked the necessary finances for the general election.

A similar pattern held for the Super PACs linked with Obama and Romney. Priorities USA Action spent $13.2 million in June, $15.7 million in July, and $24.5 million in August. And in August, it ran a highly controversial—and risky—TV ad alleging that Romney's work at Bain Capital was responsible for the cancer death of a laid-off worker's wife. This ad was reminiscent of the Swift Boat ads run against John Kerry by an outside group in 2004. The Obama campaign criticized the ad, but the ad may have reinforced the general criticism of Romney's business credentials.[98]

In contrast to Priorities USA Action, Restore Our Future spent $7.3 million in June, $8.1 million in July, and $20.2 million in August. One reason was that Restore Our Future was short of funds, because its fundraising strategy was directed at preparing for the general election.[99] But other factors central to the nature of Super PACs came into play as well. First, Super PAC spending was largely negative at a time when Romney needed to answer the charges leveled against him by Obama and to define himself in a positive way. Spies argued, "Outside groups cannot effectively run positive ads because the best positive ads feature the candidates themselves, and outside groups can't coordinate with campaigns to generate candidate-to-camera footage."[100] Then there was the necessary lack of coordination with the Romney campaign as a proper division of labor. Spies put it this way, "I think there's a legitimate argument that the Romney campaign did not counter with a positive narrative about Romney."[101]

In sum, the Super PACs that supported Romney assumed that the Romney campaign would respond to the Obama attacks as well as offer a positive message about Romney. Financial limitations aside, the Romney campaign appears to have made a major strategic error. Spencer Zwick had this take:

> There are two types of campaigns. You can run a referendum campaign, or you can run a choice campaign. The referendum campaign is the campaign that I think [the Romney campaign] thought made the most sense, which is an "Obama isn't working" message, "therefore, donate [to Romney] if you don't want four more years of this guy." That works to ignite the base, but it probably wasn't sufficient to get people to say, "Do I believe that Mitt Romney cares about me?" That's the second half of the equation, that there's nothing like negative advertising to get people excited, but I don't think it was, and that probably is not enough, or at least it wasn't enough for this election. Running, in this case, a referendum campaign on Barack Obama, I don't think was enough to win the election.[102]

By the end of the summer, Romney was benefiting from a surge in outside spending, so that "Team Romney" pulled ahead of "Team Obama" in advertising expenditures, $273 million to $239 million. But given the uncoordinated nature of outside spending, Obama still held the advantage because his campaign was in greater control of the message and campaign activities. As one journalist observed, "Just 25 percent of all the ads that are intended to benefit Romney have come from the former Massachusetts governor's campaign; outside groups, including Super PACs, have made up the difference. By contrast, 86 percent of the total advertising effort meant to boost Obama has come from the president's own campaign."[103] Thus in both financial and strategic terms, the Obama campaign held an advantage over Romney by the time of the national conventions.

The National Conventions

The 2012 nomination campaigns ended with the Republican National Convention in Tampa, Florida (August 27–30), and the Democratic National Convention in Charlotte, North Carolina (September 3–6). Both parties received $18 million in public financing funds for the conventions. The Republican and Democratic convention host committees respectively raised $55 million and $42 million in private donations. Thus the total spending for both parties was $133 million, considerably less than the $167 million spent in 2008. One reason for the decrease in private spending was a $50 million federal grant awarded to Tampa and Charlotte for convention security.[104]

Private Cash and Super PACs

The 2012 presidential nomination finances were driven by private cash and Super PACs. The final collapse of the public finance system removed previous restraints on candidate campaign spending. This lack of restraint allowed the major candidates to deploy a more comprehensive finance strategy with the general election in mind, including maximizing contributions to their own campaign committees and joint fundraising committees with their political parties, and encouraging supporters to engage in outside spending via Super PACs. In the absence of a contested primary season, the Obama campaign was better situated to exploit these opportunities, and it did so in an astute fashion. In contrast, the Romney campaign had to cope first with a competitive primary season and then with the difficulties of running against an incumbent. In addition, the Romney campaign was somewhat less skillful than its opponent.

The decay of the public financing system resulted from broad changes in the political environment of presidential campaigns. The combination of new finance rules, increased competition, and technological innovation provided candidates with strong incentives to choose private cash over public funds. A simple comparison illustrates the choice: at the end of the nomination campaign, Obama had $88 million in cash on hand, almost as much as the $91 million in public funds he did not accept. Romney was in a less favorable position, with cash on hand of $73 million, more than half of the public financing grant. But both candidates had already spent more than the grant amount in the bridge period alone; furthermore, they had excellent prospects of raising even more during the general election. And this does not include increased party and interest group spending in support of the candidates.

In this regard, Super PACs are the most recent mechanism for raising private funds outside of candidate committees. Before 2012, outside money was in part a response to the restraints imposed on candidates by contribution limits and spending limits for those accepting public funds. In 2012 Super PACs linked with specific candidates operated beyond the contribution limits, and with candidates bypassing public funding the spending limits did not act as a restraint either. Added to that was spending by other groups, such as tax-exempt organizations, which did not have contribution limits and whose donors were not disclosed. Indeed, Super PACs were in some ways less problematic than the tax-exempt groups because fuller disclosure of Super PAC activities was required. But the key feature of all these activities was independent expenditures.

Independent expenditures are evidence of a long-standing tension in federal finance law between preventing corruption and protecting political speech. On the first count, federal courts have permitted limits on campaign contributions and coordinated activities that establish a direct link between candidates and donors. But on the second count, the courts have rejected limits on spending that is not coordinated with candidates, even when it establishes an indirect link between candidates and donors. One early result of this tension was the creation of the public financing system, where candidates agreed to limit their direct and coordinated spending in return for public money. The Super PACs are an extension of this logic, with uncoordinated spending allowing for unlimited contributions.

The "independence" of such spending has been controversial. To a casual observer, the difference between supporting a candidate via contributions or via uncoordinated expenditures may appear academic—and the independence of the Super PACs' spending linked with a specific presidential candidate even less credible. However, there are extensive legal requirements that must be met to establish such independence, and these rules appear to have been followed in 2012. The impact of these requirements can be seen in the characteristics of Super PAC independent expenditures. On one hand, such expenditures tended to be against rival candidates rather than for the favored candidate. But on the other hand, such expenditures were often at cross-purposes with the favored candidate. As Stuart Stevens of the Romney campaign reported after the 2012 election, "What we discovered on our side, to our surprise and disappointment, was that there were some superb pro-Romney ads, but there was little impact on voters, not what we would have expected them to have."[105] The most important reason for the ineffectiveness of the ads "was that they were not coordinated with the campaign. They produced ads that were good as they stood alone, but they weren't directing one message."[106]

As a consequence, Super PACs were often an effective way of expanding resources in support of a candidate but an inefficient way of advancing the candidacy with voters. These characteristics help explain the uneven impact of Super PACs in the nomination contests and their modest impact during the bridge period, when the volume of campaign spending was high.[107]

Thus independence was both the key strength and the key weakness of the Super PACs. Put another way, the Super PACs were less unpredictable members of the Obama and Romney teams in 2012. Here the central role of the president's campaign finances provided greater direction to the team members, while the inability of the Romney campaign to coordinate as much activity and spending as the Obama campaign made it less effective. However, such difficulties were not unique to Romney: the Democratic team in 2004 and the Republican team in 2008 faced similar problems.[108]

In any event, 2012 saw an expansion of the scope and range of fundraising by and for the major-party nominees, and a key part of this expansion was a dramatic increase in the role of very large contributions. In this regard it is tempting to compare 2012 to 1972, the last election before the contingent and mandatory finance rules were put in place. The 1972 presidential campaign was characterized by unrestrained spending and large contributions, which contributed to scandals that led to major campaign-finance reforms.

However, the political environments of the two elections were quite different. For one thing, the primary system of 2012 was in its infancy in 1972, and the nomination calendar has had a major impact on candidate finance. In addition, the finance abuses of the Watergate era were already illegal in 1972, while the financial changes of 2012 operated under color of law.[109] If a prerequisite for campaign finance reform is a "big money" scandal, then the impetus for reform lies in the future.

The focus on large donors in 2012 threatens to obscure the important role of small donors, particularly by the Obama campaign, which expanded on its 2008 success with further innovations. But raising small donations in this fashion is expensive, requiring a large, long-term investment in personnel, infrastructure, and data collection. For many candidates, access to such resources may be more difficult than access to very large contributions—and may be just as problematic from the point of view of competitive campaigns. As Tom Edsall argued, "Early money is crucial to the long-haul development and testing of high-tech voter contact research techniques. An incumbent's built-in edge over out-party challengers, who must first spend millions to win the nomination, is now so strong that it almost guarantees two-term presidents."[110] There is surely some truth in this conclusion, especially without the restraints of the public financing system.

However, it is important to remember that Obama was able to develop his small-donor program in the context of the highly competitive 2008 primary season, and other candidates may be able to follow this path in the future. Another alternative is for the national party committees to develop this capacity, as they have done in the past with other campaign resources, from polling to voter lists. Spencer Zwick made this point with regard to the 2012 campaign, arguing that "the investment in the digital front of the campaign by the Republican Party should have been made three years ago."[111]

The 2012 experience has strong implications for the 2016 presidential nomination campaigns, when there will be an open race in both political parties. It seems likely that the major candidates will start their campaigns in the cycle, seeking to deploy a comprehensive finance strategy aimed at winning the general election. Ideally, such a strategy would involve the development of multiple organizations, including a leadership PAC and a sophisticated campaign committee aimed at high-dollar fundraising; investments and preparations for a small-donor program and preparations for joint fundraising efforts; and Super PACs led by candidate supporters. There may be further innovations in Super PAC activity as well. Taken together, these prospects forecast a 2016 presidential nomination campaign with record-breaking finances.

Notes

1. Unless otherwise noted, all 2012 finance figures come from the FEC. All 2008 and 2004 figures in this chapter are in 2012 dollars. On the 2008 nomination campaign, see John C. Green and Diana Kingsbury, "Financing the 2008 Presidential Nomination Campaigns: A Requiem for the Public Financing System?," in *Financing the 2008 Election*, edited by David B. Magleby (Brookings, 2011), pp. 86–126. For 2004, see John C. Green, "Financing the 2004 Presidential Nomination Campaigns," in *Financing the 2004 Election*, edited by David B. Magleby, Anthony Corrado, and Kelly D. Patterson (Brookings, 2006), pp. 93–125.

2. In the 2012 nomination campaign, the combination of candidate, joint fundraising, and candidate-linked Super PAC spending was $1.2 billion, 14 percent less than the $1.4 billion of the combined candidate and joint fundraising committee spending. These figures come from the tables in this chapter and from Green and Kingsbury, "Financing the 2008 Presidential Nomination Campaigns."

3. On the impact of contingent public finance regulations, see Green and Kingsbury, "Financing the 2008 Presidential Nomination Campaigns."

4. The trend toward candidate nonparticipation in public financing began in 1996 with Republican Steve Forbes's self-financed nomination campaign.

5. On the invisible primary in 2008, see Arthur C. Paulson, "The 'Invisible Primary' Becomes Visible: The Importance of the 2008 Presidential Nominations, Start to Finish," in *Winning the Presidency, 2008*, edited by William J. Crotty (Boulder, Colo.: Paradigm Publishing, 2009), pp. 87–109.

6. The bridge period was actually a little longer for the Democrats in 2012 because President Obama was nominated on September 6, 2012. Of course, Obama did not face a contested nomination either. So the bridge period dates are approximate in any event.

7. In 2008 Obama received an advisory opinion from the FEC that authorized this practice; Green and Kingsbury, "Financing the 2008 Presidential Nomination Campaigns."

8. David B. Magleby, "Electoral Politics as Team Sport: Advantage the Democrats," in *The State of the Parties: The Changing Role of Contemporary American Parties*, 6th ed., edited by John C. Green and Daniel J. Coffey (Lanham, Md.: Rowman and Littlefield, 2011), pp. 81–101.

9. Federal Election Commission, Advisory Opinion 2011-12, "Majority PAC and House Majority PAC" (http://saos.nictusa.com/saos/searchao;jsessionid= EB013FF42804D449C85A525013216427?SUBMIT=ao&AO=3268).

10. On frontloading in 2008, see Stephen J. Wayne, "When Democracy Works: The 2008 Presidential Nominations," in *Winning the Presidency, 2008*, edited by Crotty, pp. 48–69.

11. Jeff Zeleny, "Primary Calendar Stirs Republican Anxiety," *New York Times*, July 25, 2011 (www.nytimes.com/2011/07/26/us/politics/26primary.html? pagewanted=all&_r=1&).

12. For 2004, see Green, "Financing the 2004 Presidential Nomination Campaigns"; for 2008, see Green and Kingsbury, "Financing the 2008 Presidential Nomination Campaigns."

13. For 2004, see Green, "Financing the 2004 Presidential Nomination Campaigns"; for 2008, see Green and Kingsbury, "Financing the 2008 Presidential Nomination Campaigns."

14. See Green and Kingsbury, "Financing the 2008 Presidential Nomination Campaigns."

15. For each of these candidates, a mixed strategy might have been more by accident than design because of unsuccessful high-dollar fundraising.

16. On patrons in 2004, see Green, "Financing the 2004 Presidential Nomination Campaigns"; and for 2008, see Green and Kingsbury, "Financing the 2008 Presidential Nomination Campaigns."

17. Spencer Zwick, campaign finance director for Romney for President Inc., interview by David Magleby, March 15, 2013.

18. Green and Kingsbury, "Financing the 2008 Presidential Nomination Campaigns."

19. Green, "Financing the 2004 Presidential Nomination Campaigns."

20. Green and Kingsbury, "Financing the 2008 Presidential Nomination Campaigns."

21. Green, "Financing the 2004 Presidential Nomination Campaigns."

22. Green and Kingsbury, "Financing the 2008 Presidential Nomination Campaigns"; Zwick, interview.

23. Devin Dwyer, "Obama Swing State Fund Taps Wealthy to Aid Key States," *Political Punch* (blog), *ABC News*, February 3, 2012 (http://abcnews.go.com/blogs/politics/2012/02/obama-swing-state-fund-taps-wealthy-to-aid-key-states/).

24. Compiled from Federal Election Commission data.

25. In 2012 Romney raised $124 million, about 11 percent more than in his unsuccessful nomination bid in 2008, and he spent about 5 percent—about $112 million—in both cases. Green and Kingsbury, "Financing the 2008 Presidential Nomination Campaigns," p. 93.

26. Zwick, interview.

27. In 2008 McCain had ten joint fundraising committees during the bridge period.

28. Zwick, interview.

29. If the joint fundraising committees are to be included, the Obama advantage is reduced by about $15 million at the beginning of the general election campaign.

30. Green and Kingsbury, "Financing the 2008 Presidential Nomination Campaigns."

31. Campaign Finance Institute, "Money vs. Money-Plus: Post-Election Reports Reveal Two Different Campaign Strategies" (http://cfinst.org/Press/PReleases/13-01-11/Money_vs_Money-Plus_Post-Election_Reports_Reveal_Two_Different_Campaign_Strategies.aspx).

32. Green and Kingsbury, "Financing the 2008 Presidential Nomination Campaigns."

33. These "volunteer fundraisers" included those who raised funds for the Obama campaign as well as for the Obama Victory Fund 2012, in amounts of $50,000, $100,000, $200,000, $500,000, and more than $500,000. See Center

for Responsive Politics, "Barack Obama's Bundlers" (www.opensecrets.org/pres12/bundlers.php).

34. Adam Wollner, "Clinton Allies, Politicians among Obama's New Bundlers," *Open Secrets Blog*, July 20, 2012 (www.opensecrets.org/news/2012/07/obama-campaign-releases-new-bundler.html).

35. Andy Kroll, "Obama Has Attended, on Average, One Fundraiser Every 60 Hours While Running for Reelection," *Mother Jones*, August 13, 2012 (www.motherjones.com/mojo/2012/08/obama-200-fundraisers-romney-record).

36. Campaign Finance Institute, "Obama's Long-Term Small-Donor Strategy Begins to Show Dividends against Romney in August," September 6, 2012 (www.cfinst.org/Press/Releases_tags/12-09-24/Obama%e2%80%99s_Long-Term_Small-Donor_Strategy_Begins_to_Show_Dividends_against_Romney_in_August. aspx).

37. On Obama's online fundraising, see Joanne Fritz, "Online Fundraising Lessons from Obama's 2012 Campaign," March 11, 2013 (http://nonprofit. about.com/b/2013/03/11/online-fundraising-lessons-from-obamas-2012 campaign.htm); Jonathan Weisman and Danny Yadron, "Inside the Obama Money Machine," *Wall Street Journal*, November 19, 2011 (http://online.wsj.com/article/SB100014240 52970204517204577042142257818640.html); and Brian Koenig, "Obama Campaign Goes High-Tech in 2012 Reelection Effort," *New American,* April 9, 2012 (www.thenewamerican.com/tech/computers/item/11133-obama-campaign-goes-high-tech-in-2012-reelection-effort).

38. Messina quoted in Simone Baribeau, "5 Ways the Obama Campaign Was Run Like a Lean Startup," *Fast Company*, November 14, 2012 (http://www.fast company.com/3002973/5-ways-obama-campaign-was-run-lean-startup).

39. Baribeau, "5 Ways the Obama Campaign Was Run Like a Lean Startup."

40. Kyle Rush, "Meet the Obama Campaign's $250 Million Fundraising Platform," *Kyle Rush* (blog), November 27, 2012 (http://kylerush.net/blog/meet-the-obama-campaigns-250-million-fundraising-platform/).

41. Green and Kingsbury, "Financing the 2008 Presidential Nomination Campaigns."

42. Alex Pappas, "Romney Says He Raised $19 Million at Monday Fundraiser," *Daily Caller*, June 16, 2011 (http://dailycaller.com/2011/05/16/romney-says-he-raised-10-million-at-monday-fundraiser/).

43. Fredreka Schouten and Gregory Korte, "25% of Romney Bundlers Hail from Finance Sector," *USA Today*, July 18, 2012 (http://usatoday30.usatoday.com/news/politics/story/2012-07-10/romney-bundlers-finance-sector/56156 630/1).

44. The 2012 Romney donor program involved individual donors, "founding partners" (who gave $100,000), and "founding members" (who gave $50,000) as well as bundlers, "stripes" (who raised $500,000), and "stars" (who raised $250,000) in individual donations. Maggie Haberman, "Romney's

Donor Goodies," *Burns and Haberman* (blog), *Politico*, June 18, 2012 (www.politico. com/blogs/burns-haberman/2012/05/romneys-donor-goodies-123881.html).

45. This figure is estimated from Google searches of news articles about Romney fundraisers, collated by date. We also use Associated Press staff reports to tally Romney's May 29 through August 28, 2012, fundraisers; see Emily Chow, Ted Melnik, and Karen Yourish, "Presidential Campaign Stops: Who's Going Where," *Washington Post*, November 7, 2012 (http://wapo.st/2012-campaign-visits).

46. Zwick, interview.

47. Ibid.

48. Ibid.

49. David B. Magleby, "How the 2008 Elections Were Financed," in *The Change Election: Money, Mobilization, and Persuasion in the 2008 Federal Elections*, edited by David B. Magleby (Temple University Press, 2011), p. 47.

50. Green and Kingsbury, "Financing the 2008 Presidential Nomination Campaigns."

51. Green, "Financing the 2004 Presidential Nomination Campaigns."

52. For 2004, see Green, "Financing the 2004 Presidential Nomination Campaigns." For 2008, see Green and Kingsbury, "Financing the 2008 Presidential Nomination Campaigns."

53. Ibid.

54. For a profile of Restore Our Future, see Rachael Marcus, "PAC Profile: Restore Our Future," Center for Public Integrity, January 30, 2012, updated January 17, 2013 (www.publicintegrity.org/2012/01/30/7977/pac-profile-restore-our-future).

55. Dan Eggen and Chris Cillizza, "Romney Backers Launch 'Super PAC' to Raise and Spend Unlimited Amounts," *Washington Post*, June 23, 2011 (http://articles.washingtonpost.com/2011-06-23/politics/35265459_1_priorities-usa-action-american-crossroads-romney-supporters).

56. Alexander Burns, "Mitt Romney Addressing Super PAC Fundraisers," *Politico*, June 28, 2011 (www.politico.com/news/stories/0711/60143.html).

57. Michael Isikoff, "Mystery Million Dollar Donor Revealed," *NBC Today News*, August 6, 2011 (www.today.com/id/44046063/ns/today-today_news/t/mystery-million-dollar-romney-donor-revealed/#.Ug7IzD1vI5t). For a description of Restore Our Future's top donors, see Russ Choma, "Priorities USA Gains Edge with Help of New Donors," *OpenSecret Blog*, October 21, 2012 (www.opensecrets.org/news/2012/10/priorities-usa-gains-edge-with-help-of-new-donors.html).

58. Robert Draper, "Can the Democrats Catch Up in the Super-PAC Game?" *New York Times Magazine*, July 5, 2012 (www.nytimes.com/2012/07/08/magazine/can-the-democrats-catch-up-in-the-super-pac-game.html?_r=0). For a profile of Pri-

orities USA Action, see Aaron Mehta, "PAC Profile: Priorities USA Action," Center for Public Integrity, January 30, 2012, updated July 25, 2012 (www.publicintegrity. org/2012/01/30/8025/pac-profile-priorities-usa-action).

59. Jeff Mason, "Paltry Fundraising by Obama 'Super PAC' Prompted New Strategy," *Reuters,* February 21, 2012 (www.reuters.com/article/2012/02/21/us-usa-campaign-obama-superpac-idUSTRE81K02S20120221).

60. Melanie Mason, "Bill Maher Announces a $1 Million Donation to Pro-Obama Super PAC," *Los Angeles Times,* February 24, 2012 (http://articles. la times.com/2012/feb/24/news/la-pn-bill-maher-obama-super-pac-20120224). For a description of Priorities USA Action top donors, see Russ Choma, "Priorities USA Gains Edge with Help of New Donors," *OpenSecret Blog,* October 21, 2012 (www.opensecrets.org/news/2012/10/priorities-usa-gains-edge-with-help-of-new-donors.html).

61. For a profile of Winning Our Future, see Alexandra Duszak, "PAC Profile: Winning Our Future," Center for Public Integrity, January 30, 2012, updated January 17, 2013 (www.publicintegrity.org/2012/01/30/7998/pac-profile-winning-our-future).

62. For a profile of Red White and Blue PAC, see Rachael Marcus, "PAC Profile: Red White and Blue Fund," Center for Public Integrity, January 30, 2012, updated January 17, 2013 (www.publicintegrity.org/2012/01/30/8006/pac-profile-red-white-and-blue-fund).

63. For a profile of Make Us Great Again, see Aaron Mehta, "PAC Profile: Make Us Great Again," Center for Public Integrity, January 30, 2012, updated January 17, 2013 (www.publicintegrity.org/2012/01/30/8016/pac-profile-make-us-great-again).

64. For a profile of Our Destiny PAC, see Aaron Mehta, "PAC Profile: Our Destiny," Center for Public Integrity, January 30, 2012, updated January 17, 2013 (www.publicintegrity.org/2012/01/30/8019/pac-profile-our-destiny).

65. For a profile of the Revolution PAC, see Paul Abowd, "PAC Profile: Revolution," Center for Public Integrity, January 30, 2012, updated January 16, 2013 (www.publicintegrity.org/2012/01/30/8012/pac-profile-revolution); for a profile of the 9-9-9 PAC, see Paul Abowd, "PAC Profile: 9-9-9 Fund," Center for Public Integrity, January 30, 2012, updated January 16, 2013 (www.publicintegrity.org/2012/01/30/8022/pac-profile-9-9-9-fund). Michele Bachmann received support from several Super PACs established by social conservatives, but there was no clear link to Bachmann among the leadership of these organizations.

66. This section draws on James W. Ceaser, Andrew E. Busch, and John J. Pitney Jr., "The Republican Nomination Contest," in *After Hope and Change: The 2012 Elections and American Politics* (Lanham, Md.: Rowman and Littlefield, 2013), pp. 51–90.

67. On Romney's preparation for the 2012 campaign, see Newell G. Bringhurst and Craig L. Foster, *The Mormon Quest for the Presidency* (Independence, Mo.: John Witmer Books, 2011), pp. 262–74.

68. Sarah Stone, "GOP Primary Nears $80 Million Price Tag," *Campaigns and Elections Insider*, February 25, 2012 (www.campaignsandelections.com/campaign-insider/306572/gop-primary-nears-80-million-price-tag.thtml). On Iowa advertising spending in 2008, see "2012 Iowa Caucus.biz" (www.iowacaucus.biz/IA_CAUCUS_MONEY.html).

69. Jeff Zeleny, "Romney Shifts in Iowa, Playing to Win Quickly," *New York Times*, November 19, 2011 (www.nytimes.com/2011/11/20/us/politics/mitt-romney-shifts-in-iowa-playing-to-win-quickly.html?_r=1&ref=jeffzeleny).

70. Sasha Issenberg, "Anatomy of a Narrow Victory," *Slate*, January 4, 2012 (www.slate.com/articles/news_and_politics/victory_lab/2012/01/romney_s_iowa_win_it_took_a_lot_more_than_money_.html.Issenberg).

71. Ruth Marcus, "Super PACs Are a Dangerous New Weapon," *Washington Post*, January 3, 2012 (www.washingtonpost.com/opinions/super-pacs-are-a-dangerous-new-weapon/2012/01/03/gIQAfGVDZP story.html).

72. In 2013 Bachmann faced an investigation of her presidential campaign finances. Ben Jacobs, "Michele Bachmann Investigation Gets House Ethics Committee Extension," *Daily Beast*, September 13, 2013 (www.thedailybeast.com/articles/2013/09/12/michele-bachmann-investigation-gets-house-ethics-committee-extension.html).

73. Stone, "GOP Primary Nears $80 Million Price Tag."

74. Ariel Sabar, "GOP Bellwether Shows a Tangled Race," *Christian Science Monitor*, August 2, 2007 (www.csmonitor.com/2007/0802/p01s02-uspo.html?page=1).

75. Stone, "GOP Primary Nears $80 Million Price Tag."

76. Ibid.

77. Paul Blumenthal, "Mitt Romney Florida Primary Comeback Fueled by Deep Pockets, Big Advertising Spending," January 28, 2012 (www.huffington-post.com/2012/01/28/mitt-romney-florida-primary-newt-gingrich-super-pac_n_1239002.html).

78. Stone, "GOP Primary Nears $80 Million Price Tag."

79. Jonathan Martin, "Romney Worked the CPAC Straw Poll," *Burns and Haberman* (blog), *Politico*, February 12, 2012 (www.politico.com/blogs/burns-haberman/2012/02/romney-worked-the-cpac-straw-poll-114267.html).

80. Katy Bachman, "Super Tuesday TV Spending Not So Super," *Adweek*, March 8, 2012 (www.adweek.com/news/political-ads/super-tuesday-tv-spending-not-so-super-138803).

81. Thomas B. Edsall, "In Political Campaigns, Do You Get What You Pay For?," *Opinionator* (blog), *New York Times*, April 10, 2013 (http://opinionator.blogs.nytimes.com/2013/04/10/in-political-campaigns-do-you-get-what-you-pay-for/?smid=tw-NYTOpinionator&seid=auto).

82. Charles R. Spies, counsel and treasurer of Restore Our Future, interview by David Magleby, December 21, 2012.

83. Peter Overby, "Pro-Romney Super PAC Spent Big on Super Tuesday," *NPR*, March 7, 2012 (www.npr.org/2012/03/07/148137446/superpac-spent-heavily-before-super-Tuesday).

84. Christi Parsons and Kathleen Hennessey, "Obama Volunteers Adapt to Reality of 2012," *Los Angeles Times*, August 23, 2012 (http://articles.latimes.com/2012/aug/23/nation/la-na-obama-volunteers-20120823).

85. This observation comes from Ian P. Schwarber, who worked for the Obama campaign in Ohio.

86. Romney campaign official, interview by David Magleby, December 12, 2012.

87. Ibid.

88. Edsall, "In Political Campaigns, Do You Get What You Pay For?"

89. Chris Cillizza, "Obama Allies Attack Mitt Romney in Michigan," *The Fix* (blog), *Washington Post*, February 22, 2012 (www.washingtonpost.com/blogs/the-fix/post/obama-allies-attack-mitt-romney-in-michigan/2012/02/22/gIQACnmJTR_blog.html).

90. Sean Sweeney, senior strategist for Priorities USA, interview by David Magleby, February 11, 2013.

91. Green, "Financing the 2004 Presidential Nomination Campaigns."

92. Edsall, "In Political Campaigns, Do You Get What You Pay For?"

93. Zwick, interview.

94. Ibid.

95. Melanie Mason, "Romney Campaign Took $20 Million Loan, Still Owes $11 Million," *Los Angeles Times*, September 18, 2011 (http://articles.latimes.com/2012/sep/18/news/la-pn-mitt-romney-fundraising-loan-20120918).

96. Green, "Financing the 2004 Presidential Nomination Campaigns."

97. Neil Newhouse, cofounder of Public Opinion Strategies, interview by David Magleby, December 27, 2012.

98. Sweeney, interview.

99. Spies, interview.

100. Ibid.

101. Ibid.

102. Zwick, interview.

103. Dominico Montanaro, "Political Campaign Ad Spending Tops $500 Million," *First Read*, August 16, 2012 (http://firstread.nbcnews.com/_news/2012/08/16/13319834-political-campaign-ad-spending-tops-500-million).

104. On the Republican convention spending, see John Clarke, "Republican National Convention Could Bring Tampa $173 Million," *Forbes*, August 18, 2012 (www.forbes.com/sites/johnclarke/2012/08/18/republican-national-convention-could-bring-tampa-173-million/). On the Democratic convention spending, see *Tourism Economics*, "2012 Democratic National Convention Economic Impact," January, 2013 (http://crva.com/files/docs/DNC%20Economic%20Impact%20Study.pdf).

105. Edsall, "In Political Campaigns, Do You Get What You Pay For?"

106. Ibid.

107. Ibid.

108. For 2004, see Green, "Financing the 2004 Presidential Nomination Campaigns." For 2008, see Green and Kingsbury, "Financing the 2008 Presidential Nomination Campaigns."

109. See Hebert E. Alexander, *Financing the 1972 Election* (Lexington, Mass.: D. C. Heath, 1976).

110. Edsall, "In Political Campaigns, Do You Get What You Pay For?"

111. Zwick, interview.

FOUR   *Financing the 2012 Presidential General Election*

CANDICE J. NELSON

Although overall spending by the Republican and Democratic candidates and by the parties and groups supporting them in the 2012 presidential election was relatively even on both sides, that was not the case during the general election. The Obama campaign outraised the Romney campaign by almost $100 million dollars during this period.[1] Spending by the Republican Party and outside groups helped the Romney campaign offset some of the Obama fundraising advantage, but the Obama campaign had direct control over more money. In Romney's case he was more dependent on his Super PAC and other allied groups, meaning he had less control over where money was spent and what it was spent on. Obama was also able to take greater advantage of the discounted advertising rates given to candidates but not to outside groups.

As noted earlier in this volume, Super PACs continued to play an important role in the 2012 general election. However, the financial advantage the Romney campaign had in Super PAC support was tempered by the campaign's inability to coordinate with its allied Super PACs. The Super PACs that opposed Obama were not consistently presenting reinforcing messages, as highlighted by Bill Burton at Harvard after the election: "Crossroads and Restore focused a lot on jobs and debt, but if you look at what AFP [Americans for Progress] was doing with Solyndra and all these other attacks, and you've got the Romney campaign doing welfare reform and the war on religion."[2] In addition, because Super PACs are best suited to advertising, Romney-affiliated Super PACs could not make up for the Obama campaign's advantage in developing and supporting an aggressive ground game. Although the Republican National Committee (RNC) and Romney mounted a more active voter mobilization effort in 2012 than the committee had with McCain in 2008, they still fell well short of the Obama voter mobilization in battleground states in 2012. One experienced observer noted that he had never seen a presidential campaign as "unflinchingly devoted" to field operations as the Obama campaign was.[3]

The Obama campaign also made a strategic investment in building a database of potential supporters and in using data analytics and metrics to more efficiently target fundraising appeals and media buys and to enhance the success of its field operation.[4] This chapter examines these factors in the financing of the 2012 presidential election.

General Election Spending

Table 4-1 compares candidate, party, and independent group expenditures in the general election in 2012 with such expenditures in the previous two presidential elections. As pointed out in the introduction, this was the first presidential election since the Federal Election Campaign Act of 1972 (FECA) established public funding of elections that neither major-party candidate accepted public funding in the general election.[5] Both the amounts spent by the candidates and the overall spending in the election reflect that change. More than $1 billion was spent by candidates, political parties, and independent groups in the 2012 general election, exceeding the $722 million spent by the same array of participants in the 2008 election.

When spending by parties and independent groups is included, overall support for Governor Romney's campaign efforts exceeded that of President Obama by about $121 million ($650 million in support of Romney, compared with $528 million in support of Obama). The reverse is true if we look only at candidate expenditures. The Obama campaign itself spent over $132 million more than the Romney campaign;[6] the Obama campaign spent $382.7 million, compared with $249.9 spent by the Romney campaign. The Obama campaign had a spending advantage throughout 2012. As the previous chapter points out, the Obama campaign raised more than $441 million between January 1, 2011, and August 31, 2012, whereas the Romney campaign raised $283.5 million during the same period.[7] At the start of the general election, the Obama campaign had $88.7 million cash on hand, compared with Romney's $50.4 million, an almost $40 million advantage.[8] Party spending played a minimal role in the general election, but spending by Super PACs and

Table 4-1. *Campaign Finances, 2004, 2008, and 2012*
Presidential General Elections
Millions of dollars

	2004 Election		2008 Election		2012 Election	
	Bush	Kerry	Obama	McCain	Obama	Romney
Candidate						
Candidate-public funding	74.6	74.6	0	84.1	0	0
Candidate-private funding	0	0	336.9	0	382.7	249.9
Candidate-GELAC[a]	12.2	8.9	0	46.4	0	0
Candidate total	86.8	83.5	336.9	130.5	382.7	249.9
Party						
Coordinated expenditures	16.1	16.0	6.4	18.9	2.8	1.0
Independent expenditures[b]	18.2	120.3	1.1	53.5	0	19.9
Hybrid advertising expenditures[c]	22.9	12.0	0	28.9	0	20.0
Victory Funds[d]	0.1	0.3	18.5	16.0	54.4	79.5
Party total	57.3	148.6	26.0	117.3	57.2	120.4
Groups and political committees						
Independent expenditures[e]	7.6	35.2	38.5	26.8	81.0	278.5
Electioneering communications[f]	36.8	18.0	6.0	9.2	0	0
Communication costs	1.3	23.0	29.8	1.0	7.3	0.7
Group total	45.7	76.2	74.3	37.0	88.3	279.2
Total	189.8	308.3	437.2	284.8	528.2	649.5

Source: Based on data reported to the FEC and the CMAG. Unless noted otherwise, figures represent funds spent in the period from the date of the national nominating convention through the end of the election.

a. Total amount deposited in McCain's GELAC account. Of this amount, $16.9 million had been spent by the end of the election year.

b. All Democratic and Republican National Committees' independent expenditures, including disbursements made before the national nominating conventions. Total for each candidate is expenditures in support of the candidate and against his opponent.

c. Figures include only the share of hybrid spending that can be attributed to the party, since the monies spent by the candidate are included in the candidate's funds. In 2004, Bush and the RNC spent a total of $45.8 million on hybrid advertising, while Kerry and the DNC spent $24 million. In 2008, McCain and the RNC spent a total of $57.9 million. In 2012, the RNC and Romney spent $20 million on hybrid advertising (Rick Wiley, political director of the Republican National Committee, interview by David Magleby, February 11, 2013) and the DNC and Obama spent nothing (see Emily Miller, "Obama's Cash Crunch; RNC Has the Edge in a Key Monetary Battle," *Washington Times*, October 26, 2012, p. B2).

d. Transfers to affiliated committees and offsets to operating expenditures are deducted from the joint fundraising committee disbursement totals to avoid double counting.

e. Total for each candidate is expenditures in support of the candidate and against his opponent.

f. Totals for 2008 do not include the $2.6 million spent by The One Campaign on advertisements that referenced both Obama and McCain.

other independent groups vastly exceeded independent spending in the previous two presidential elections and was heavily skewed to assist Romney. Almost $200 million more was spent independently in support of Romney or in opposition to Obama ($278.5 million) than was spent in support of Obama or in opposition to Romney ($81 million).

Table 4-2. *Receipts and Disbursements, 2012 Presidential
General Election*[a]
Millions of dollars

Candidate and party	Receipts	Disbursements
Democratic Party: Obama	297.2	382.7
Republican Party: Romney	199.9	249.9

Source: Based on disclosure filings reported to the FEC (www.fec.gov/finance/disclosure/candcmte_info.shtml).
a. Data are from September 2012 through December 2012.

Candidate Spending

As noted, the Obama campaign exceeded the Romney campaign in both
receipts and expenditures in the general election (see table 4-2). The
$132 million difference in the amounts spent by the two campaigns gave
the Obama campaign a substantial strategic advantage. First, the campaign had more money under its direct control. It was not reliant on other
groups, for example, the Democratic National Committee (DNC), to
decide how best to spend the money to advance Obama's candidacy. Second, candidates, not political parties or outside groups, are eligible for the
lowest unit rate in political advertising. This means the Obama campaign
got more bang for its buck in terms of campaign spending. One attendee
at a postelection briefing, who was comparing Obama and Romney television advertising, explained it this way: "The Obama guys put more lead
on the target and were buying their bullets cheaper."[9]

Jim Margolis, a media consultant for the Obama campaign, described
this advantage in more detail at the postelection conference at Harvard
University.

> So we spent about twice as much out of OFA [Obama for America]
> as the Romney people did out of the Romney for President cam-
> paign. And the difference there is we are getting the lowest unit rate
> time. . . . And so we got a rate that was often, as you got into the
> end of the campaign, half—even sometimes a third—of what the
> Super PACs were paying for that advertising.[10]

In addition, the Obama campaign turned to its data analytics team to
inform its ad buying. "The campaign used a program called 'the opti-

mizer' that linked data from its voter bases, focus groups, and television ratings to determine how to reach people who do not typically see campaign ads."[11] One campaign official described the campaign's ad buying:

> We were able to put our target voters through some really complicated modeling to say, O.K., if Miami-Dade women under 35 are the targets [here is] how to reach them. . . . As a result, the campaign bought ads to air during unconventional programming, like "Sons of Anarchy," "The Walking Dead," and "Don't Trust the B---- in Apt. 23," skirting the traditional route of buying ads next to local news programming.[12]

The same campaign official, when asked to compare ad buying in 2008 and 2012, said, "On TV we were able to buy 14% more efficiently . . . to make sure we were talking to our persuadable voters." One of the biggest financial investments the Obama campaign decided to make was to build

> a holistic, totally in-house digital operation that [was] the largest department in the campaign headquarters. [The campaign] hired a number of nonpolitical tech innovators, software engineers, and statisticians, invested in cutting edge technology that [scaled] the website to fit the screen of any device, and developed a complex symbiosis between the campaign and Facebook.[13]

In the end, the Obama campaign had 33 million Facebook friends, compared with the Romney campaign's 12 million.[14] The campaign also rigorously tested e-mails. Amelia Showalter, the campaign's director of digital analytics, describes the process: "We did extensive A-B testing not just on the subject lines and the amount of money we would ask people for, but on the messages themselves and even the formatting."[15] In *Bloomberg Businessweek*, Joshua Green reported that "the campaign would test multiple drafts and subject lines—often as many as 18 variations—before picking a winner to blast out to tens of millions of subscribers."[16]Alex Gage, the CEO of Target Point Consulting, whose firm worked for the Romney campaign, compared the technologies of the two campaigns: "Obama's re-election campaign is the only one doing cutting-edge work with data. . . . President Obama's re-election team consist[ed] of statisticians, predictive modelers, data miners, experts, mathematicians, software developers, general analysts, and organizers. . . . The Romney campaign . . . did not have data scientists, mathematicians, predictive modelers, or statisticians."[17]

Campaign Advertising

As the previous chapter shows, the Obama and Romney campaigns had very different strategies with respect to campaign advertising. The Obama campaign chose to begin defining Romney during the summer with a series of ads attacking Romney's tenure at Bain Capital, whereas the Romney campaign chose to hold its advertising until the fall. At the post-election conference at Harvard University's Institute of Politics, Obama campaign strategist David Axelrod and Romney campaign strategist Stuart Stevens described their respective strategies. "We gambled, and we gambled on front-loading,"[18] said Axelrod, while Stevens's perspective was, "It was really a $20 to $40 million decision, and [we decided] that we'd rather have $20 to $40 million to spend in October."[19]

The Obama campaign's early effort to define Romney paid off in the general election; Romney was never able to escape the perception that he was an out-of-touch businessman who did not understand the issues facing the majority of Americans. In exit polls following the election, 53 percent of respondents thought Romney's policies would generally favor the rich, whereas just one-third (34 percent) of respondents believed his policies would favor the middle class. When asked who was more in touch with "people like you," 53 percent of respondents cited Obama, compared with 43 percent who thought Romney was more in touch.[20]

Although American Crossroads tried to counter the Obama campaign's attack on Romney's record at Bain, spending more than $9 million on ads in 9 states, the Super PAC spending was just not as effective as the message from the Obama campaign. Neil Newhouse, a pollster for the Romney campaign, makes this point in comparing the spending of the two campaigns. "Our side in general relied much more heavily on Super PACs because it was available and they did a great job, but it was less impactful than it would have been had the Romney campaign itself had the money to spend as Obama did."[21]

The Super PACs that supported Romney also expected that the Romney campaign would focus on the positive messaging for Romney, while the Super PACs would take care of the negative attacks on Obama. Charles R. Spies, the counsel and treasurer of Restore Our Future, a Super

PAC that supported the Romney campaign, described the expectations: "I think everybody thought the campaign was going to do positives. . . . We primarily saw our focus as continuing to define the failed Obama academy and making clear that Obama's policies weren't working."[22]

Yet some people affiliated with Romney Super PACs felt the Romney campaign was not as effective as it could have been in driving the campaign's positive message. One person interviewed for this project reflected, "I was surprised they did not do more. . . . There were a lot of positive elements to his story that never got told."[23]

Candidate Fundraising

Because neither major-party nominee accepted public funding in the general election, both had to devote time to fundraising. In 2008, though Obama declined public funding, McCain did not, so though Obama needed to spend time fundraising, it did not take his campaign long to exceed the $84 million in public funds the McCain campaign had to spend in the general election.[24] The Obama campaign raised $150 million in September 2008 alone.

That was not the case in 2012. Unshackled by the restrictions of public funding, both candidates competed for an advantage in fundraising. Often, the competition for funds occurred in states with large pockets of wealthy donors, such as New York, California, and Texas, none of which were battleground states in 2012. In practice, that meant both candidates had to take time away from campaign events in battleground states for fundraising events in nonbattleground states. This had not been the case since public funding was inaugurated in the 1976 general election. The following description of both candidates' campaign schedules illustrates the role of fundraising in the 2012 general election and its toll on campaign events.

> With less than seven weeks remaining until election day, the Republican presidential nominee spent his morning at a Salt Lake City finance event before a scheduled trip to Dallas for a private fundraising dinner.
>
> Entrenched in the most conservative state in the nation before landing deep in the heart of Texas, the entirety of Romney's day will have been spent hundreds of miles from the nearest swing state. . . .

Over the last seven days, Romney's public events have included just two rallies: one with supporters at a campaign office in Florida, and a speech to the United States Hispanic Chamber of Commerce in California.

During the same time frame, he has attended seven private fundraisers and had two days with no events scheduled at all, choosing instead to prepare for the three upcoming debates with President Obama and conducting one TV interview.

In all, Romney has spent only nine of the 19 days since the conclusion of the Republican National Convention campaigning in battleground states. . . .

President Obama has also kept his foot on the fundraising gas pedal as autumn approaches.

When Romney's campaign plane touches down in Dallas on Tuesday night, for instance, Obama will be on his way to attend a pair of Manhattan fundraisers.[25]

Not only did Obama need to raise money to compete against Romney, he also needed to raise money to compete against Super PACs and other independent expenditure groups. As reported in the previous chapter, almost $96 million was spent by Super PACs and other independent expenditure groups against Obama during the primary season and over the summer. In fact, one of the Obama campaign's most successful fundraising e-mails during the summer was one with the subject line, "I will be outspent." The e-mail, sent in June, brought in more than $2.6 million dollars, performing better than seventeen similar fundraising e-mails.[26] As table 4-3 shows, $227 million was spent by Super PACs and other independent expenditure groups against Obama in the general election. President Obama did not attend his last fundraising event until mid-October; only then could he "turn his focus entirely to campaigning in the swing states, aides say, wasting no time on private fundraisers that have sometimes filled his schedule over the past few weeks."[27] Romney also continued fundraising into the final month of the campaign; his last fundraising events were held in Palm Beach, Florida, on October 20.[28]

The way the Obama and Romney campaigns raised money also differed. Simply put, the Obama campaign raised more of its money in small donations than did the Romney campaign. As table 4-4 shows, the Obama campaign raised 64 percent of its money in the general election in amounts of $200 or less, whereas the Romney campaign raised just

Table 4-3. *Outside Money, 2012 Presidential General Election*[a]

	Candidates	
	Obama	Romney
SuperPAC independent expenditures		
For	16,588,662	14,142,866
Against	149,737,977	47,616,152
Other group independent expenditures		
For	7,646,807	37,225,065
Against	77,368,224	9,181,104
Internal communication costs		
For	5,483,419	568,545
Against	162,545	1,856,985
Electioneering communication costs		
For	0	0
Against	0	0

Source: Compiled from Federal Election Commission data.

a. Figures represent funds spent from September 1, 2012, through the end of the election. Expenditures reported as for or against a candidate are self-reported by the groups making the expenditures.

13 percent of its donations in these smaller amounts. Conversely, 61 percent of the Romney campaign's general election money came from maximum donations of $2,500, compared with 13 percent of the Obama campaign's donations. According to Spencer Zwick, the Romney campaign's finance chairman, the campaign built its fundraising program around maxed-out donors. "We built that maxed-out base by marketing maxed-out pricing, so what we did when we created a donor program, when we marketed raising programs, we would market it around what was initially the $2,500 per person maxed-out."[29]

Another way to look at the respective contributions to the Obama and Romney campaigns is to compare itemized and unitemized contributions (see table 4-5). The Federal Election Commission requires federal campaigns to disclose their donors once they contribute an aggregate amount of $200 or more to a campaign. Between September 1 and December 31, 2012, the Obama campaign raised more than twice as much as the Romney campaign in unitemized donations (Obama, just over $71 million; Romney, just over $33 million).[30] Because unitemized donations represent donors who contribute less than $200, this is another measure of the ability of the Obama campaign to repeatedly attract greater numbers of small donations.

Table 4-4. *Individual Donors, 2012 Presidential General Election*[a]
Dollars

	Candidates	
	Obama	Romney
Itemized individual donors (number)	253,130	176,619
Net individual contributions	466,271,952	258,137,307
Less than $200		
Amount	297,624,523	33,299,117
Percent	64	13
$201–$999		
Amount	71,209,327	35,339,929
Percent	15	14
$1,000–$2,499		
Amount	34,566,936	31,517,233
Percent	7	12
$2,500 or more		
Amount	62,871,166	157,981,028
Percent	13	61

Source: Compiled from Federal Election Commission data.

a. Data from September through December 2012. Totals represent contributions from individuals minus refunds. The percentages shown are the percentage of net individual primary contributions given by donors in each category. Obama's and Romney's amounts include donor contributions to their joint fundraising committees.

Strategically, these differences in campaign resources meant the Obama campaign had many more donors whom it could solicit over and over again, because the donors had not reached their contribution limits. The campaign also used the metrics it developed for its advertising and field programs to increase fundraising capabilities. The database the campaign developed allowed it to target donors based on their age, interests, and socioeconomic backgrounds. For example, the campaign found that "$3 was a 'magic number.' Asking supporters for that small donation to win a chance to attend a fundraiser with the president and George Clooney or Sarah Jessica Parker generated tens of thousands of responses—people from whom the campaign can collect highly valuable data and then go back to."[31] One of the Obama campaign's most successful fundraising programs was its Quick Donate program. This program allowed donors, after their first contribution to the campaign, to simply indicate for subsequent contributions the amount, without having to also reenter their credit card information. Quick Donate donors ended up giving about four times as

Table 4-5. *Itemized and Unitemized Individual Contributions to Presidential Candidates, 2012 General Election*

	September 1–30, 2012	October 1–17, 2012	October 18– November 26, 2012	November 27– December 31, 2012
Obama				
Itemized	63,283,768	36,208,412	41,620,462	161,158
Unitemized	33,069,328	18,268,563	19,802,184	271,790
Total	96,353,096	54,476,975	61,422,646	432,948
Romney				
Itemized	29,512,946	26,406,646	21,035,195	63,850
Unitemized	12,403,804	11,688,103	9,153,738	53,470
Total	41,916,749	38,093,749	30,188,933	117,320

Source: Federal Election Commission (http://query.nictusa.com/pres/).

much as other small contributors.[32] Also, because the campaign developed technology to fit smart phones, tablets, and other electronic devices, donors were able to contribute in ways not possible four years before. According to Obama campaign manager Jim Messina, "More than 40 percent of all our donors are new, and a lot of them are coming in because of things like this [smart phones]."[33]

Table 4-5 is also instructive in illustrating the amounts of money each campaign raised during the general election. In both itemized or unitemized donations, the Obama campaign raised more money than the Romney campaign. In September alone, a key month for finalizing planning for the final campaign air and ground operations, the Obama campaign raised almost $100 million, more than twice the $41.9 million raised by the Romney campaign.

Party Spending

The Democratic and Republican Parties can advance the candidacies of their presidential nominees in four ways: direct contributions to the candidates, coordinated expenditures on behalf of the nominees, independent expenditures in support of the nominee or in opposition to his or her opponent, and joint fundraising committees. National party committees can contribute $5,000 to presidential candidates, and state, district, and local party committees can contribute another $5,000. Although the

DNC spent almost three times what the RNC spent in coordinated expenditures, the amounts themselves were exceedingly small; the DNC spent $2.8 million in coordinated expenditures, while the RNC spent just $1 million.

The biggest difference in expenditures by the two national committees was in independent expenditures. The DNC made no independent expenditures on behalf of the Obama campaign or in opposition to Governor Romney,[34] whereas the RNC spent $43.6 million in independent expenditures. There were also some notable differences in the joint fundraising committee activity in the 2012 general election. Joint fundraising committees allow the campaigns and the parties to jointly raise money and then share the amounts raised between the parties and the candidate. Joint fundraising committees can also be an efficient way to raise money from wealthier donors, because donors can write one check to the committee, rather than several checks to the candidate, the national party, and the state party. For example, in the 2012 general election, an individual could contribute $45,800 to a joint fundraising committee, combining the allowed $5,000 contribution to a candidate ($2,500 in the primary and $2,500 in the general),[35] $30,800 to a national party committee, and $10,000 to a state, district, or local party committee. This was exactly the strategy the Romney campaign used in the general election. According to Matt Waldrip, the Romney campaign's deputy national finance director, "[The campaign] just made the strategic decision to break this down into two 'asks': one was a primary and then one was a general. The primary max out was $2,500 and the general max out was the full contribution amount that you could ask for from the joint fundraising committee."[36] The RNC, the Romney campaign, and the state Republican parties raised about $313 million in joint fundraising, compared with about $341 million raised by the DNC, the Obama campaign, and the Democratic state party committees. However, about $35 million more was transferred from joint fundraising committees to the Obama campaign than was transferred to the Romney campaign. As was pointed out above, this meant that the Obama campaign had more of that money under its direct control.

Independent Expenditures and Super PACs

Super PACs were the most important new addition to campaign finance in the 2012 election. Just as Super PACs played an important role in the Republican primary, they continued to play a role in the general election.

As table 4-3 shows, Super PACs and other independent groups support-ing Governor Romney spent twice as much money, $51 million, in sup-port of Romney, compared to just $24 million spent by Super PACs and other independent expenditure groups in support of Obama. Groups self-report whether their independent spending is for or against a candidate, though how groups categorize the spending (for or against a candidate) is at the discretion of the group. The vast majority of spending related to President Obama was in opposition to him. Super PACs spent almost $150 million, and other independent expenditure groups spent another $77 million, in opposition to Obama. In contrast, only $57 million was spent by Super PACs and other independent groups against Romney.

Table 4-6 lists the twenty-eight groups that spent more than $1 million in independent expenditures in the 2012 general election. The indepen-dent expenditures could have been by a Super PAC funded by unlimited contributions or a traditional PAC funded by limited contributions. Of the twenty-eight groups, just eight were pro-Democratic. Moreover, the total spent by the eight pro-Democratic groups was just over $72 million, about $10 million less than the nearly $82 million spent by American Crossroads, a pro-Republican Super PAC, alone.

However, though the Romney campaign seemed to benefit from Super PAC and other outside spending, such spending was not as efficient as the spending by the Obama campaign itself. The following observation by Neil Newhouse, Romney's campaign pollster, illustrates the problems Super PACs faced: "It makes the [Super PAC] money, to some extent, less effective . . . because they pay higher rates for advertising, they're not always on message with where the campaign wants to go, they don't nec-essarily anticipate the strategic direction the campaign's headed in."[37]

Super PAC spending is not only less efficient than candidate spending, it is also more limited. Most Super PACs concentrate their efforts on paid media, particularly broadcast advertising, and much of that advertising is negative. Charles Spies, the counsel and treasurer of Restore Our Future, makes this point:

> Super PACs are very good at negative definition of your opponent. That's the easiest thing for an outside group to do and has the dual benefit of the negative message not having to come from the candi-date. . . . What Super PACs are not, I think, equipped to do is posi-tively defining candidates. . . . Just having an outside group trying to drive a positive message is very difficult.[38]

Table 4-6. *Independent Expenditures by Top Groups, 2012 Presidential General Election*[a]

Group	Total expenditures	Partisan classification[b]
American Crossroads	81,825,519	Republican
Restore Our Future	60,163,810	Republican
Priorities USA Action	42,990,224	Democratic
Crossroads Grassroots Policy Strategies	22,146,280	Republican
American Future Fund	19,201,429	Republican
National Rifle Association	17,918,863	Republican
Americans for Prosperity	13,298,158	Republican
Service Employees International Union	10,900,070	Democratic
Ending Spending Action Fund	9,910,670	Republican
Americans for Responsible Leadership	8,799,450	Republican
Planned Parenthood	8,249,773	Democratic
Americans for Job Security	8,228,538	Republican
Republican Jewish Coalition	6,332,629	Republican
The 60 Plus Association	3,229,634	Republican
Fair Share Action–Fair Share Alliance	2,956,025	Democratic
Workers' Voice	2,674,242	Democratic
National Right to Life	2,339,348	Republican
Conservative Majority Fund	1,777,276	Republican
America's Next Generation	1,769,671	Republican
League of Conservation Voters	1,759,488	Democratic
Focus on the Family Action	1,536,057	Republican
RightChange.com Inc.	1,520,000	Republican
Florida Freedom PAC	1,472,115	Democratic
American Federation of State, County, and Municipal Employees	1,383,984	Democratic
Super PAC for America	1,362,213	Republican
Hispanic Leadership Fund	1,333,899	Republican
Local Voices	1,266,266	Democratic
Restore America's Voice PAC	1,168,967	Republican

Source: Compiled from Federal Election Commission data (ftp://ftp.fec.gov/FEC).

a. Expenditures made in support of or in opposition to presidential candidates in excess of 1 million during the general election period beginning August 28, 2012. Expenditures for all national affiliates of an organization are combined, but expenditures for the state affiliates are excluded.

b. The partisan classifications were determined by the author based on each group's stated intent, the partisan orientation of their contributors (if data available), or newspaper accounts of the group's activity.

Super PACs and other outside groups are also not very good at field and get-out-the-vote activities, what is commonly called "the ground game." Again, Charles Spies commented on the strengths and weaknesses of Super PACs: "The second thing that I have not seen an outside group, whether it's a Super PAC or a 501(c)(4), do effectively is the ground game. That goes all the way back to [America Coming Together] in 2004. . . . I

Table 4-7. *Individual Contributions to Super PACs, 2012 Presidential General Election*[a]

| | Candidates | | |
Contribution	Obama	Romney	Total
$2,500 or less			
Number	1,108	1,091	2,199
Percent	78	74	
$2,501–5,000			
Number	93	69	162
Percent	7	5	
$5,001–100,000			
Number	151	244	395
Percent	11	17	
$100,001–500,000			
Number	45	47	92
Percent	3	3	
$500,001–1,000,000			
Number	16	10	26
Percent	1	1	
Greater than $1,000,000			
Number	5	6	11
Percent	< .05	< .05	< .05
Total	1,418	1,467	2,885

Source: Compiled from Federal Election Commission data.

a. Data from September 2012 through December 2012. Includes only Super PACs that were directly affiliated with each candidate. The data represent contributions from donors as reported to the FEC by the Super PACs. An individual who gave five separate $1,000 contributions would show up five times in the $2,500 or less column and not in the $2,501 to 5,000 column.

think they found that using paid staff to do get out the vote activities was not as effective as the organic and organized campaign volunteers of the Bush effort."[39]

Finally, table 4-7 breaks out individual contributions to candidate-related Super PACs. Although much was made in the press about wealthy individuals giving substantial donations to Super PACs, in fact, 76 percent of contributions to Super PACs were $2,500 or less. Six percent of Super PAC donations were between $2,501 and $5,000, 14 percent were donations of between $5,001 and $100,000, and only slightly more than 4 percent were donations of more than $100,000. Twenty-six donors gave between $500,001 and $1 million to Super PACs, and just eleven donors gave more than $1 million to these PACs.

Conclusion

The Obama campaign had a strategic fundraising advantage in the 2012 general election. It outraised and outspent the Romney campaign by more than $1 million. Because it had more money under its control, campaign spending, particularly on advertising, was more efficient, and the campaign was able to stretch its campaign dollars further. Moreover, the campaign's decision to invest in cutting-edge technology and sophisticated modeling metrics enabled it to target its fundraising and advertising in ways that had not been done in previous elections.

Although Super PACs and other independent groups that supported Romney tried to offset their financial disadvantage, their spending was less efficient. The cost of running ads was higher, and they could only guess what advertising would be helpful to the Romney campaign. In the end, the Obama campaign's general election financing was more focused, more efficient, and more successful than that of the Romney campaign.

Super PACs will most likely be part of the presidential election landscape for the foreseeable future. Charles R. Spies describes Super PACs as "essential. . . . It's a tool that levels the playing field. . . . If you don't have one you're basically defenseless."[40] By the summer of 2013, Republicans announced a new Super PAC, America Rising, to do opposition research for other Super PACs and to compete with American Bridge 21st Century, which was formed by Democrats after the 2010 election and was active in 2012.[41] Speaking at the postelection conference at the Harvard University Institute of Politics, Spies observed that "until the McCain-Feingold law is repealed or at least modified and you're able to get money into political parties and campaigns, you are going to have outside groups having a disproportionate influence."[42]

Super PACs will continue to play a role in presidential elections, but public funding will not. The amount of money candidates can raise will continue to dwarf the amount of public funds available to them, so presidential candidates will continue to fund their campaigns with private donations, as both major-party candidates did in 2012.

Presidential candidates also try to learn from past campaigns. The success of the Republican Party's 72 Hour Task Force in the 2004 presidential election led the Democratic Party to rethink how it approached its ground game in 2008. The Obama campaign's success in turning out African Americans, Latinos, and young people in 2008 led its 2012 campaign to develop analytics to further refine its approach to voter identification, turnout, fundraising, and advertising. The success of the Obama campaign's metrics in 2012 led the Republican Party, by the summer of 2013, to put together a team to develop its own data system to emulate and, the party hoped, improve on the Obama data metrics for the 2014 and 2016 elections.[43]

Every presidential campaign in the modern era has brought innovation into campaign funding, and the 2012 election was no different. Super PACs became the newest vehicle for raising and spending money, the public funding system implemented by FECA in 1976 became completely irrelevant, and campaigns continued to devise new ways to effectively raise and spend money. The latest twist in campaign finance came in the spring of 2014, with the Supreme Court's decision in *McCutcheon* v. *Federal Election Commission*. The first test of the implications of this decision will occur during the 2014 midterm elections, but the decision will also impact the 2016 presidential elections, as contributors will be able to contribute up to the maximum allowable per candidate and to as many federal candidates as they wish.

Notes

1. The difference between the Obama for America and Romney for President campaign committee receipts during the general election was $100 million; see Federal Election Committee, "Candidate and Committee Viewer" (www.fec.gov/finance/disclosure/candcmte_info.shtml).

2. The Institute of Politics, John F. Kennedy School of Government, Harvard University, *Campaign for President: The Managers Look at 2012* (Lanham, Md.: Rowman and Littlefield, 2013), p. 149.

3. Mike Lux, cofounder and president of Progressive Strategies, L.L.C., interview by David Magleby, January 14, 2013.

4. Lois Romano, "Obama's Data Advantage," *Politico*, June 9, 2012 (www.politico.com/news/stories/0612/77213.html).

5. Although the Federal Election Campaign Act of 1972 established public funding of presidential campaigns, it was not until the 1976 presidential election that public funding took effect.

6. The difference between the combined Obama campaign and joint fundraising committees and the combined Romney campaign and joint fundraising committees during the general election period was $132 million; see Federal Election

Commission, "Candidate and Committee Viewer" (www.fec.gov/finance/disclo sure/candcmte_info.shtml).

7. Federal Election Commission, "Candidate and Committee Viewer," September 25, 2013 (www.fec.gov/finance/disclosure/candcmte_info.shtml).

8. Ibid.

9. Tom Hamburger, "In Election Postmortems, Romney's TV Advertising Strategy Comes Under Fire," *Washington Post*, December 12, 2012, p. A6.

10. Institute of Politics, *Campaign for President*, pp. 132–33.

11. Michael Kranish, "Mitt Romney Was Hesitant to Reveal Himself," *Nation* (blog), *Boston Globe*, December 23, 2012 (www.bostonglobe.com/news/nation/ 2012/12/23/the-story-behind-mitt-romney-loss-presidential-campaign-president-obama/OeZRabbooIw0z7QYAOyFFP/story.html).

12. Michael Scherer, "How Obama's Data Crunchers Helped Him Win," America's Choice 2012: Election Center, *CNN Tech*, November 8, 2012 (www. cnn.com/2012/11/07/tech/web/obama-campaign-tech-team).

13. Romano, "Obama's Data Advantage."

14. Robert Draper, "Can the Republicans Be Saved from Obsolescence?" *New York Times*, February 14, 2013 (www.nytimes.com/2013/02/17/magazine/can-the-republicans-be-saved-from-obsolescence.html?pagewanted=all&_r=0).

15. Joshua Green, "The Science behind Those Obama Campaign E-mails," *Bloomberg Businessweek* (www.businessweek.com/articles/2012-11-29/the-science-behind-those-obama-campaign-e-mails).

16. Ibid.

17. Alex Gage, founder and CEO of Target Point, interview by David Magleby, December 6, 2012.

18. Institute of Politics, *Campaign for President*, p. 135.

19. Ibid., p. 192. See also Karen Tumulty, "Analyzing the Whys of Winning and Losing," *Washington Post*, December 4, 2012, p. A5.

20. "President: Full Results," *CNN Politics*, "America's Choice 2012: Election Center," December 10, 2012 (www.cnn.com/election/2012/results/race/president).

21. Neil Newhouse, cofounder of Public Opinion Strategies, interview by David Magleby, December 27, 2012.

22. Charles R. Spies, counsel and treasurer for Restore Our Future, interview by David Magleby, March 31, 2013.

23. Off-the-record interview with David Magleby, May 14, 2013.

24. For a discussion of Obama's fundraising strategies in 2008, see Candice J. Nelson, "Strategies and Tactics of Fundraising in 2008," in *Campaigns and Elections American Style,* 3rd ed., edited by James A. Thurber and Candice J. Nelson (Boulder, Colo.: Westview Press, 2010), pp. 93–103.

25. Scott Conroy, "Fundraising Trumps Rallies in Romney's Schedule," *RealClearPolitics*, September 18, 2012 (www.realclearpolitics.com/articles/2012/09/ 18/fundraising_trumps_rallies_in_romneys_schedule_115487.html).

26. Green, "The Science behind Those Obama Campaign E-mails."

27. Devin Dwyer, "Obama Attends 'Final' Campaign Fundraiser," *Political Punch* (blog), *ABC News*, October 11, 2012 (http://abcnews.go.com/blogs/politics/2012/10/obama-attends-final-campaign-fundraiser/).

28. "Presidential Campaign Stops: Who's Going Where," Campaign 2012, *Washington Post*, November 7, 2012 (www.washingtonpost.com/wp-srv/special/politics/2012-presidential-campaign-visits/).

29. Spencer Zwick, campaign finance director for Romney for President, Inc., interview with David Magleby, March 15, 2013.

30. The exact amounts were $71,411,865 for the Obama campaign and $33,299,115 for the Romney campaign. Calculated from the Federal Election Commission, Presidential Reports, "2012 Report Year: October Monthly, Pre-General, Post-General, and Year-End" (http://query.nictusa.com/pres/).

31. Romano, "Obama's Data Advantage."

32. Michael Scherer, "Inside the Secret World of Quants and Data Crunchers Who Helped Obama Win," *Time*, November 7, 2012 (http://swampland.time.com/2012/11/07/inside-the-secret-world-of-quants-and-data-crunchers-who-helped-obama-win/print/).

33. Romano, "Obama's Data Advantage."

34. The lack of independent expenditures by the DNC may have stemmed from the lessons learned by David Axelrod and David Plouffe during the 2004 presidential campaign. The DNC hired their firm to produce the committee's independent expenditures, but because they could not coordinate with the Kerry campaign, the spending was "inefficient" (David Plouffe, *The Audacity to Win* [Viking, 2009], p. 257). This experience was an important part of the Obama campaign's decision in 2008 to opt out of the public financing system in the general election, thus giving the campaign more control over spending, rather than having to rely on the DNC for key aspects of the campaign. For a detailed description of the Obama campaign's decisionmaking on the relative strategic considerations of public financing versus opting out, see Plouffe, *The Audacity to Win*, pp. 256–63.

35. In March 2007 the FEC issued an advisory opinion allowing the Obama campaign to solicit funds for the general election during the primaries. Federal Election Commission, Advisory Opinion 2007-3, issued March 1, 2007.

36. Matt Waldrip, deputy national finance director for Romney for President, Inc., interview by David Magleby, March 12, 2013.

37. Newhouse, interview.

38. Spies, interview.

39. Ibid.

40. Ibid.

41. Rachel Weiner, "America Rising: Mitt Romney Staffer Starting Opposition Research Group," *Post Politics* (blog), *Washington Post*, March 21, 2013

(www.washingtonpost.com/blogs/post-politics/wp/2013/03/21/america-rising-mitt-romney-staffer-starting-opposition-research-group/); see also Matea Gold, "2016 Is Now for Outside Groups," *Washington Post*, June 23, 2013, p. A1.

42. Institute of Politics, *Campaign for President*, pp. 156–57.

43. Micah Cohen, "From Campaign War Room to Big-Data Broom," *Bits* (blog), *New York Times*, June 19, 2013 http://bits.blogs.nytimes.com/2013/06/19/from-campaign-war-room-to-big-data-broom/?_r=0).

FIVE   *Financing the 2012*
         Congressional Elections

PAUL S. HERRNSON,
KELLY D. PATTERSON, AND
STEPHANIE PERRY CURTIS

Congressional elections naturally take a back seat to the presidential election, and 2012 was no exception. The news media lavish attention on presidential candidates and their campaigns. Voters are inundated with coverage of the candidates' strategies, standing in the polls, fundraising, and efforts to capture support in battleground states. Congressional elections, by contrast, are mostly local affairs that rarely make national headlines and often receive only minimal coverage in the local news. Occasionally a bitter or competitive congressional campaign captures the attention of the broader public, but these occurrences are the exception rather than the rule.

However, commentators and the public alike had several reasons to pay attention to the dynamics of the 2012 congressional cycle, if not the individual races. First, the 2012 elections occurred in the wake of redistricting. States redrew the congressional boundaries, a process that always interjects uncertainty into the outcomes of some previously safe seats and leaves more than a few incumbents nervous. Second, at the outset of the 2012 election cycle, Republicans believed they had an opportunity to win control of the Senate.[1] Republicans hoped that, with control of both chambers of Congress, they could stymie the agenda of President Obama, should he win a second term.[2] Democrats and allied interest groups sought to build a firewall of at least forty-one seats in the Senate to block actions of a possible Republican president and GOP majority in both houses of Congress.[3] Finally, the elections unfolded in a less regulated campaign finance environment. As Anthony Corrado shows in chapter 2 of this volume, court decisions and rulings by the Federal Election Commission (FEC) created new opportunities for candidates, parties, and interest groups to shape the flow of money into congressional elections.

The financing of the 2012 congressional elections provides a glimpse into the dizzying world of regulations, court cases, and strategic behavior that constitute the current campaign environment. Understanding the financing of these elections requires an examination of candidate, party, and interest group organizations, all of which can take on a variety of forms and engage in different practices. The efforts of individuals, who provide most of the funds collected by most Senate and many House candidates, also are important. The current environment provides a mix of incentives for individuals and organizations to contribute to candidates or coordinate their independent spending efforts with a variety of entities, which is an increasingly common tactic among interest groups. Of course, some groups work completely alone, taking an entirely independent path.[4] Consequently, any examination of the role of money in congressional elections requires a look at the principal sources of money and the institutions that disburse that money.

The Strategic Context

Presidential campaigns always pose a problem for congressional elections in terms of media coverage and money. As the most powerful among the constitutional offices, the presidency demands and receives the lion's share of media attention. When it comes to finances, there is only so much money that most individual donors, parties, and groups can raise and spend, which results in a competition for relatively small amounts of money. Of course, there are a few deep-pocketed individuals and groups that spend in the tens of millions of dollars.

Normally, incumbents in congressional elections do not have problems raising the money they need. Given their policymaking influence, visibility, and strong likelihood of reelection, they are prime targets for a variety of donors. Not surprisingly, challengers to an incumbent face the largest hurdles. Their lack of experience, public recognition, and political clout make them questionable investments for donors, especially donors who seek political access. Candidates for open seats typically raise large sums. Many bring significant political experience to the campaign, and because the lack of an incumbent typically heightens competition, an open-seat contest is viewed by many donors as an opportunity to spend their money where it will have the greatest impact on who serves in Congress.[5]

Presidential incumbents who run during times of high unemployment, low economic growth, and diminished consumer confidence normally do not win reelection.[6] Recognizing this, the Obama campaign took nothing for granted, as discussed in chapters 3 and 4. It engaged in aggressive fundraising to make sure it had the resources to wage a vigorous campaign in all of the battleground states. A similar calculation infused the Republicans. The Romney campaign, sensing that the president was vulnerable, aggressively raised money and sought to build a competitive campaign organization. The hypercompetitive environment led to a financial arms race that limited the resources available to candidates for other offices.

Although the presidential election was shaping up to be a high-profile donnybrook, the 2012 election seemed relatively tame compared with previous election cycles. Few individuals believed that Democrats had a chance to regain the House.[7] Republican hopes for winning the Senate waned as weak Republican nominees emerged in states like Indiana and Missouri.[8] Political prognosticator Charlie Cook rates contests for the U.S. Senate and U.S. House, among other contests, as solid Republican, solid Democratic, likely Republican, likely Democratic, lean Republican, lean Democratic, or toss-up. As candidates entered the last stages of the campaign, Cook pegged 192 House seats as safe for Republicans and 158 safe for the Democrats.[9] Of the nine Democratic seats rated as toss-ups, Democrats won seven. Of the twenty Republican seats rated as toss-ups, Republicans won seven and lost thirteen. Both parties held on to the majority of their seats rated as leaning toward or likely to vote for their party by the Cook Political Report. Such results confirmed two truisms about politics. First, incumbents generally win at a high rate: if most of a party's incumbents run again, that normally bodes well for the party. The second truism follows from the first: redistricting efforts often protect incumbents. The 2012 cycle was the first cycle after the redistricting process had finished in the states.

Predictably, the party that controlled the state redistricting process eased the way for the success of its party in congressional elections. This meant that the huge gains made by Republicans in state legislatures across the country would pave the way for protecting Republican members of Congress. Democrats controlled thirty-two state houses before the 2010 election. Afterward, the numbers flipped, and Republicans controlled thirty-two state houses. Republicans held only 43 percent of state legislative seats before the 2010 elections, but after the elections their representation surged to 54 percent. This meant that Republican candidates fared better in states like North Carolina, where in 2010 they won both chambers of the legislature for the first time in over a century.[10] Similar results played out across the nation, where the legislative results of 2010 shaped the 2012 congressional results. In Ohio, a state that would lose two seats in reapportionment, Republicans protected their own. Democrats did well in states like Illinois, where they were able to maintain control of both chambers of the legislature.

Incumbents also fared well in the Senate in 2012. In this chamber, however, the Democrats clearly enjoyed better results. Republicans did not defeat a single Democratic incumbent, whereas Democrats defeated Republican incumbent Scott Brown in Massachusetts and also won a formerly Republican-held open seat in Indiana. Democrats also benefited from Angus King's victory in the previously Republican-held open seat in Maine (King, elected as an Independent, caucuses with the Democrats). Republicans picked up the open seat in Nebraska, which had been Democratic. What appeared at first to be a difficult cycle resulted in an increased majority for the Democratic Party.[11]

Sensing limited opportunities, interest groups sought to participate in the relatively few congressional races where they could most likely have an effect. The Tea Party, which played such a prominent role in the 2010 midterm elections, managed again to influence the tenor and course of several races.[12] Although they did not have the impact they had in 2010, Tea Party groups managed to help nominate and fund candidates who courted the Tea Party vote. These loosely affiliated groups continued their strident criticism of the economic and social policies of the Obama administration and sought to rally individuals who expressed a preference for small government, a free-market economy, and conservative stances on social issues.[13] Liberal groups, such as labor unions, the League of Conservation voters, and NARAL Pro-Choice America, countered that the economy favored the rich and that conservative groups sought to ruin the environment and to restrict abortion rights and other moral choices. Overall, the issue agenda of the 2012 cycle differed little from 2010.[14] What mattered, however, was the presence of a presidential campaign that nationalized the conversations about campaign issues.

The groups under the umbrella of the Tea Party and labor unions were only a few of the dozens of groups that participated in the 2012 congressional elections. The cycle unfolded with a set of regulations in place that for the first time in 2010 made possible independent spending by Super PACs (also known as independent expenditure–only committees). Other groups, including 501(c) organizations and traditional political action committees (PACs), though less the center of media attention, played important roles. Section 501(c) groups are governed by rules that enable them to withhold disclosure of their financial backers. Crossroads GPS and Americans for Prosperity, both of which are 501(c)(4) groups, are examples of groups that propped up candidates and issues on the conservative side. Priorities USA, a Super PAC, and Patriot Majority USA, which was organized as both a Super PAC and a 501(c)(4), were among the groups that sustained causes on the left.[15] Overall, the amount of money flowing into the campaign arena, and the means by which it flowed, amazed veteran observers, probably baffled attentive voters who followed the campaigns, and frustrated less interested individuals whose lives were inundated by televised campaign ads and by unsolicited political mail, mass telephone calls, and e-mails.

Perhaps one of the best examples of how interest groups, parties, and candidates would act in this new regulatory campaign environment is the 4th Congressional District in the state of Utah. The 4th District is a new district created in the wake of the redrawing of congressional boundaries. With reapportionment, Utah received a fourth seat, and speculation quickly turned to the shapes the districts would take. With an overwhelming number of Republican voters with whom to work, legislators created four Republican-leaning districts and put incumbent Democrat representative Jim Matheson on the defensive.[16] Matheson chose to run in the 4th District, even though he did not live in it. The district contained enough moderate and Democratic voters from Salt Lake County to give him a better chance of winning. His opponent, Mia Love, a mayor from Saratoga Springs, Utah, burst onto the national scene because of her unique story.[17] The daughter of Haitian immigrants, she defeated better-known state legislators who also sought the Republican nomination. The significance of this race resulted in large amounts of money from the national parties and interest groups flowing into the district. The national party committees gave close to $1 million to Love, and interest groups contributed more than $2.5 million. Members of Congress donated $63,750, and contributions from individuals totaled nearly $2 million. Matheson received more than $2.8 million from interest groups, more than $600,000 from the national parties, close to half a million from individual donors, and $57,500 from other members of Congress.[18] Both of the candidates, and the networks of parties and groups that supported them, sought to leverage the rules to gain an advantage. In the end, after a plethora of ads, endorsements, and debates, Matheson prevailed by 768 votes.[19]

On the Senate side, the Virginia race was heated from the start. In 2006 Democrat Jim Webb narrowly defeated Republican incumbent George Allen by a margin of 0.6 percent in the biggest upset of the 2006 elections. Webb announced that he would not run for reelection in 2012, and former governor of Virginia and Democratic National Committee (DNC) chair Tim Kaine stepped in as the Democratic candidate.[20] Allen threw his hat back in the ring and won the Republican nomination.[21] Money flowed into this race from every direction. Interest groups spent more than $13.5 million on behalf of Kaine, while other groups spent more than $25.6 million for Allen. Individual donors and the national parties stepped in to even out the spending in this competitive race. Individuals contributed nearly $16.1 million and national parties contributed or spent just over $9 million to help Kaine, while Allen received $11.2 million from donors and benefited from close to $7 million in national party committee contributions and expenditures. Allen's hopes were dashed when he lost by 6 percent of the vote.[22]

Campaign Contributors

In some respects the 2012 cycle looked quite similar to other election cycles. Issues and the intensity of campaigns seemed familiar. The motivations of individual donors, parties, and interest groups were probably the same as in previous election cycles. Individual donors participated because of concerns related to political access, issues, ideology, and the pleasure some get from participating in the process.[23] Interest groups also pushed their agendas and wanted to make sure that congressional candidates were aware of the interest groups' support.[24] As usual, political parties sought to maximize the number of congressional seats they held.[25] They wanted their candidates at all levels of government to succeed, but their resources flowed to the elections where they could have the greatest impact.

Political Parties

Party committees want to win as many offices as possible; this overriding aim shapes all subsequent decisions as to where money and other resources should go. The Democratic Congressional Campaign Committee (DCCC) and the National Republican Congressional Committee (NRCC) play the lead role in devising the parties' national strategies in House elections. They advise House candidates on campaign strategy and assist in hiring campaign consultants, raising money, conducting issue and opposition research, and encouraging contributions from PACs and individuals.[26] The congressional campaign committees are particularly helpful in assisting with the fundraising of freshman lawmakers, incumbents in jeopardy of losing their seats, and nonincumbents in competitive elections.[27] In recent years, they have played a critical role in redistributing the wealth from party leaders and other safe incumbents to candidates involved in races that are too close to call.[28] The Democratic Senatorial Campaign Committee (DSCC) and the National Republican Senatorial Committee (NRSC) perform similar roles in Senate elections. The DNC and the Republican National Committee are typically less involved in congressional elections, but their voter registration and mobilization efforts can influence the outcomes of these contests.[29]

Under the Bipartisan Campaign Reform Act (BCRA), the national, congressional, and state party committees can each contribute $5,000 to a House candidate in the general election; the parties' national and senatorial campaign committees can contribute a combined total of $43,100 (in 2012) in direct contributions to a Senate candidate; and state party committees can contribute an additional $5,000 to candidates for the House and Senate.[30] Parties provide additional assistance to candidates through coordinated expenditures.[31] These transactions, which offer both parties and candidates the opportunity for input, usually pay for public opinion polls, television and radio ads, issue and opposition research, fundraising, and other campaign activities.[32] The limits for national party coordinated expenditures are indexed for inflation. In 2012 national parties could make a total of $45,600 in coordinated expenditures in House elections and between $91,200 and almost $2.6 million in Senate elections, depending on the size of the state's voting-age population.[33] State party committees are authorized to spend the same amounts in coordinated expenditures in House and Senate elections as the parties' national organizations. Party organizations also can make unlimited independent expenditures to expressly advocate the election of their candidates or the defeat of those candidates' opponents.[34] These expenditures must be made without the knowledge or consent of the candidate, the candidate's campaign organization, or any other group working in cooperation or

Figure 5-1. *Party Receipts, 2012 Federal Elections*[a]

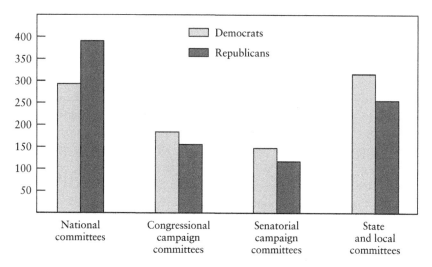

Millions of dollars

Source: Federal Election Commission, "National Party Committee Data Summaries (1/1/11–12/31/12)" (www.fec.gov/press/summaries/2012/ElectionCycle/NatlPartyYE.shtml).
  a. Funds in parties' federal accounts; excludes funds transferred among party committees.

coordination with a candidate, including some other part of the party (see chapter 2).

In 2012 the national parties vigorously raised funds to sustain all these types of activities. The Republicans have traditionally enjoyed a fundraising advantage over the Democrats because of their ability to tap into a deeper pool of wealthy and upper-middle-class donors and because of their superior direct-mail fundraising operation.[35] However, the Democrats have begun to close the gap in recent years. The DNC, the DCCC, and the DSCC all improved their direct-mail donor bases and introduced other fundraising innovations. Their Internet-based fundraising programs were relatively effective. As figure 5-1 shows, by the 2012 cycle the Democratic congressional and senatorial campaign committees had raised more than their Republican counterparts. It is somewhat unusual that the DCCC fundraising surpassed that of the NRCC. Usually, the party that controls the House (the Republicans in 2012) enjoys substantial fundraising advantages. Even Democratic state and local committees raised more money than Republican state and local committees. Only the DNC did not raise as much as its Republican counterpart during the 2012 elections.

Figure 5-2. *Party Contributions, Coordinated Expenditures, and Independent Expenditures, 2012 Congressional Elections*

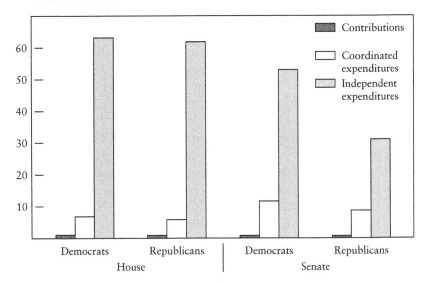

Source: Compiled from Federal Election Commission data.

The relatively low ceilings for party contributions and coordinated expenditures, combined with BCRA's prohibitions against party soft money–financed issue advocacy ads, have encouraged the parties to increase their independent expenditures since the act became law following the 2002 election (see figure 5-2). The 2012 cycle continued this trend. Because campaign finance law prohibits parties from coordinating or communicating their independent spending strategies with the candidates, candidate campaign organizations, or others working with a candidate—including party committees that advise or contribute to candidates—planning these expenditures requires substantial organizational investment. The parties must form special, segregated groups for the purpose of directing this spending. These groups have to hire their own teams of staff and consultants, purchase their own polls and other research, and create and disseminate their own TV, radio, mail, and other advertisements. These requirements increase the actual costs of making independent expenditures considerably over those associated with routine contributions and coordinated expenditures. Nonetheless, campaign finance law renders independent expenditures a necessary vehicle for a party committee to invest huge sums in individual races.

Independent expenditures also come with some risk: the advertisements disseminated may be inconsistent with the message being communicated by the candidate the party is trying to help, or they might alienate that candidate's supporters, mobilize the opponent's supporters, or put the candidate at some other disadvantage. Nevertheless, in 2012, as in previous cycles, party strategists focused independent expenditures on states or districts where they thought such spending could influence the outcome of a race. Given the high value associated with each seat gained or lost in the House and Senate in the 2012 elections, and the legal limits imposed on other party spending, party officials may have been willing to incur the additional costs and risks associated with independent expenditures. The largest amount of party-independent expenditures spent in one race was in the highly competitive Virginia Senate contest. The DSCC spent more than $7.8 million attacking Republican George Allen, and the NRSC spent more than $5.7 million attacking Democrat Tim Kaine. Independent expenditures allow the parties to concentrate substantial resources in key races; the party money spent on behalf of Kaine helped influence voters and secure his win.[36]

Of course, the cash contributions and independent expenditures of formal party organizations do not constitute the full range of party efforts. Party organizations provide promising candidates with assistance in campaign management, fundraising, research, communications, and a host of other specialized election activities. In addition, party-connected committees, consisting of politicians' principal campaign committees (including retired members of Congress or those not up for reelection in 2012) and leadership PACs (including PACs sponsored by nonfederal politicians) collected and redistributed roughly $58 million to candidates in the 2012 House and Senate elections (see table 5-1).[37] This figure only slightly exceeds the almost $56 million raised in 2008 and the $54 million collected in 2006. Members of the GOP were considerably more involved in this activity than were the Democrats. Leading among Republican donors were the Senate Conservatives Fund, affiliated with Senator James DeMint (R-SC) and Every Republican Is Crucial PAC, sponsored by House Majority Leader Eric Cantor (R-VA), each of which contributed in excess of $2 million. First among the leadership PACs connected to House Democrats was AmeriPAC: The Fund for a Greater America. Associated with House Minority Whip Steny Hoyer (D-MD), this com-

Table 5-1. *Party-Connected Contributions, 2012 Congressional Elections*[a]

Dollars

	House		Senate	
Source	Democrats	Republicans	Democrats	Republicans
Leadership PACs	10,402,693	18,227,973	7,020,618	6,669,341
Candidates	5,420,130	6,291,762	435,296	1,755,410
Congressional retirees and members not up for reelection	485,739	554,849	365,057	117,970
Nonfederal-politician-sponsored PACs	41,895	322,273	13,500	197,100
Total	16,350,457	25,396,857	7,834,471	8,739,821

Source: Compiled from FEC and Center for Responsive Politics data.

a. Figures are for contributions from leadership PACs, congressional candidates, retired members, members of Congress not up for reelection in 2012, and PACs sponsored by nonfederal politicians to candidates in all congressional elections, including those in primaries, runoffs, and uncontested races.

mittee contributed almost $1.5 million to Democratic congressional candidates. Senate Majority Leader Harry Reid's (D-NV) Searchlight Leadership Fund ranked first among Democratic Senators, contributing $376,500.[38]

The distribution of these party-connected contributions to candidates of both parties for the House and Senate bear similarities and differences in the distribution of contributions and coordinated expenditures by party organizations. The major similarity is that candidates involved in competitive elections received more funds of both types than candidates in one-sided contests. The major difference is that more party-connected money than party organization money flowed to incumbents, including incumbents in uncompetitive races, than to challengers. The differences in the distributions of these two types of funds can be attributed to the differing perspectives of the individuals who allocate them. Party leaders are authorized to use party resources to pursue their party's collective goals, which in elections means maximizing the number of seats under the party's control. Party members who contribute to other candidates are concerned with advancing both the party's collective interests and their own private benefits. These private benefits include running for higher office, winning a congressional leadership race, claiming a valued committee assignment, or swaying the legislative votes of congressional colleagues.[39] Party members pursue their party's collective interests by following their party's lead in contributing to candidates in competitive elections. They pursue private benefits by contributing to the politicians most likely to be in a position to help them, which mainly includes incumbents, most of whom have a very high probability of reelection.[40]

The existence of party-connected committees signifies three important points about the roles of parties in congressional elections. First, analyses that rely solely on disbursements made by formal party organizations underestimate the parties' role in the financing of congressional elections. Second, party committees influence the contributions of individuals and other organizations, including those sponsored by members of Congress.[41] Third, the pro-incumbent bias of contributions by party-connected committees suggests that members of Congress contribute to other candidates to advance both their party's collective goals and their individual goals.[42]

Party activity in congressional elections also includes substantial voter mobilization efforts. Parties make mass telephone calls, send targeted e-mails, carry out door-knocking campaigns, and undertake other efforts to register voters and turn them out to the polls. In presidential election years, most of this activity is carried out to influence the presidential election. Still, some funds are allocated specifically to mobilize voters in key House and Senate districts. State and local party committees organize most party voter mobilization efforts, but money from the parties' national, congressional, and senatorial campaign committees has traditionally helped to fund those efforts.[43]

Interest Groups

Interest groups also assume significant roles in campaigns. From the mid-1970s through the 1990s, traditional PACs (also referred to as multicandidate committees) were responsible for all interest group contributions and virtually all independent expenditures in federal elections. As noted in chapter 1, to qualify as a traditional PAC a group must raise money from at least fifty individual donors and spend it on at least five federal candidates. Federal regulations limit individual contributions to PACs at $5,000 or less a year, and corporations, unions, and other groups are prohibited from contributing to a PAC. Most PACs provide direct contributions to specific candidates; some disseminate information that favors or opposes a candidate or help identify and mobilize voters. The FEC categorizes traditional PACs according to the sponsoring organization or, in some cases, the lack thereof. Leadership PACs, classified above

Figure 5-3. *PAC Contributions and PAC Independent Expenditures, 2012 Congressional Elections*

Millions of dollars

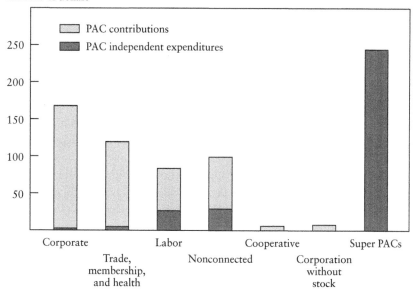

Source: PAC contributions from Federal Election Commission, "Political Action Committee (PAC) Summaries (1/1/11 –12/31/12)" (www.fec.gov/press/summaries/2012/ElectionCycle/PACYE.shtml); PAC and Super PAC independent expenditures compiled from Federal Election Commission data.

as party-connected committees, are a subset within the FEC's category for nonconnected PACs.

There are also six categories of traditional PACs (see figure 5-3). Of the traditional PACs, the largest expenditures were made by corporate PACs, amounting to more than $167 million, 99 percent of which were candidate contributions. Trade, membership, and health groups spent the second highest amount at more than $119 million, with candidate contributions making up 97 percent of the total. Traditional nonconnected PACs also made significant independent expenditures, but they allocated substantially more in the form of campaign contributions given directly to candidates; they contributed more than $70 million to congressional candidates during the 2012 election cycle. They also made an additional $28.5 million in independent expenditures. Super PACs made $244 million in independent expenditures in the 2012 congressional races.

Election-oriented interest groups use what are generally referred to as ideological, access-oriented, or mixed strategies when spending money in House and Senate elections.[44] Most of these PACs are classified as non-connected PACs by the FEC because they have no sponsoring organization. These PACs generally contribute to maximize the number of House and Senate members in office who share their policy views, often on such salient issues as abortion rights, business regulation, and the environment. These PACs distribute most of their resources to candidates in competitive contests but occasionally make contributions to encourage the careers of promising politicians. Some of their contributions go to leadership PACs, who later redistribute the funds to incumbents and other candidates in close races.[45] Nonconnected PACs concentrate on advancing issues linked to fundamental values that officeholders are seldom willing to compromise on. Planned Parenthood and National Right to Life are two prominent nonconnected PACs that were heavily involved in the 2012 congressional races.

Access-oriented PACs view elections pragmatically.[46] Their main goal is to gain access to members of Congress who are in a position to influence regulations, appropriations, taxes, or treaties that affect the policy environment in which the PAC's sponsor operates. These groups consider campaign contributions an important tool for reaffirming or strengthening their relationships with influential lawmakers. They recognize that contributions can foster goodwill in representatives and senators, making it easier for the group's lobbyists to influence the legislative process.

Political action committees that follow access strategies are likely to contribute most of their money to incumbents, especially to members of the House and Senate who occupy party leadership posts, who chair or are members of important committees or subcommittees, or who are recognized leaders in specific policy areas. Because these PACs are interested in influencing congressional policy decisions more than election outcomes, they are not typically concerned about the competitive aspect of elections. In fact, some access-oriented PACs distribute contributions well before an upcoming election and support incumbents who face no or minimal opposition. Procedural control of Congress, which influences a legislator's ability to get things done, does have a substantial impact on the flow of money from access-oriented PACs. Thus the recent switches in control from Democrats to Republicans in 1994, then back again to Democrats in 2006 and back to the GOP in 2010 had a major impact on the flow of these funds.[47] Corporate and other business PACs with dealings before Congress, such as AT&T and Microsoft, make up the largest share of this group. For example, corporate PACs contributed the most money to Utah Republican incumbent Orrin Hatch during his 2012 U.S. Senate race. Hatch has served as the chair or ranking minority member of five senate committees over the course of his six terms in office. With the $2.2 million corporate PACs spent on Senator Hatch (in contributions and independent expenditures), the uncompetitive Utah Senate race received the second-highest combined total of corporate money given to candidates in a single race—all this with only $500 contributed to Democratic challenger Scott Howell.[48]

The last group of PACs, mostly labor unions, follow mixed strategies. They make some contributions to candidates who share their views and some to incumbents with whom they wish to maintain access. In the first case, most of the contributions go to candidates in close races, and in the second case, to powerful incumbents. The most money labor PACs spent on one race in 2012, in excess of $3.4 million, was in the open-seat Wisconsin Senate contest, where Republican Tommy Thompson ended up losing a close match to Democrat Tammy Baldwin. Labor contributed only $13,500 to Thompson but made over $2.8 million in independent expenditures attacking him. By contrast, labor gave Baldwin $348,000 in contributions and made more than $202,000 in independent expenditures supporting her. Janice Hahn (CA-44) who ran against another Democratic incumbent (Laura Richardson), Steny Hoyer (MD-5), George Miller (CA-11), and Nancy Pelosi (CA-12), four powerful Democratic incumbents, were the major beneficiaries of labor PAC spending in uncompetitive races. These organizations spent $442,556; $304,140; $295,675; and $291,500, respectively, in their contests.[49] In elections where PAC decisionmakers are conflicted because the incumbent is in a position to influence the group's legislative priorities but the challenger is more supportive of the group's interests, most PACs that follow mixed strategies contribute solely to the incumbent, but a few also contribute to the challenger.

Contributions in House races followed this pattern in the 2012 cycle. Corporate PACs, which tend to share the antitaxation and antiregulation views of Republicans, gave about 68 percent of their donations to Republicans, regardless of the competitiveness of their races (see table 5-2). Trade associations did about the same at 70 percent. Similarly, nonconnected PACs distributed about 56 percent of their House contributions to Republicans. In contrast, labor union PACs made 90 percent of their

Table 5-2. *PAC Contributions, 2012 House Elections*[a]

Percent, except as indicated

	Corporate	Trade, membership, and health	Labor	Nonconnected	Leadership	Cooperative	Corporation without stock
Competitive							
Incumbents							
Democrats	8	9	18	11	12	13	10
Republicans	32	32	5	26	31	26	35
Challengers							
Democrats	1	1	20	7	13	1	2
Republicans	1	2	<.05	3	11	2	2
Open seats							
Democrats	1	1	9	3	5	2	1
Republicans	3	3	<.05	4	10	3	2
Uncompetitive							
Incumbents							
Democrats	21	18	35	21	4	20	23
Republicans	31	31	4	21	9	29	22
Challengers							
Democrats	<.05	<.05	2	<.05	<.05	<.05	<.05
Republicans	<.05	<.05	<.05	<.05	<.05	<.05	1
Open seats							
Democrats	1	1	6	2	2	2	1
Republicans	1	2	<.05	2	3	2	1
Total (dollars)	102,045,761	48,258,141	39,798,780	45,290,513	22,473,491	3,387,188	4,433,982

Source: Compiled from FEC data.

a. See table 5-4 for cell *n* values and other information, including definitions of competitive and uncompetitive races. Some columns may not add to 100 percent because of rounding. Super PACs are not included in this table because they are prohibited from making candidate contributions.

House contributions to Democrats. The 35 percent of their funds that were contributed to Democratic incumbents in lopsided contests were presumably given to party leaders, committee chairs, and policy entrepreneurs who were in positions to influence the legislative process. The overall distribution of PAC money favored members of the House majority, with Republicans receiving 57 percent of the total funding.

The pattern for Senate races looks quite different, largely because Democrats controlled the Senate, and that control seemed all the more secure as the cycle evolved. First, corporate donations favored the Republicans in competitive races and advantaged the Democrats in uncompetitive races (see table 5-3). Trade associations follow the same pattern as corporations, and labor unions contribute almost exclusively to Democrats.

The allocations of PAC dollars in the 2012 congressional elections thus underscore the differences in the two parties' constituencies. Republican general election candidates in both chambers raised substantially more PAC dollars from corporate and trade association PACs ($188 million), with 65 percent going to Republicans during the 2012 election cycle. Labor unions contributed less than one-quarter of the amount given by corporate and trade association PACs ($46 million), with 91 percent going to Democrats. Labor has been a faithful ally of the Democratic Party since the 1930s, and labor PACs have been consistent supporters of Democratic candidates for more than five decades, including twelve years marked by near-continuous Republican congressional majorities. But in comparison with other PACs, labor has been playing a smaller role. In 2012 labor PACs made 14 percent of all PAC contributions in House and Senate races combined, which is down from 16 percent in 2008 and 18 percent in 2004. Meanwhile, the Republican Party has been able to draw substantial support from corporations and trade association PACs, even before 1995 and after 2006, when it was in the legislative minority. Moreover, the relative contributions made by these PACs has been growing. Corporate and trade PACs accounted for 56 percent of all PAC contributions in 2012, down from 65 percent in 2008 and 63 percent in 2004. Both parties have strong supporters among nonconnected PACs. Most of these demonstrate their fealty to one party by consistently supporting only its candidates.

Besides PACs and Super PACs, other outside groups are involved in electing and defeating congressional (as well as presidential) candidates. Those designated as 501(c) organizations and 527 committees, as well as corporations, labor unions, trade associations, and other groups, make

Table 5-3. PAC Contributions, 2012 Senate Elections[a]

Percent, except as indicated

	Corporate	Trade, membership, and health	Labor	Noncommected	Leadership	Cooperative	Corporation without stock
Competitive							
Incumbents							
Democrats	16	16	25	18	17	18	16
Republicans	13	13	1	7	8	7	9
Challengers							
Democrats	1	2	10	7	4	3	3
Republicans	7	9	1	8	12	4	9
Open seats							
Democrats	5	5	29	13	17	11	9
Republicans	17	18	1	14	17	18	18
Uncompetitive							
Incumbents							
Democrats	26	25	25	22	13	31	23
Republicans	12	10	1	7	5	5	8
Challengers							
Democrats	<.05	0	<.05	0	0	0	0
Republicans	<.05	<.05	<.05	1	3	<.05	2
Open seats							
Democrats	1	1	.5	2	2	2	1
Republicans	1	1	<.05	2	2	1	1
Total (dollars)	27,284,692	10,614,358	6,523,999	12,831,876	10,899,244	598,295	1,104,013

Source: Compiled from FEC data.

a. See table 5-4 for cell *n* values and other information, including definitions of competitive and uncompetitive races. Some columns may not add to 100 percent because of rounding. Super PACs are not included in this table because they are prohibited from making candidate contributions.

Figure 5-4. *Outside Spending by Different Interest Group Entities, 2012 Congressional Elections*[a]

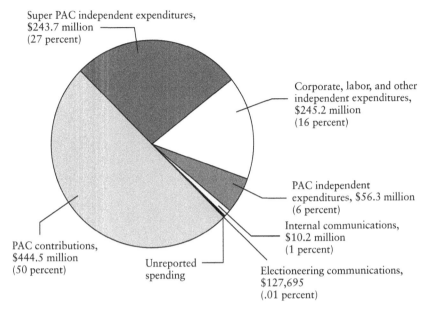

Super PAC independent expenditures, $243.7 million (27 percent)

Corporate, labor, and other independent expenditures, $245.2 million (16 percent)

PAC independent expenditures, $56.3 million (6 percent)

Internal communications, $10.2 million (1 percent)

PAC contributions, $444.5 million (50 percent)

Unreported spending

Electioneering communications, $127,695 (.01 percent)

Source: Compiled from FEC data.
a. "Corporate, labor, and other independent expenditures" includes independent expenditures reported to the FEC by 527 committees and 501(c) organizations, or funds obtained directly from corporation, union, or other group treasuries.

political expenditures independently of, rather than coordinated with, candidates' committees. In 2012 there was better coordination among outside groups, including the timing of ad buys and field resources.[50] Outside interest groups spent most of their money on independent expenditures in congressional races, but they also spent relatively small amounts on electioneering communications and internal communication costs (see figure 5-4). PAC campaign contributions to candidates accounted for half of the $900 million in reported interest group spending in the 2012 congressional elections, and PAC independent expenditures made up 6 percent. Independent expenditures financed by Super PACs, 527 committees, or 501(c) organizations, or by funds obtained directly from corporation, union, or other group treasuries accounted for 43 percent. The internal political communications that organizations distribute to their members made up about 1 percent. Electioneering communications financed by 501(c) groups and 527 committees constituted an estimated .01 percent.

Table 5-4. *Outside Spending, 2012 Congressional Elections*[a]

Dollars, except as noted

	House[b]		Senate[b]	
	Democrats	Republicans	Democrats	Republicans
Competitive				
Incumbents	21,650,213	49,367,280	44,084,708	12,312,075
	(32)	(84)	(6)	(3)
Challengers	44,758,909	17,556,794	13,955,685	39,936,726
	(84)	(32)	(3)	(6)
Open seats	14,356,890	9,339,158	46,162,555	60,583,779
	(27)	(27)	(8)	(8)
Uncompetitive				
Incumbents	851,564	2,565,466	1,965,101	1,433,374
	(93)	(87)	(9)	(2)
Challengers	47,707	1,039,512	6	1,490,379
	(87)	(93)	(2)	(9)
Open seats	1,333,115	1,371,699	815,374	898,920
	(28)	(28)	(1)	(1)
Total	82,998,398	81,239,909	106,983,429	116,655,253
N	(351)	(351)	(29)	(29)

Source: Compiled from FEC and Center for Responsive Politics data.

a. Figures are for major-party candidates in two-party contested general elections (Democrats versus Republicans), excluding incumbent versus incumbent contests. Sample sizes (number of candidates) are in parentheses. Incumbents in competitive races are defined as those who lost or who won by 20 percent or less of the two-party vote. Incumbents in uncompetitive races are incumbents who won by more than 20 percent of the two-party vote. Challengers in competitive races are those who won or who lost by 20 percent or less of the two-party vote. Challengers in competitive races are those who lost by more than 20 percent of the two-party vote. Open seats in competitive races are those whose election was decided by 20 percent or less of the two-party vote. Open seats in uncompetitive race are those whose election was decided by more than 20 percent of the two-party vote.

b. Outside spending comprises independent expenditures, electioneering communications, and internal communications of PACs, Super PACs, 527 committees, 501(c) organizations, corporations, unions, or other groups.

The final category in figure 5-4, unreported spending, is a place holder for interest group expenditures that are not publicly disclosed. These unreported issue advocacy ads take place within thirty days of primary elections and sixty days of general elections.

In total, more outside money was spent on Republican candidates in the Senate than Democrats, while spending was essentially equal in the House for the two parties (see table 5-4). Open-seat candidates in competitive Senate races received the highest proportion of money spent on Senate hopefuls. Republicans in this category received 27 percent of the total outside money spent on Senate races, and Democrats received 21 percent. The largest amount of outside group money spent in a Senate race (just over $39 million) was in the open-seat Virginia race. Democrat Tim Kaine had more than $13.5 million spent on his behalf or against his opponent,

George Allen; and outside groups spent more than $25.6 million for Allen and against Kaine.[51] Outside groups spent the highest proportion of their money (30 percent) on Republican incumbents in House races. Democratic challengers received 27 percent of the outside money spent in House races. The most outside money spent in one House race (nearly $7 million) was in the Ohio 16th Congressional District, where Democratic incumbent Betty Sue Sutton faced Republican incumbent Jim Renacci. Outside groups spent $4.3 million for Renacci (who won by 4 percent of the vote) and against Sutton, and $5 million for Sutton and against Renacci.

Individuals

Individuals historically have constituted the largest source of campaign money in congressional elections, and 2012 was no different from its predecessors. During the 2012 election cycle, individual donors gave approximately $880 million to all primary and general election candidates for the House and the Senate, or 59 percent of all congressional campaign receipts. Individuals are also major sources of funds to PACs and party committees. Some large contributors are plugged into networks that include one or more political organizations and may consider communications they receive from those networks when selecting candidates for contributions, but most individual donors give small amounts to one or a few candidates and tend to support those candidates routinely. Indeed, studies of prior elections found that 36 percent of all donors who give $200 or more in an election cycle typically contribute to only one candidate. Another 56 percent contribute to two to five candidates, and only 8 percent contribute to more than five.[52] Moreover, most individual contributions to congressional candidates do not travel very far: three-fourths of all contributions were made to a candidate in the donor's state, and in the case of House races, 70 percent went to a candidate in the donor's district or a neighboring district.[53]

The Bipartisan Campaign Reform Act set the total amount for contributions to congressional candidates at $2,000 (adjusted for inflation) per candidate in each stage of the election (primary, general, and runoff if one is held). In 2012 the limit for each stage was $2,500, meaning that donors in most cases could give a maximum of $5,000 to a candidate, if they contributed during both the primary and general elections. This law also substantially raised the aggregate limit an individual can contribute to federal candidates, party committees, and PACs. Thus BCRA created new opportunities for wealthy individuals to contribute to congressional candidates. A significant number of donors took advantage of those opportunities, and this influenced the distribution of individual contributions. At the top end, 31 percent of all individual contributions to House candidates competing in general elections races were made in amounts of $2,400 or greater, and 61 percent of those contributions, comprising $93.4 million, were given to incumbents (see table 5-5). At the bottom end, only 21 percent of all individual contributions came in amounts of less than $200, with 58 percent of those going to incumbents.

Incumbents, particularly Republicans in competitive races, received most of the individual contributions across the different contribution amounts. However, there are some notable differences in the flow of individual contributions. More contributions of less than $200 went to candidates in competitive elections than did contributions of any other size. The distribution of small contributions favored Republican incumbents in competitive races. The Republican advantage across all the categories is most likely a result of the differences in the two parties' constituencies. Individuals who believe they have the disposable income to contribute any sum to a campaign are often well educated, relatively wealthy, and connected to the business world—three of the demographic traits associated with voters who identify with the Republican Party.[54] Most appear to be motivated by policy considerations rather than ideological ones. Some of the large contributions that flow to incumbents from individuals may also be the product of social incentives such as the opportunity to meet candidates or simply be part of the inner circle.[55]

The patterns for individual contributions to Senate candidates, shown in table 5-6, bear some similarities to and some differences from individual contributions to candidates for the House. The biggest similarities are that candidates of both chambers raised most of their individual contributions in the form of large donations, and most of these were given to incumbents. Forty percent of all individual contributions to Senate candidates in typical races were made in amounts of $2,400 or greater, and 45 percent of those contributions were given to incumbents. The biggest difference is that the Democrats, not the Republicans, raised most of the contributions given in amounts of $200 or more. Another difference concerns the flow of small contributions. Democratic challengers in competitive elections collected the lion's share of these in races for the Senate; these funds were more evenly distributed in races for the House. This suggests that many contributors who gave small amounts, presumably mostly Democratic donors, appeared to respond to the possibility of picking up

Table 5-5. *Individual Contributions, 2012 House Elections*[a]

Percent, except as indicated

	Less than $200	$200–749	$750–999	$1,000–2,399	$2,400 or more	Total
Competitive						
Incumbents						
Democrats	6	9	7	9	7	8
Republicans	37	22	24	25	28	28
Challengers						
Democrats	19	17	13	11	10	14
Republicans	3	6	5	6	8	6
Open seats						
Democrats	5	7	5	5	3	5
Republicans	1	5	6	6	8	5
Uncompetitive						
Incumbents						
Democrats	9	13	15	14	12	12
Republicans	6	12	15	16	14	12
Challengers						
Democrats	2	2	1	1	1	1
Republicans	4	2	2	2	2	2
Open seats						
Democrats	4	3	4	3	3	4
Republicans	1	2	3	3	3	2
Total (dollars)	106,181,247	111,601,731	3,449,199	121,656,113	152,297,293	495,185,583
Share of total individual contributions	21	23	1	25	31	100

Source: Compiled from individual contributions data provided by the FEC.

a. See table 5-4 for cell *n* values and other information, including definitions of competitive and uncompetitive races. Some columns may not add to 100 percent because of rounding.

Table 5-6. *Individual Contributions, 2012 Senate Elections*[a]

Percent, except as indicated

	Less than $200	$200–749	$750–999	$1,000–2,399	$2,400 or more	Total
Competitive						
Incumbents						
Democrats	13	17	24	19	13	15
Republicans	1	9	8	9	14	9
Challengers						
Democrats	29	13	8	9	6	13
Republicans	9	10	12	10	16	12
Open seats						
Democrats	22	18	13	14	11	15
Republicans	9	14	10	13	16	14
Uncompetitive						
Incumbents						
Democrats	11	11	16	16	13	13
Republicans	<.05	2	4	5	5	3
Challengers						
Democrats	<.05	<.05	<.05	<.05	<.05	<.05
Republicans	6	3	3	3	3	3
Open seats						
Democrats	0	2	2	2	2	1
Republicans	0	1	1	1	2	1
Total (dollars)	77,149,707	68,400,966	2,450,818	89,068,393	155,097,326	392,167,210
Share of total individual contributions	20	17	1	23	40	100

Source: Compiled from individual contributions data provided by the FEC.

a. See table 5-4 for cell *n* values and other information, including definitions of competitive and uncompetitive races. Some columns may not add to 100 percent because of rounding.

Republican-occupied Senate seats. Individuals who had the capacity to make larger contributions, presumably more Republicans, responded just as strongly by donating to Republicans to keep Democrats from establishing a filibuster-proof Senate majority. These patterns are exemplified in the Massachusetts Senate contest, where Democratic challenger Elizabeth Warren raised the largest amount in contributions of less than $200 (over $21.7 million) of any Senate race, and Republican incumbent Scott Brown raised the most from donors who spent $2,400 or more (over $18.2 million).[56]

The Money Chase

Money, perhaps next to a candidate's talents, is the critical resource for conducting an effective campaign.[57] Without money, candidates can do very little in districts where they need to reach hundreds of thousands of voters or in states where they need to reach millions of voters. For this reason, candidates spend time and money in pursuit of more money. On average, House candidates spend 9.4 percent of their campaign budgets on fundraising.[58] Incumbents allocate a larger portion of their budgets and spend significantly more in actual dollars on fundraising and overhead than nonincumbents. These differences can be explained by the fact that virtually every House incumbent relies on one or more paid professionals—a political consultant, campaign aide, or both—who specialize in fundraising. The same is true for roughly nine out of ten nonincumbents in competitive House races. By contrast, fewer than 50 percent of the challengers in lopsided House races hire a campaign professional for fundraising.[59] Not surprisingly, practically every Senate campaign, regardless of incumbency or competitiveness, places its fundraising in the hands of professionals.[60]

Given the importance of money, it is not surprising that incumbents learn to be effective fundraisers, and raising money becomes part of their routine even in years when there is no election. Because of their connections and policymaking influence, incumbents can rely on previous donors for continued support and can attract many large contributions. Incumbents in House elections raise almost equal amounts from PACs and individuals (see figure 5-5). Challengers, on the other hand, rarely raise as much as incumbents and must rely more heavily on donations from individuals (see chapter 1).

Senators also enjoy important fundraising advantages over their challengers, but these are not nearly as substantial as those enjoyed by House

Figure 5-5. *Source of House Candidates' Receipts, 2012 Congressional Elections*[a]

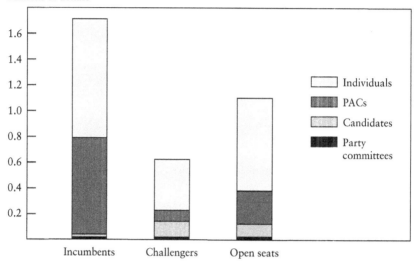

Millions of dollars

Source: Compiled from FEC data.
a. Bars represent average receipts for general election candidates in major-party contested races. Party committee contributions include coordinated expenditures. Candidate contributions include candidates' loans to their own campaigns.

members. This is because senators typically face more politically experienced challengers.[61] More often than not, senators square off against challengers who are known in the state or who have previously been elected to the House or a statewide or local office. The size and diversity of most state electorates provide most challengers with a base of support from which to launch a campaign. In 2012 senators depended more on PAC contributions than their challengers did but did not rely on PACs nearly as much as their House counterparts (see figure 5-6). Another major difference between the House and Senate is that candidates for the upper chamber, particularly open-seat contestants, depended much more on individual contributions.

Winners and Losers

What impact did campaign spending have on the outcomes of the 2012 congressional elections? Usually, the candidates who raised and spent the most money won, and most of these candidates were incumbents. Because

Figure 5-6. *Source of Senate Candidates' Receipts, 2012 Congressional Elections*[a]

Millions of dollars

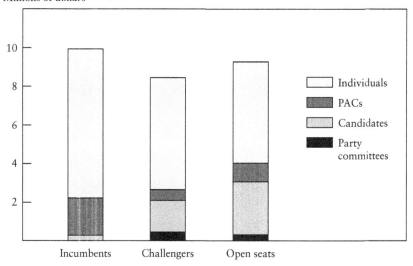

Source: Compiled from FEC data.
a. Bars represent average receipts for general election candidates in major-party contested races. Party committee contributions include coordinated expenditures. Candidate contributions include candidates' loans to their own campaigns.

most members of Congress have political clout and a high probability of electoral success, they are able to raise large sums of money, which they use to deter strong challengers and stage professional campaigns.[62] Generally speaking, advantages in name recognition, superior press relations, their opponent's weaknesses, and other factors help to explain most incumbents' success. Nevertheless, not every incumbent was successful in 2012. In the House primary races, thirteen House incumbents were defeated, and another twenty-seven lost their general elections.

One House member who was defeated was Allen West, the Republican incumbent in Florida's 22nd Congressional District, who decided after Florida's redistricting process to run in the more Republican-friendly 18th Congressional District. After facing a primary opponent whom he did not consider significant enough even to debate, he won the Republican nomination with 74.4 percent of the vote and then faced Democratic newcomer Patrick Murphy in the general election. West raised a total of $19.3 million in the 2011–12 election cycle to compete against Murphy's $4.7 million. Murphy, a newcomer to public office, ran a successful campaign, painting

West as an extreme Republican who represented Washington gridlock. Despite West's millions of campaign dollars raised from organizations such as the conservative political advocacy group Americans for Prosperity, and after several demands for a recount, West lost the reelection bid by 1,904 votes.

Notwithstanding their losses, Democratic and Republican House incumbents enjoyed reelection rates of 97 and 91 percent respectively in 2012. One senator, Richard Lugar (R-IN), a thirty-six-year incumbent, lost his renomination bid, and his seat then fell to a Democrat, and another Senate incumbent—Republican Scott Brown of Massachusetts—was defeated in the general election.

Conclusion

The financing of the 2012 congressional elections bore several similarities to the previous election cycles. Even with changes in the ways in which money could be spent, some of the same fundraising and spending patterns appear as in earlier contests. Party committees, party-connected committees, and ideological PACs, which are strongly committed to electing candidates who share their partisan affiliations or policy views, continued to pour most of their resources into close elections. Access-oriented PACs, ideological PACs, and to some extent labor PACs continued to favor House incumbents, especially members of the majority party—largely because of the incumbents' influence over policymaking and their excellent reelection prospects. Republicans did slightly better in House races, largely because they held the majority. The Democratic Party fared much better in Senate elections. Expecting to lose seats, the Democrats capitalized on the nominating and campaign blunders of the Republicans and actually increased their margin in the Senate.

Despite its similarities to previous election cycles, the 2012 cycle was unique because of the growth of outside spending. Parties and interest groups alike used independent expenditures, electioneering communications, and other forms of spending to influence the outcome of congressional races. What seemed to be a chaotic campaign environment became even more difficult for voters to navigate because of the ability of parties and groups to communicate directly with voters about their choices. Voters seemed to be at a loss as to whether the messages came from the candidate, the party, an outside interest group, or some combination of all three. Some candidates, mainly those in hotly contested races, expressed dismay at the loss of control over messaging, but that loss was a long time in the making and seems to have reached a crescendo in 2012. Freed from some of the regulatory boundaries of BCRA, those who had the where-withal and the desire to participate in elections were able to do so using a variety of spending mechanisms. In an environment where parties, and especially interest groups, can collect and spend sums from sources and in amounts prohibited to candidates, they can compete with candidates to influence voters. The world of congressional elections will probably be even more rough-and-tumble in the future than it was in 2012.

Notes

1. Russell Berman, "Republicans Hope to Win Trifecta in 2012," *The Hill,* August 27, 2012 (http://thehill.com/conventions-2012/gop-convention-tampa/245349-no-tamping-gop-hopes-of-winning-the-trifecta).

2. Michael Brenan Dougherty, "George Will: Forget Beating Barack This Year, Win the Senate and Thwart His Agenda from Congress," *Business Insider,* March 2, 2012 (www.businessinsider.com/george-will-forget-beating-barack-this-year-win-the-senate-and-his-agenda-from-congress-2012-3).

3. Navin Nayak, senior vice president of the League of Conservation Voters, interview by David Magleby, May 14, 2013.

4. Paul S. Herrnson, *Congressional Elections* (Washington: CQ Press, 2012), esp. pp. 146–50 and 168–69.

5. Ibid., pp. 174–202.

6. Bureau of the Census, "Population Characteristic (P20) Reports and Detailed Tables," Department of Commerce, May 8, 2013 (www.census.gov/hhes/www/socdemo/voting/publications/p20/index.html).

7. Nate Silver, "Do Democrats Have a Shot at the House?," *FiveThirtyEight* (blog), *New York Times,* June 23, 2012 (http://fivethirtyeight.blogs.nytimes.com/2012/06/23/do-democrats-have-a-shot-at-the-house/?_r=0).

8. Josh Kraushaar, "How Weak Candidates Could Cost the GOP Control of the Senate," *Atlantic,* July 11, 2012 (www.theatlantic.com/politics/archive/2012/07/how-weak-candidates-could-cost-the-gop-control-of-the-senate/259692/); Nate Silver, "FiveThirtyEight Forecast: G.O.P Senate Hopes Slipping," *FiveThirtyEight* (blog), *New York Times,* September 18, 2012 (http://fivethirtyeight.blogs.nytimes.com/2012/09/18/fivethirtyeight-forecast-g-o-p-senate-hopes-slipping/).

9. *Cook Political Report,* "2012 House Race Ratings for November 5, 2012" (http://cookpolitical.com/house/charts/race-ratings/5105).

10. Joshua Miller and Shira Toeplitz, "Redistricting a Winner for GOP and Democrats," *CQ Weekly,* November 12, 2012 (http://library.cqpress.com/cqweekly/weeklyreport112-000004173936), pp. 2247–50.

11. Kyle Trugstad, Abby Livingston, and *Roll Call* staff writers, "Democrats Overcome Odds, Dominate Senate Elections," *CQ Weekly*, November 12, 2012 (http://library.cqpress.com/cqweekly/weeklyreport112-000004173931), pp. 2228–30.

12. Jonathan Mummolo, "Nimble Giants: How National Interest Groups Harnessed Tea Party Enthusiasm," in *Interest Groups Unleashed*, edited by Paul S. Herrnson, Christopher J. Deering, and Clyde Wilcox (Washington: CQ Press, 2013), pp. 193–212; Janie Lorber, "Tea Party Returns with Refills," *CQ Weekly*, November 12, 2012 (http://library.cqpress.com/cqweekly/weeklyreport112-000004173913), p. 2196.

13. "The Tea Party and Religion," Pew Forum on Religion and Public Life, February 23, 2011 (www.pewforum.org/Politics-and-Elections/Tea-Party-and-Religion.aspx).

14. Gallup Poll conducted October 15–16, 2012 (www.gallup.com/poll/158123/satisfaction-stable.aspx).

15. Eliza Newlin Carney, "Politicking Under Cover," *CQ Weekly*, September 17, 2012 (http://library.cqpress.com/cqweekly/weeklyreport112-000004152999), pp. 1872–80.

16. Lisa Riley Roche, "Matheson: There's No Question I'm a Target in Redistricting," *Deseret News*, August 30, 2011 (www.deseretnews.com/article/705389999/Matheson-Theres-no-question-Im-a-target-in-redistricting. html?pg=all).

17. Jennifer Steinhauer, "Utah Mayor Hopes Star Turn, and Romney's Star Power, Lift Her to the House," *New York Times*, October 30, 2012 (www.nytimes.com/2012/10/31/us/politics/mia-love-mayor-in-utah-seeks-path-to-congress.html?_r=0).

18. Data compiled from the Federal Election Commission (ftp://ftp.fec.gov/FEC/).

19. "Election Results," *Huffington Post*, November 9, 2012 (http://elections.huffingtonpost.com/2012/results#house-races).

20. Catalina Camia, "Sen. Jim Webb Won't Run for Reelection in 2010," *USA Today*, February 9, 2011 (http://content.usatoday.com/communities/onpolitics/post/2011/02/jim-webb-senate-2012-/1).

21. David Catanese, "Allen E-mails Supporters; Webb Reacts," *Essential Intelligence from the Campaign Trail* (blog), *Politico*, January 24, 2011 (www.politico.com/blogs/davidcatanese/0111/Allen_emails_supporters.html).

22. Data compiled from FEC.

23. Peter L. Francia and others, *The Financiers of Congressional Elections* (Columbia University Press, 2003), pp. 42–68.

24. See, for example, *Interest Groups Unleashed*, edited by Herrnson, Deering, and Wilcox.

25. See, for example, Herrnson, *Congressional Elections*, pp. 101–35.

26. Ibid., pp. 91–135.

27. Ibid., pp. 118–21.

28. Ibid., pp. 109–11; Herrnson, "The Roles of Party Organizations, Party-Connected Committees, and Party Allies in Elections," *Journal of Politics* 71, no. 4 (2009): 1207–24; Eric S. Heberlig and Bruce A. Larson, *Congressional Parties, Institutional Ambitions, and the Financing of Majority Control* (University of Michigan Press, 2012), esp. pp. 95–134.

29. Herrnson, *Congressional Elections*, p. 97.

30. Party committees can also contribute $5,000 to candidates in primaries and runoff elections. However, they rarely make financial contributions until the general election.

31. Federal Election Commission, *Federal Election Commission Campaign Guide: Political Party Committees*, August 2013 (www.fec.gov/pdf/partygui.pdf).

32. See, for example, Herrnson, *Congressional Elections*, 105–07.

33. The limits for coordinated expenditures in states that have only one House district are twice the level in states with two or more House members. The upper limit in 2012 was for the California Senate race.

34. *Colorado Republican Federal Campaign Comm. v. Federal Election Commission,* 518 U.S. 604 (1996).

35. See, for example, Francia and others, *The Financiers of Congressional Elections,* 36-39.

36. Data compiled from FEC.

37. On party-connected committees see, for example, Herrnson, "The Roles of Party Organizations, Party-Connected Committees, and Party Allies in Elections."

38. Center for Responsive Politics, "Leadership PACs," March 25, 2013 (www.opensecrets.org/pacs/industry.php?txt=Q03&cycle=2012).

39. Damon M. Cann, *Sharing the Wealth* (State University of New York Press, 2008).

40. Herrnson, "The Roles of Party Organizations, Party-Connected Committees, and Party Allies in Elections"; Marian L. Currinder, "Leadership PAC Contribution Strategies and House Member Ambitions," *Legislative Studies Quarterly* 28, no. 4 (2003): 551–77; Eric Heberlig, Marc Hetherington, and Bruce Larson, "The Price of Leadership: Campaign Money and the Polarization of Congressional Parties," *Journal of Politics* 68, no. 4 (2006): 992–1005.

41. D. E. Apollonio and Raymond J. La Raja, "Who Gave Soft Money? The Effect of Interest Group Resources on Political Contributions," *Journal of Politics* 66, no. 4 (2004): 1134–54.

42. See especially Heberlig and Larson, *Congressional Parties, Institutional Ambitions, and the Financing of Majority Control.*

43. See, for example, Herrnson, *Congressional Elections*, pp. 121–24.

44. For a discussion of PAC giving strategies, see Theodore J. Eismeier and Philip H. Pollock III, *Business, Money, and the Rise of Corporate PACs in American Elections* (New York: Quorum Books, 1988); Craig Humphries, "Corporations, PACs, and the Strategic Link between Contributions and Lobbying Activities," *Western*

Political Quarterly 44, no. 2 (1991): 357–72; and Frank J. Sorauf, *Inside Campaign Finance: Myths and Realities* (Yale University Press, 1992).

45. Diana Dwyre and others, "Committees and Candidates: National Party Finance after BCRA," in *The State of the Parties*, 6th ed., edited by John C. Green (Lanham, Md.: Rowman and Littlefield, 2006).

46. Ibid.

47. Thomas J. Rudolph, "Corporate and Labor PAC Contributions in House Elections: Measuring the Effects of Majority Party Status," *Journal of Politics* 61 no. 1 (1999): 195–206; Gary W. Cox and Eric Mager, "How Much Is Majority Status in the U.S. Congress Worth?" *American Journal of Political Science* 93, no. 2 (1999): 299–309.

48. Incumbents in uncompetitive races are defined in this chapter as incumbents who won by more than 20 percent of the two-party vote. Data compiled from FEC.

49. Ibid.

50. Nayak, interview.

51. Data compiled from FEC.

52. Francia and others, *The Financiers of Congressional Elections*, p. 23.

53. Ibid., p. 107.

54. Ibid., pp. 27–31.

55. Ibid., p. 52.

56. Data compiled from FEC.

57. Walter J. Stone and L. Sandy Maisel, "The Not-So-Simple Calculus of Winning: Potential U.S. House Candidates' Nomination and General Election Chances," *Journal of Politics* 65, no. 4 (2003): 951–77.

58. Herrnson, *Congressional Elections*, p. 87.

59. Ibid., pp. 78–81.

60. Ibid., pp. 89–90.

61. Jonathan S. Krasno, *Challengers, Competition, and Reelection: Comparing Senate and House Elections* (Yale University Press, 1994).

62. Jonathan S. Krasno and Donald Philip Green, "Preempting Quality Challengers in House Elections," *Journal of Politics* 50 (1988): 920–36; Peverill Squire, "Preemptive Fundraising and Challenger Profile in Senate Elections," *Journal of Politics* 53, no. 4 (1991): 1150–64.

SIX

Party Money in the 2012 Elections

DIANA DWYRE AND ROBIN KOLODNY

Although many commentators predicted that political parties in America would be weakened by the passage of the Bipartisan Campaign Reform Act of 2002 (BCRA), American parties proved their ability to adapt to changing legal, technical, economic, and political circumstances. Despite receiving minimal press, political parties continued to play a pivotal role in the financing and conduct of the 2012 elections. Parties received little attention in part because of the media obsession with Super PACs—their creation and their activities in the 2012 elections. Owing to a fundamental misunderstanding of the term *corporation* and the avenues already available to corporations to spend money in campaigns, many assumed that Super PACs would channel undocumented money spent directly by corporations to further their corporate interests.[1] Instead, many Super PACs became shadow party organizations, similar to what was witnessed in the era of soft-money issue advocacy strategies by political parties (1998–2002). Here, we explore both conventional and unconventional tactics used by the political parties in the 2012 federal elections.

A Changed Campaign Finance Regulatory Landscape: How Have Parties Fared?

In 2012 the parties continued to operate under BCRA, just as they had in 2008. Yet two major court decisions, *Citizens United v. Federal Election Commission* and *SpeechNow.org v. Federal Election Commission*, as well as six Federal Election Commission (FEC) advisory opinions, led to a dramatic change in the money landscape because of the emergence of Super PACs.[2]

Super PACs, sometimes called independent expenditure–only committees, can raise and spend unlimited amounts of money but must disclose the amount and source of all donations. Most contributions to Super PACs in 2012 came from individuals, not from other PACs or corporations (see chapter 7). Some contributions to Super PACs came from section 501(c) organizations, and since 501(c) organizations do not have to disclose their donors, the original source of donations is not known.[3] Initial experimentation in the 2010 midterm election campaigns led to a full-scale rollout of Super PACs in 2012 (see chapter 7). The most prominent of these Super PACs were new incarnations of previous 527 and 501(c)(4) organizations, with prominent former political party operatives at the helm. While technically working independently of political party organizations, Super PAC operations clearly mirrored political party campaigning.

The 2012 elections also effectively witnessed the end of the presidential public finance system for the nomination and general election stages of the campaign. Neither major-party candidate accepted public money in the primary or general election, save for the funding available for the two major parties' nominating conventions. Although we might assume that candidate-controlled funding for presidential races might lead to further distance between presidential nominees and their parties in fundraising, this did not prove to be the case in 2012. Both presidential candidates formed joint fundraising committees with their respective national parties; these committees collectively raised $953 million in the 2012 presidential election.[4] In 2008, by contrast, Barack Obama and John McCain raised only $449 million through joint fundraising efforts.[5] If anything, candidates and party organizations innovated even further with new forms of joint and hybrid fundraising and spending than before.

The Relative Influence of Party Money

The first thing to note about party fundraising totals is that in inflation-adjusted dollars, neither party dramatically improved its overall receipts; indeed, both seemed to have lost ground. Figure 6-1 shows total party receipts from 1998 until 2012—hard and soft money until 2004 and then hard money only from 2004 until 2012. Hard-money contributions to parties are limited in amount and can only be given by individuals, PACs, and some other groups. Before BCRA, the parties could collect unlimited soft-money donations from these sources as well as from unions and corporations. This figure shows a steep rise in receipts by both parties in 2000, the height of soft-money fundraising. Then there is a steady decline in post-BCRA overall receipts in inflation-adjusted dollars, with some recovery in 2008. Figure 6-2 shows only hard-money totals over the same period. Although the decline in party receipts is not nearly as dramatic, it is nevertheless clear that federal political party organizations have seen their real receipts decline since 2004.

Two other interesting items to note from these figures are that in the 2010 cycle, Democrats took in more than Republicans overall, and that in 2012 both parties were at parity in resources at roughly $806 million each. Previously, Republicans had a substantial advantage in soft money from 1998 to 2002 and in hard money for the six elections from 1998 through 2008. That advantage appears to now be gone.

However, as chapters 3 and 4 in this volume clearly demonstrate, the profound changes in presidential general election funding practices are responsible for the real decline in party purses. With both major-party presidential candidates now refusing the public money to which they are entitled, the candidates not only continue to raise funds throughout the fall election (had they accepted general election public funds, they could not have done this), but they expect to raise significantly more than they would receive in public money. Barack Obama raised $337 million in 2008 for the general election, compared with the general election public grant of $84 million that he turned down, which McCain accepted.[6]

For candidates who accept public funding, the prohibition against presidential fundraising means that after the nominating conventions, the only way presidential nominees can continue raising campaign funds is to direct donors to give to their joint fundraising committee. This committee, often called a victory committee, is established by a candidate and his or her political party, usually with the national party committee and a mix of state party committees, to raise funds for all participants to be distributed according to a predetermined formula. In 2008 McCain raised an additional $221 million with various joint fundraising committees, while Obama's joint fundraising totaled $228 million.[7] But since McCain had accepted the public funds, he was limited in how he could use the money raised through joint fundraising, and $30 million was left unspent.[8] Given how much a presidential candidate can raise for his or her own campaign and through joint fundraising, it is not surprising that both Mitt Romney and Obama declined the public funding grant in 2012.

Figure 6-1. *Total Federal Party Hard and Soft Money, Election Years, 1998–2012*[a]

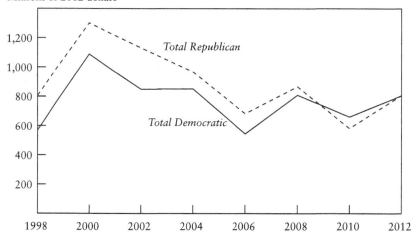

Millions of 2012 dollars

Source: Federal Election Commission, "National Party Committee Data Summaries (1/1/11–12/31/12)" (www.fec. gov/press/summaries/2012/ElectionCycle/NatlPartyUE.shtml).
a. Only hard money from 2004 to 2012.

Figure 6-2. *Federal Party Hard Money, Election Years, 1998–2012*

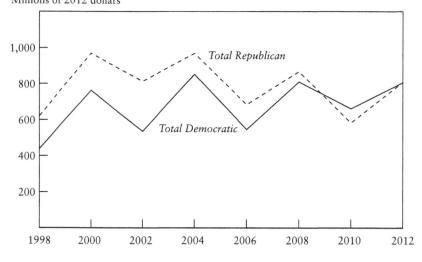

Millions of 2012 dollars

Source: Federal Election Commission, "National Party Committee Data Summaries (1/1/11–12/31/12)" (www.fec. gov/press/summaries/2012/ElectionCycle/NatlPartyYE.shtml).

Both raised record amounts and pursued joint fundraising in the general election with their respective national party committees.

Parties help their presidential nominees in other ways as well. Shortly after the enactment of BCRA in 2002, the FEC approved new rules that allowed national party committees—the DNC and RNC—to make unlimited hard-dollar independent expenditures on behalf of presidential candidates. Both parties' congressional campaign committees had been making independent expenditures since a 1996 Supreme Court ruling in *Colorado Republican Party* v. *Federal Election Commission.*[9] Before those rules took effect in January 2003, the FEC had treated the RNC and the DNC as if they were equivalent to the principal campaign committee or authorized committee of its presidential candidate and therefore unable to act independently of it. The later act, BCRA, rejected this distinction; thus beginning with the 2004 election, rules were changed to allow party committees to make independent expenditures on behalf of presidential candidates.[10] So donors were now confident that these party committees would help their presidential candidates.

Parties, their presidential nominees, Super PACs, and section 501(c) groups are often competing for the same donors' dollars. Yet the contribution limits and full disclosure requirements associated with giving to the RNC and DNC may make contributing to them less attractive compared with the potential to make unlimited contributions to a Super PAC that is dedicated to helping elect its preferred presidential candidate. Although competition between candidates, party committees, Super PACs, and 501(c)s exists, most maxed-out donors want to give to the candidates and are urged by candidates to also give to their party committees. Super PACs and 501(c) organizations acknowledge that they also urge donors to contribute first to candidates and party committees because of the more favorable rules for campaign expenditures for these groups and because of the ability of candidates and party committees to coordinate (see chapter 1).

The National Committees and the Presidential Candidates

Overall, the RNC outraised the DNC in 2012 (see table 6-1), yet these aggregate amounts mask much of the fundraising and spending done by the parties with and for their candidates. For example, both presidential candidates made use of victory committees to conduct joint fundraising with their parties. Romney and Obama each raised nearly half a billion

Table 6-1. *National Party Committee Receipts, by Source, Election Years, 2000–12*[a]
2012 dollars, except as indicated

	2000	2002	2004	2006	2008	2010	2012
Democratic National Committee							
Total receipts	210,773,719	119,158,260	491,315,055	148,999,139	277,304,551	236,270,988	290,440,506
Total contributions from individuals	149,592,116	70,941,675	406,405,258	134,337,989	144,517,077	207,521,295	119,221,793
Itemized	79,321,799	48,239,861	200,997,484	83,370,243	88,191,920	108,767,024	75,860,221
Unitemized as share of total from individuals (percent)	53.0	68.0	49.5	62.1	61.0	52.4	63.6
Contributions at the maximum permitted	14,720,000	867,347	52,673,147	4,278,132	44,013,467	23,168,000	6,581,257
Maximum as a share of individual total (percent)	9.8	1.2	13.0	3.2	30.5	11.2	5.5
Contributions from federal candidates	1,971,549	70,297	29,238,756	1,252,703	28,571	6,674,315	0
Contributions from PACs	3,470,765	1,402,441	3,691,417	1,697,270	2,329,308	0	1,588,057
Transfers from affiliated committees	3,243,425	8,713,915	27,732,739	1,268,428	106,165,484	2,861,736	135,124,025
Democratic Senatorial Campaign Committee							
Total receipts	65,503,159	76,970,129	107,726,973	138,242,555	173,551,656	136,361,519	145,906,977
Total contributions from individuals	23,342,412	25,712,114	70,197,086	99,353,560	111,905,072	86,928,017	104,183,372
Itemized	11,211,864	12,402,145	25,734,378	27,912,141	26,241,919	36,040,028	49,615,777
Unitemized as share of total from individuals (percent)	48.0	48.2	36.7	28.1	23.5	41.5	47.6
Contributions at the maximum permitted	2,186,667	2,576,531	14,793,439	11,408,542	29,109,275	11,712,000	14,439,327
Maximum as a share of individual total (percent)	9.4	10.0	21.1	11.5	26.0	13.5	13.9
Contributions from federal candidates	1,510,800	2,322,684	17,785,793	13,459,212	21,957,463	11,263,579	10,802,363
Contributions from PACs	5,745,503	6,004,026	7,632,739	9,010,950	11,433,011	11,224,696	10,584,303
Transfers from affiliated committees	17,769,929	19,476,962	7,406,113	6,835,362	10,166,931	15,039,073	3,406,579

Democratic Congressional Campaign Committee

Total receipts	43,283,305	52,302,251	113,288,186	159,446,899	187,851,412	172,522,160	183,843,039
Total contributions from individuals	21,437,023	24,747,839	61,657,226	94,754,022	96,721,937	93,925,088	131,707,585
Unitemized	13,243,365	14,287,605	30,618,830	35,980,110	32,879,512	39,471,048	71,036,725
Unitemized as share of total from individuals (percent)	61.8	57.7	49.7	38.0	34.0	42.0	53.9
Contributions at the maximum permitted	1,386,667	1,020,408	8,110,571	5,997,665	16,741,471	11,712,000	12,460,188
Maximum as a share of individual total (percent)	6.5	4.1	13.2	6.3	17.3	12.5	9.5
Contributions from federal candidates	4,489,019	15,473,684	29,110,947	37,990,317	50,140,906	37,886,525	25,499,258
Contributions from PACs	6,381,401	5,302,358	7,833,746	8,296,888	10,563,058	9,756,113	9,542,101
Transfers from affiliated committees	2,311,929	5,087,806	1,330,558	2,582,952	6,061,278	9,827,827	2,667,813

Republican National Committee

Total receipts	328,107,337	258,197,240	476,808,507	276,773,511	455,819,594	206,670,234	390,216,923
Total contributions from individuals	257,575,227	190,785,040	425,721,654	243,113,197	302,704,345	175,303,581	222,679,264
Unitemized	121,403,348	131,285,344	190,877,101	128,529,833	162,272,735	119,820,766	125,427,594
Unitemized as share of total from individuals (percent)	47.1	68.8	44.8	52.9	53.6	68.4	56.3
Contributions at the maximum permitted	16,880,000	3,801,020	73,936,817	912,301	39,895,736	3,936,000	28,694,454
Maximum as a share of individual total (percent)	6.6	2.0	17.4	0.4	13.2	2.2	12.9
Contributions from federal candidates	74,733	204,401	32,416,177	1,451,464	93,012	0	0
Contributions from PACs	2,173,473	896,791	3,609,769	2,470,793	2,300,406	1,521,745	2,994,176
Transfers from affiliated committees	15,011,999	4,491,224	8,421,085	5,238,214	137,511,823	9,590,055	149,081,183

(continued)

Table 6-1. *National Party Committee Receipts, by Source, Election Years, 2000–12*[a] (Continued)
2012 dollars, except as indicated

	2000	2002	2004	2006	2008	2010	2012
National Republican Senatorial Committee							
Total receipts	81,973,307	92,948,423	95,966,570	101,153,060	100,666,037	118,209,715	117,045,859
Total contributions from individuals	45,332,943	52,983,063	73,889,968	74,275,934	75,730,500	81,532,988	76,222,525
Unitemized	25,722,833	25,805,296	36,450,768	27,933,438	30,852,306	34,845,933	26,283,802
Unitemized as share of total from individuals (percent)	56.7	48.7	49.3	37.6	40.7	42.7	34.5
Contributions at the maximum permitted	240,000	408,163	7,442,284	2,428,929	14,038,380	15,296,000	20,590,440
Maximum as a share of individual total (percent)	0.5	0.8	10.1	3.3	18.5	18.8	27.0
Contributions from federal candidates	3,947,073	2,068,011	4,673,961	5,304,100	2,968,200	4,494,987	1,206,400
Contributions from PACs	5,369,833	5,364,925	9,373,309	9,908,706	9,366,995	10,788,304	11,496,884
Transfers from affiliated committees	13,500,564	16,900,338	3,114,509	7,773,902	7,269,534	10,231,893	16,843,383

National Republican Congressional Committee

Total receipts	126,346,197	144,392,888	225,661,605	200,797,998	126,145,808	140,820,125	155,724,614
Total contributions from individuals	89,346,668	100,989,004	177,227,289	123,943,915	79,869,856	74,316,179	59,163,662
Unitemized	46,271,949	50,603,625	60,498,007	44,562,494	34,232,166	35,865,378	24,953,607
Unitemized as share of total from individuals (percent)	51.8	50.1	34.1	36.0	42.9	48.3	42.2
Contributions at the maximum permitted	640,000	229,592	4,586,877	212,870	2,993,070	5,824,000	8,580,600
Maximum as a share of individual total (percent)	0.7	0.2	2.6	0.2	3.7	7.8	14.5
Contributions from federal candidates	19,755,728	17,955,503	29,462,061	34,423,213	25,830,694	33,675,039	44,675,712
Contributions from PACs	6,124,184	5,945,906	10,444,383	12,755,792	9,957,015	11,055,732	13,472,783
Transfers from affiliated committees	6,830,253	16,212,691	2,625,554	19,481,777	2,477,468	7,656,500	22,667,800

Sources: Data compiled from disclosure filings reported to the Federal Election Commission (www.fec.gov/finance/disclosure/candcmte_info.shtml). Data adjusted for 2012 dollars using Robert Sahr's conversion factor (http://oregonstate.edu/cla/polisci/individual-year-conversion-factor-tables).

a. Table presents federal or "hard" money only. Total receipts include other items not listed in table which include, but are not limited to, offsets to operating expenditures and loans received. Unitemized contributions from individuals are those that total $200 or less in a calendar year from a single person. The maximum contribution from individuals was changed from $20,000 a year to $25,000 per year for the 2004 election cycle, and $26,700 in 2006, $28,500 in 2008, $30,400 in 2010, and $30,800 in 2012. Transfers from affiliated committees include transfers from the joint fundraising committees of the presidential campaigns.

dollars with their victory committees to distribute to their own campaigns and to state and national party committees.

Barack Obama raised $716 million through his personal campaign organization, Obama for America (OFA),[11] and an additional $460 million through his two victory committees, Obama Victory Fund and Swing State Victory Fund.[12] Early in the election cycle, Obama appeared at Obama Victory Fund joint fundraising events asking for $35,800 in hard-money contributions—$30,800 for the DNC (the maximum that a donor could give to a national party committee) and $5,000 for Obama for America (the maximum candidate contribution for the primary and general elections).[13] Even with this sort of event, Obama spent most of his time fundraising for OFA rather than for the DNC. This reflected a strategy to target donors at all giving levels. Only donors who max out to a candidate became targets for joint committee solicitation. As noted in chapter 1, this is because contributions to candidates, and to a lesser extent to parties, are strategically more valuable in a campaign than money given to interest groups.

Mitt Romney's approach to joint fundraising with the RNC was based in part on the need and desire to resuscitate the party organization in the aftermath of the 2008 election. In January 2011, RNC chair Michael Steele was ousted amid allegations of financial mismanagement and poor oversight associated with the behavior of several RNC employees and their requests for reimbursement for questionable expenses.[14] Reince Priebus became the RNC chair for the 2012 cycle, and he successfully retired more than $23 million in debt. The RNC raised $390.2 million for 2011–12, $100 million more than the DNC. Romney's approach was also influenced by his campaign's targeting of maxed-out donors for contributions to his campaign. One way for these donors to provide additional assistance was for them to contribute to Romney's joint fundraising committee, Romney Victory, which raised $493 million.[15] Romney raised $446 million for his own campaign.[16]

Another reaction to the RNC leadership and financial challenges was the creation of American Crossroads as an alternative for major donors who had lost confidence in the post-McCain RNC.[17] Karl Rove, George W. Bush's former political adviser, is famously associated with American Crossroads and Crossroads GPS, an affiliated 501(c)(4) organization. Ed Gillespie, a longtime Republican Party operative and former chair of the RNC, joined Rove and stated publicly that Crossroads was the alternative for past RNC loyalists.[18]

The RNC and DNC are each entitled to spend hard money in coordination with the presidential campaigns of their nominees. This amount is
limited, based on the national voting age population multiplied by $0.02
and a cost of living adjustment.[19] The full limit for 2012 was
$21,684,200. The RNC used a special fund called the Presidential Trust
to raise and spend this money. The Presidential Trust originated in 2004
to raise money for the coordinated expenditure allotment that the RNC
can spend on behalf of its presidential candidate as soon as he or she
secures the nomination. In September 2011, the RNC appointed the eventual vice presidential nominee, Representative Paul Ryan, as head of the
fund, and by March 2012, before Mitt Romney had secured the GOP
presidential nomination, the Presidential Trust had the allowed
$21.6 million on hand and ready to spend.[20] In all federal races the RNC
spent $22.3 million in coordinated expenditures in 2012, whereas the
DNC spent $20.8 million.

Moreover, both presidential candidates were supported by single-
candidate Super PACs, which were not permitted to coordinate with the
candidate or his party: Restore Our Future backed Mitt Romney, and Priorities USA Action supported Barack Obama's reelection. The RNC also
benefited from the extensive fundraising done by American Crossroads,
the Super PAC started by Karl Rove. The former RNC political director
Rick Wiley said that Rove worked closely with big donors, encouraging
them to send the most usable hard dollars first to their candidate, next to
the RNC and state party "federal" committees if possible, and finally to
Super PACs.[21] Indeed, the top contributors to American Crossroads also
directed the maximum contribution ($30,800) to GOP national party
committees. Most of these big contributors, such as Sheldon and Miriam
Adelson and Bob Perry, gave the maximum amount to the RNC, and with
control of the Senate seriously in contention, they also maxed out to the
National Republican Senatorial Committee.[22]

State parties may have federal accounts to which donors can give money
to help fund federal races. The annual limit for such a contribution to any
single state party is $10,000, and such a contribution would have counted
toward an individual's aggregate contribution limit to political parties,
which was $74,600 in 2012. However, owing to the 2014 Supreme Court
decision in *McCutcheon* v. *Federal Election Commission* the aggregate limit
is removed, allowing an individual to give up to $10,000 to all fifty state
parties each election cycle as well as the maximum allowable contribution
to each of the three national party committees and all federal candidates.[23]

Party leaders may establish joint fundraising committees with federal candidates as well as national and state party committees, to which individuals could write a single check of as much as $3.7 million.[24]

The Hill Committees

Looking at receipts according to committee puts a different perspective on the data. The DNC and RNC are dominant, as would be expected for a presidential election year. There are four additional federal party committees, one for each party in each chamber of Congress, charged with assisting in the election or reelection of members of that party to the U.S. House of Representatives or the U.S. Senate in hopes of maintaining or securing majority status: the National Republican Senatorial Committee (NRSC), the National Republican Congressional Committee (NRCC), the Democratic Senatorial Campaign Committee (DSCC), and the Democratic Congressional Campaign Committee (DCCC). For ease of reference and to distinguish these four committees from the RNC and DNC, we refer to them collectively as the Hill committees, meaning the committees associated with Capitol Hill. These committees are headed by a sitting member of the party in that chamber. In 2012 the committees were led by Senator John Cornyn (NRSC), Senator Patty Murray (DSCC), Representative Pete Sessions (NRCC), and Representative Steve Israel (DCCC). These committees engage in candidate recruitment, opposition research, and fundraising. They may also engage in significant independent campaigning on behalf of their candidates, which they tend to do in very competitive races.[25]

Sometime between the 2006 and 2008 elections, the Democratic Hill committees overtook their Republican counterparts in receipts. Since the 2008 elections, Democrats have stayed ahead of their Republican counterparts (see figures 6-3 and 6-4). The biggest difference is between the DCCC and the NRCC. From 1998 through 2006 the NRCC outraised the DCCC by an average of $81 million per election cycle. Since 2006 the DCCC has outraised the NRCC by an average of $41 million in inflation-adjusted dollars. On the eve of the 2012 election, the DCCC trumpeted its fundraising prowess over the NRCC on the web, emphasizing the role of a large grassroots donor base and extensive fundraising efforts by House Minority Leader Nancy Pelosi. Outside observers also attributed the DCCC's continued fundraising advantage while in the minority to superior information regarding small donors maintained from the 2006

Figure 6-3. *Hard-Money Receipts to National Party Committees, Election Years, 1998–2012*

Millions of 2012 dollars

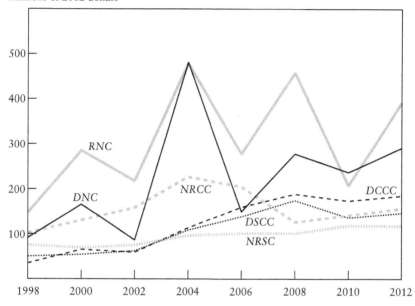

Source: Federal Election Commission, "National Party Committee Data Summaries (1/1/11–12/31/12)" (www.fec. gov/press/summaries/2012/ElectionCycle/NatlPartyYE.shtml).

and 2008 cycles and to Pelosi's dedication to returning the Democrats to majority status in the House.[26] On the Senate side, the DSCC has consistently led the NRSC since the 2000 cycle. Of the four Hill committees, the NRSC's fundraising operation has been the most stagnant. Officials of that committee cite the long-standing reluctance of incumbent Republican senators to transfer funds to the committee. Rob Jesmer, the executive director of the NRSC, stated that the committee "certainly asked [senators] for money" but that "they don't want to give money." As a substitute, the NRSC "utilized members to try to help us raise money by going to events for us."[27]

Figure 6-4 illustrates the effect that the BCRA soft-money ban has had on party receipts overall. Because these line plots use constant 2012 dollars, it is evident that in value terms, five of the six party committees have experienced a real drop in receipts, though not as extreme as might be

Figure 6-4. *Hard- and Soft-Money Receipts of National Party Committees, Election Years, 1998–2012*

Millions of 2012 dollars

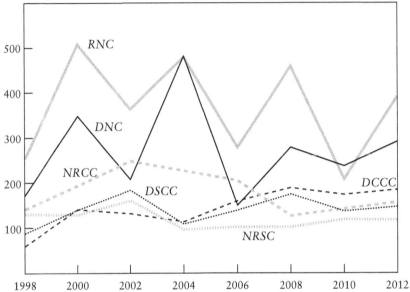

Source: Federal Election Commission, "National Party Committee Data Summaries (1/1/11–12/31/12)" (www.fec.gov/press/summaries/2012/ElectionCycle/NatlPartyYE.shtml).

expected, and one committee, the DCCC, has actually increased its receipts. The RNC's biggest haul of the decade was in 2000, before BCRA, but the DNC's best performance was in 2004, after BCRA and on par with the RNC. In 2008 the RNC's receipts held steady but the DNC's dropped, due to Obama's decision to refuse public money in the general election. Obama raised money through the full election cycle for his campaign but not as much for the DNC. In 2012 the RNC was still ahead of the DNC, but not by as large a margin as in 2008. It is clear that since 2004, when BCRA went into effect, the Democrats have been much more competitive with the Republicans in terms of fundraising. Figure 6-4 also shows that the DSCC outraised the NRSC from 2004 through 2012. The NRCC outraised the DCCC in 2004 and 2006 but not in 2008 or since. A decade ago, few would have predicted the dominance of the Democrats in fundraising, but the trends indicate that Democrats have succeeded beyond even their expectations.

Party Fundraising

To fully understand the activities of the national parties we must take a more detailed look at each party committee's fundraising environment, techniques, and results. In the next few sections, we examine the various sources of party receipts and the ways that the parties adapted to the changing campaign finance legal and regulatory landscape and to the 2011–12 political environment. We then examine how the parties spent their money.

Individual Contributions to Party Committees

Party committees can raise funds from individual contributors, federal candidates and lawmakers, PACs, and other party committees. As noted, the vast majority of party funding comes from individuals (see table 6-1). Although BCRA banned party soft money, it also significantly raised and indexed to inflation the limits on hard money individual contributions to party committees, which has helped the national parties make up for the loss of unlimited soft-money donations. For the 2012 elections, an individual could give $30,800 a year to any national party committee, with an overall limit on contributions of $117,000 over the two-year election cycle. Up to $70,800 of this overall limit could be given to all PACs and parties. Individuals could give $5,000 to a single candidate for the primary and general election combined and up to a total of $46,200 to candidates overall.

Despite the claim that BCRA would decimate America's political parties, that has not been the case in terms of money raised. The peak in fundraising for most party committees has occurred since BCRA. For the DNC, the RNC, and the NRCC, the post-BCRA peak came in 2004, whereas for the DSCC and the DCCC it was in 2008 and for the NRSC in 2010. In terms of total inflation-adjusted receipts, the three Democratic Party committees more than doubled their 2000 receipts in 2004, and the growth was even greater for the DNC. For the Democratic Hill committees, the upward trajectory of post-BCRA fundraising continued so that by 2008 both the DSCC and the DCCC had tripled what they raised in 2000. The NRCC saw a substantial drop in receipts in 2008 and increases in 2010 and 2012. The NRSC, as noted, has seen a more linear progression in receipts over time.

MAXED-OUT DONORS. The Bipartisan Campaign Reform Act allows individuals to contribute much more to party committees than to candidates or PACs. All the national party committees raised some of their money from maxed-out donors, those who contributed the maximum of $30,800. In 2012 the RNC collected far more from maxed-out donors ($28.7 million) than the DNC ($6.6 million). Since neither party's presidential nominee took public funds in 2012, the presidential candidates did not need to use the national committees to continue their fundraising in the fall of the election season; they could continue to approach their donors until each had reached the maximum donation of $2,500 for the primary election and an additional $2,500 for the general election.

Since much of Obama's money came from small contributors, he could keep returning to these donors to ask for more. Because Romney relied more on big givers, many of whom had reached the $5,000 contribution limit fairly early in the election season, he could not do the same. Therefore, in 2012, the major parties' presidential candidates had different fundraising relationships with their national committees than they had in the past. Romney engaged in far more joint fundraising with the RNC than Obama did with the DNC, which helps explain why the RNC raised so much more from big donors than the DNC. However, both parties' national committees took in less from big donors in 2012 than they had in 2008, especially the DNC, which raised $44 million in 2007–08 this way but only $6.6 million for the 2012 election (in adjusted 2012 dollars—see table 6-1). Some big Obama donors did not max out to the DNC in 2012 but instead directed money to other party committees and Super PACs. For example, Victor Elmaleh maxed out to Obama for America, gave less than the maximum to the DNC, contributed $100,000 to Majority PAC (a Super PAC whose purpose is to protect the Democrats' majority in the Senate), and donated between $3,000 and $10,000 to each of a few state party committees in presidential battleground states.[28] The drop in big-donor giving to the DNC is also a reflection of the Democrats' superior ability to raise more from small contributors. The RNC raised $39.9 million from maximum givers in 2008 and $28.7 million in 2012. For the Republicans, this trend arose, in part, because the RNC was dealing with $23 million in debt, and as the 2012 RNC political director Rick Wiley noted, "A major donor doesn't want to give their dollars to help retire debt."[29]

The DNC actually raised less from maxed-out contributors than the party's two Hill committees in 2012. The DSCC raised $14.4 million from these big contributors, 13.9 percent of its individual contributions, but far less than it raised from maxed-out donors in 2008 ($29.1 million). Its GOP counterpart, the NRSC, raised $20.6 million at the maximum level, a full 27 percent of all individual contributions, and more than it raised in 2008 ($14 million) and 2010 ($15.3 million). The DCCC took in $12.5 million from maxed-out contributors, generally less than it had collected in previous cycles, but more than the $8.6 million the NRCC collected, which was nevertheless a big increase for the GOP committee over previous elections.

SMALL DONORS. Far more of the parties' individual contributions in 2012 came from small donors, who contributed $200 or less. (These small contributions are identified in the table as unitemized contributions.) Although the RNC raised far more money overall than the DNC in 2011–12, almost 64 percent of the DNC's and 56 percent of the RNC's receipts from individuals came from these small donors. Yet both the DNC and RNC raised less from individuals in 2012 than they had in 2008. Indeed, since neither party's presidential nominee took public funds for the general election, the parties did not have to do as much fundraising for their nominees after they were selected.

The Democratic Hill committees continued to raise most of their funds from individuals, taking in a good deal more from small contributors than they had in 2008 and 2010. For example, the DCCC raised more than half of its money from small contributors (54 percent), and the DSCC was at almost 48 percent. The NRSC also relied heavily on small individual contributions, but it raised less from small donors in 2012 (35 percent) than it had in 2008 and 2010. Although the NRCC raised less from small donors than in 2008 and 2010, a full 42 percent of its individual contributions were less than $200 each.

After BCRA, both parties worked hard to find more contributors with whom they could have direct contact via phone and mail and especially online. Since the 1970s the Republicans had dominated fundraising from individuals. The party was unable to raise much from PACs in the 1970s since the Democrats controlled both chambers of Congress and had the incumbency advantage, so the GOP turned to individual contributors. The RNC chair, Bill Brock, and other GOP party leaders developed extensive voter lists and an aggressive direct-mail fundraising operation.[30] Their efforts were very successful. The Democrats did not begin to catch up with the Republicans until after 2002, when the end of soft money made it necessary to come up with new ways to raise money.

The Democrats' voter lists did not rival the Republican Voter Vault operation until 2004, when some Democratic Party allies created a limited liability corporation called Catalist to build a massive voter list and create targeting capabilities that would be available to any Democratic paying customer, not just the party committees. Democratic presidential candidates Hillary Clinton and Barack Obama both bought Catalist data in 2008, as did the party committees and allied interest groups.

Using Catalist data and data from other sources such as magazine subscriptions, car registrations, and hunting licenses, the 2012 Obama campaign developed its own database, Project Narwhal, named after a predatory whale. The Obama team used the new list to target voters to contribute, to volunteer, and to vote. Campaign workers added even more detail to the list gathered from in-person, phone, e-mail, and online contacts. Although all Democratic candidates can access the party's lists, Obama's "database adds . . . more fine-grained analyses of what issues matter most to voters and how best to motivate them to donate, volunteer, and vote."[31] The list is still controlled by the now defunct Obama campaign, and as of spring 2013, only the new Obama 501(c)(4) advocacy group, Organizing for Action (OFA), created to advance the president's policy agenda, has been permitted to use the list.

The Democrats have more than closed the voter list gap between them and the GOP; the Republicans are now trying to catch up with the Democrats. In 2011 the RNC privatized its voter file as well and handed it over to Data Trust, a dual entity of a trust and a for-profit corporation directed by former GOP party leaders.[32] Like Catalist, Data Trust data can be accessed by candidates, parties, and outside groups. These GOP organizations can use and share data on the platform, and Data Trust, not the RNC, maintains and updates the files. These stepped-up GOP efforts helped the RNC take in $125.4 million in small contributions for 2012, but this is less than it had raised in small contributions for the 2008 elections (see table 6-1). The DNC collected $75.9 million, also less than it had raised in small donations in previous elections since 2004.

Both parties are likely to continue to pursue small contributions because the cost of such appeals is low when made online, via e-mail, on social networking sites such as Facebook or Twitter, or with a text message. Therefore, efforts to add to and enhance Catalist, Data Trust, and other lists will also continue as parties, candidates, and others search for new potential donors.

Contributions from Candidates and Lawmakers

Political parties have long turned to their elected members for party dues to help the party maintain or secure majority status in Congress. Candidates and former candidates or officeholders may transfer unlimited amounts from their own campaign accounts to a party committee. Representative Tom Cole of Oklahoma, a former NRCC chair, explained the advantages of raising money from fellow members of Congress: "There are no fundraising costs associated with raising $30,000 from a direct transfer or from an individual contribution that a member secures. That's all profit."[33] Both parties' House campaign committees have been particularly adept at raising money from their members in recent election cycles. For 2012 the DCCC collected $25.5 million from federal candidates, down from $50 million in 2008 and $38 million in 2010. Ranking committee and subcommittee members especially, who were in line to become committee and subcommittee chairs if the Democrats took control of the House, were expected to pay their dues and then some. Indeed, party leaders consider a member's contribution to the party effort when deciding whom to support for top committee posts. Some House Democrats put off paying their DCCC dues because their states' redistricting was delayed so they did not know where they would be running and against whom. Others faced tough primaries or strong GOP challengers and felt they had less to give to the DCCC.[34] In 2012 the NRCC surpassed the DCCC in member contributions for the first time since 2006 by raising $44.7 million from GOP House members, with more than a quarter of that total (almost $12 million) coming from House Speaker John Boehner. Member transfers to the DSCC were $10.8 million in 2012, down from almost $22 million in 2008 and $11.3 million in 2010 but still roughly ten times the number of dollars GOP members transferred to the NRSC in 2012 ($1.2 million). Members also ask their individual and PAC contributors to make contributions to their party committees.

President Obama did not transfer any money from either his campaign account or his joint fundraising accounts to the DCCC or DSCC during the 2011–12 election cycle, a departure from the past two election cycles, when Obama and the DNC gave the Hill committees a combined $30 million for each election.[35] Romney, on the other hand, transferred $7.4 million to the NRCC and $7.4 million to the NRSC from his joint fundraising committee.

PAC Contributions

Contributions from traditional political action committees usually constitute a small portion of the national party committees' receipts (see table 6-1). Indeed, PACs give most of their money directly to candidates.

A PAC may contribute $15,000 per calendar year to a national party committee within the overall limits discussed above. During the 2011–12 election cycle, political action committees gave $423.1 million to presidential, Senate, and House candidates, but only $106.4 million to the national party committees.[36]

Republican Party committees collected more from PACs ($28 million) than Democratic committees ($21.7 million) for the 2012 election, after the two parties were near parity in money raised from PACs from 2002 to 2008.[37] Most of this GOP advantage in raising PAC funds is from the Hill committees, especially the NRCC. In 2012 the NRCC raised $13.5 million from PACs, while the DCCC raised $9.5 million. In the same year the NRCC surpassed any prior cycle in PAC receipts. In 2006 the committee raised $12.8 million from PACs, the best year for the committee in the past decade before the increase in 2012. Corporate PAC donations had begun to trend toward House Republicans in 2010, when they regained the majority. Not only did the PAC community bank on Republican retention of the House, but also PACs were directed by Romney to support the party organizations.[38] Still, PACs are a relatively minor source of funds for most national party committees. Much more is coming in to the national party committees from affiliated committees, and, in recent elections, that is mostly from joint fundraising committees.

Joint Fundraising

As discussed above, joint fundraising committees are formed by a candidate or group of candidates and some mix of federal and state parties. Joint fundraising can be a major source of funding for the national parties. The DNC and the RNC especially have benefitted from joint fundraising in presidential election years. For instance, in 2012 the DNC collected more from joint fundraising efforts (approximately $128 million) than from individual contributors who gave directly to the DNC ($119 million).

These victory committees are not party committees, or PACs, or candidate committees. Participating candidates and party committees who will receive the proceeds of the joint fundraising are named when the joint fundraising committee is established with an FEC Statement of Organization. Once contributors max out to a presidential or other candidate, joint fundraising is the most effective way to raise and spend money, because it allows the candidate to have some control over how the money is spent, whereas candidates have no control over money spent by Super PACs and other outside groups.

Big-ticket joint fundraising events feature presidential or other candidates, high-profile officials, and often celebrities. In May 2012, for example, the actor George Clooney hosted an Obama Victory Committee event at his Studio City home, featuring President Obama as the "special guest."[39] At these types of events, a donor writes one big check, and the money is distributed according to a predetermined formula.

Joint fundraising committees allow a contributor to donate the maximum $5,000 to a candidate for federal office, plus an additional $30,800 to a national party committee, usually the DNC or the RNC, which will spend most of that money to help elect the party's presidential nominee. A contributor to a joint fundraising committee may give the full $30,800 to the national party and may also contribute up to $40,000 to state parties. Thus joint fundraising allows individual contributors to give an aggregate sum of $75,800 at one event or in one contribution to influence one contest. Transfers from the joint fundraising committees are included in the "transfers from affiliated committees" row in table 6-1 (as are other transfers from, for example, state parties and candidate committees). As noted, these aggregate limits were declared unconstitutional in *McCutcheon v. Federal Election Commission. McCutcheon* now allows party leaders to "set up a joint fundraising committee with their presidential nominee, congressional candidates and state affiliates to accept nearly $3.7 million from an individual in each election cycle."[40]

Obama set up two joint fundraising committees, both designed to focus on presidential battleground states. The bigger operation, the Obama Victory Fund 2012, established in April 2011, raised $452.9 million from individual contributors, 79 percent of it coming from contributors who gave more than $200.[41] Yet many of these contributors made a number of relatively small donations ($1 to $1,000), and far fewer gave the maximum $35,800. The Obama Victory Fund was established to transfer funds to Obama for America, the DNC, and state Democratic Party committees in ten presidential battleground states—Colorado, Florida, Iowa, Nevada, New Hampshire, North Carolina, Ohio, Pennsylvania, Virginia, and Wisconsin—and it raised $456 million in 2011–12. Of the $337.4 million transferred to the various participants, 54 percent ($181.7 million) went to Obama for America, 37 percent to the DNC ($126.2 million), and the remaining 9 percent ($29.5 million) to the ten participating state party committees.[42] No Obama Victory Fund money was transferred to the DCCC or the DSCC.

Obama's Swing State Victory Fund was established later, in December 2011, to "allow supporters who would like to contribute to individual state efforts to elect the president and Democrats up and down the ballot," according to an Obama campaign official.[43] Most of the contributors made large donations, above $5,000. The Swing State Victory Fund was established to direct funds to eleven state party committees, again in battleground states—Colorado, Florida, Iowa, Michigan, Nevada, New Hampshire, North Carolina, Ohio, Pennsylvania, Virginia, and Wisconsin. This victory committee raised $4.5 million, far less than the Obama Victory Fund, and $4.2 million was transferred to the state party committees in the eleven battleground states, with Florida and Ohio getting the largest transfers. No Swing State Victory funds were sent to the Obama campaign or to any of the national party committees.

The Romney Victory Committee was established by the Romney campaign and the RNC in April 2012 to direct money to Romney's campaign, select state parties, the RNC, and, to a lesser extent, the Republican Hill committees. Interestingly, Romney's state party victory committee participants were not in battleground states. Instead, all state party transfers went to party committees in Idaho, Massachusetts, Oklahoma, and Vermont. So, once contributors maxed out to the Romney campaign and the RNC, they could give to these state party committees. Once it reached these state parties, some of the money was then redistributed to other state parties in presidential battleground states.[44] For instance, $9.2 million was transferred from the Romney Victory Committee to the Massachusetts Republican Party, and $8.8 million was then transferred from the Massachusetts Republican Party to GOP party committees in select battleground states—Colorado, Florida, Iowa, Ohio, and Virginia.[45]

Why did Romney use these four state party committees rather than transfer the money directly to battleground state parties, as Obama did? The Romney campaign had close relationships with the leaders of these four state parties, giving Romney more control over how the funds would be spent. As *Roll Call's* David Drucker reported, "State parties in contested battlegrounds that need the money might spend it on activities not approved by team Romney in Boston or the RNC, while a poorly managed party might squander the funds altogether."[46] A national Republican fundraiser agreed: "I guarantee the reason they're asking for those [states] is [that] they can control them."[47] Washington, D.C., political finance lawyer Matthew Sanderson, who was legal counsel to Romney's Massachusetts leadership PAC, noted, "There's no legal reason to choose those four state parties over others. . . . My educated guess is that they chose those four because they trust those four party chairs to honor any requests for disbursing funds to battlegrounds as needed."[48]

The Romney Victory Committee raised $491.6 million, and virtually all of these funds came from individuals, 90 percent of whom gave more than $200 and many of whom gave the maximum contribution. Of the $340 million transferred to affiliated committees, 43 percent ($146.5 million) went to Romney for President, 42 percent ($141.9 million) was sent to the RNC, 4 percent ($7.4 million each) was given to the NRCC and the NRSC, and as noted, 11 percent ($36.8 million) was split evenly between the Idaho, Massachusetts, Oklahoma, and Vermont Republican committees. NRSC executive director Rob Jesmer again noted that fundraising was very competitive in 2012, as most people prefer to give to the presidential candidate, but 2012 was "a lot better than previous cycles, as the Romney campaign actually played ball. . . . So we got the money that [we] probably would not have gotten . . . out of the Romney joint fundraising, which was helpful to us."[49] The NRSC and NRCC received far more from joint fundraising than their Democratic counterparts, and more than they had in previous election cycles. For example, in addition to the $7.4 million the NRSC received from the Romney Victory Committee, it also received $4.7 million from Massachusetts U.S. Senate candidate Scott Brown's victory committee, and more from a number of smaller joint fundraising committees. The NRCC benefited from $10.9 million in joint fundraising with Speaker John Boehner and smaller amounts from other Republican House leaders and members.

Other House and Senate candidates also established joint fundraising committees with the party committees. For example, the DSCC and various female candidates for the Senate formed seven committees around the country called Women on the Road to the Senate: 12 and Counting. Separate committees were set up for New York City, Washington, D.C., Boston, the San Francisco Bay Area, Denver, Los Angeles, and Seattle. Each committee was established with a common core of sitting women senators and was designed to help them and other Democratic women who were running for the Senate. These were relatively small operations, with only the Bay Area, Los Angeles, and Seattle committees raising more than $200,000.

In the House, the GOP also set up the Freshman Class Joint Fundraising Committee in October 2011. Although twelve House members participated, only four of them were in truly competitive races. The committee raised and spent only $55,800, giving $32,000 of it to the twelve
members who created the committee.[50] Interestingly, the members in the
most competitive races did not receive the largest contributions.[51]

Party Spending

Political party organizations may assist their candidates by making direct
contributions to them, making coordinated expenditures on their behalf,
or launching independent expenditure campaigns to promote their candidacies. Both direct contributions and coordinated expenditures assume
close contact between the candidate and the party organization. For this
reason, the amounts allowed in the law are limited. Independent expenditures are presumed to occur without the candidate's knowledge and
consent and therefore are unlimited. The party committees use different
campaign vendors for independent expenditures than for coordinated
expenditures. Party staff who work on independent expenditures do not
communicate with staff who work on the contribution or coordinated
expenditure activities. All of this is done to preserve the "independence"
of independent expenditures. As this election cycle was marked by the
entrance of Super PACs, it is important to note that coordination between
party committees and Super PACs is strictly forbidden.

Contributions

Political party organizations may make contributions of up to $5,000
in each election to any federal candidate. This limit has not changed since
the enactment of the Federal Election Campaign Act (FECA) in 1974,
and it is not indexed for inflation, with the exception of contribution limits to U.S. Senate candidates, which have been indexed for inflation since
BCRA, beginning in 2004.[52] A contribution may be in the form of cash,
or it may be something else of value to the candidate; the latter is considered an "in-kind" contribution. This means that the donor must estimate
a cash value for the donation, an amount that will be counted against the
limit. In the case of party organizations, it is common for in-kind donations to be for the use of fundraising assistance (for example, phone
banks or the use of technical production facilities at the Washington
offices of the national committees) or the candidate's portion of joint

campaigning costs. Also, polls conducted by the national party organizations and then shared with one or more candidates are listed as in-kind contributions.

In recent years, candidates for federal office have not expected much in the way of contributions from the party committees. Indeed, as table 6-2 shows, the number of House and Senate candidates who received contributions declined by more than half in 2012 compared with 2008 and 2010. Interestingly, in 2012, the overall amount of money or in-kind services donated stayed about the same as in 2010 or increased only slightly. This means that fewer candidates are receiving the maximum allowed contribution, and most candidates receive nothing or very little. For example, in 2012, the DSCC contributed to only fourteen of the thirty-three contested U.S. Senate races, and the NRSC contributed to only fourteen. Twelve of these races, all of which were on the list of toss-up "leaning-toward" races, had contributions from both parties, effectively canceling each other out.[53] The most precipitous decline in the number of candidates who received party contributions in 2012 was among House Republicans, of whom only 69 received contributions from the NRCC compared with an average of 252 per cycle for the 1996–2010 period. In the 1980s and early 1990s, candidates for Congress typically expected the full party contribution as a matter of course. Two things have changed that expectation. First, the parties are far more strategic about targeting resources to only the most competitive races, so candidates in safe seats (particularly incumbents) are told not to expect any automatic donations. Rather, party committees concentrate their resources on the most competitive contests through independent expenditures. Second, the lack of adjustment in the value of the donation for U.S. House candidates means that the contribution is quite small and will continue to decrease over time in terms of its value to the campaign. It seems petty to press for this contribution when the party organizations have the potential to spend millions of dollars in competitive contests, which in a given year might be in that member's own district. In the end, party contributions did not amount to much in the 2012 election cycle.

Coordinated Expenditures

The 1974 FECA also provides for a particular type of political party spending referred to as coordinated expenditures. Coordinated expenditures are expenditures made by parties for goods or services that benefit a candidate, with funds that the party committee and the candidate work

Table 6-2. *Party Committee Contributions to Candidates, Election Years, 1996–2012*[a]
2012 dollars, except as indicated

	1996	1998	2000	2002	2004	2006	2008	2010	2012
Democratic National Committee	48,572	9,710	14,077	12,755	14,581	13,667	51,866	29,135	75,250
Democratic Senatorial Campaign Committee	790,630 (34)	440,141 (22)	438,040 (25)	522,832 (22)	843,864 (22)	679,727 (23)	595,522 (19)	788,632 (27)	646,500 (15)
Democratic Congressional Campaign Committee	1,154,889 (432)	654,231 (277)	775,581 (311)	814,888 (253)	546,181 (209)	2,799,426 (220)	1,094,319 (268)	595,932 (268)	863,217 (213)
Republican National Committee	719,646	626,741	550,000	480,022	306,188	520,364	559,163	63,967	264,437
National Republican Senatorial Committee	1,412,958 (36)	644,851 (28)	574,445 (25)	581,603 (28)	987,724 (22)	394,968 (18)	143,923 (24)	1,111,684 (29)	775,800 (18)
National Republican Congressional Committee	1,855,066 (333)	1,104,752 (246)	952,771 (254)	1,047,091 (246)	798,981 (235)	419,767 (227)	784,747 (213)	665,646 (264)	639,090 (69)
Total Democrat	3,551,120	3,868,585	5,293,808	2,809,411	2,200,005	4,427,212	2,502,078	2,130,586	2,346,949
Total Republican	7,022,592	5,018,365	3,591,860	6,480,099	3,236,056	1,847,950	5,929,930	2,508,065	2,586,653

Sources: Federal Election Committee, "National Party Committee Data Summaries (1/1/11–12/31/12)" (www.fec.gov/press/summaries/2012ElectionCycle/NatlPartyYE.shtml); Center for Responsive Politics, "Political Parties Overview" (www.opensecrets.org/parties/index.php). Conversion factor from Robert Sahr (http://oregonstate.edu/cla/polisci/individual-year-conversion-factor-tables); 2012 amounts calculated by authors.

a. Figures in parentheses are the number of recipient candidates. The totals for each party include state and local contributions, which are not shown.

together to decide how to spend. For example, one of the Hill committees could pay for a poll or for the filming of a campaign ad that will benefit the candidate. Political parties, by their very definition, have a direct relationship with the candidates who run for office under their party's label. For this reason, political parties are expected to discuss election issues and strategies with their candidates. To prevent parties from serving as potential "corrupt conduits" for special interests by passing interest group contributions directly on to candidates, parties are encouraged to spend money to help their candidates by providing knowledge and support, but in limited amounts through coordinated expenditures.[54]

Coordinated expenditures are paid for with limited hard-dollar contributions and can only be spent up to limits set by the law, with adjustments for inflation every two-year cycle. The Federal Election Campaign Act provided a formula for the national committee and state committee to each contribute $10,000 (times a cost of living adjustment) for congressional candidates. Through what are called agency agreements, a state party's coordinated expenditure has normally been made by the relevant Hill committee as an agent for both the national committee and the relevant state committee, effectively doubling the impact of these coordinated expenditures. For 2012 the DCCC and the NRCC were able to allocate coordinated expenditures of up to $45,600 per race for each of these committees. If the DCCC or NRCC received agency agreements for both the national and state party committees, then they could spend double that amount, up to $91,200. In 2012 only 9.7 percent of all Democratic federal coordinated expenditures came from state and local party committees, and only 4.3 percent of all Republican coordinated expenditures came that way.[55]

The DCCC made coordinated or independent expenditures in 114 U.S. House races and 3 U.S. Senate races. The Senate races were in New York, North Dakota, and Pennsylvania. Coordinated expenditures were made in 78 of these races. Of these 78 races, 8 had coordinated spending of $10,000 or less, 11 received spending between $10,001 and $45,600, and 59 received spending of more than $45,601 (up to the limit of $91,200). The NRCC chose only 81 House races and 2 Senate races (New York and Arizona) for campaign spending. They made coordinated expenditures in all but one of these targeted races. Of these 80 races, 18 received spending of $10,000 or less, 10 received spending between $10,001 and $45,600, and 54 received spending of more than $45,601 (up to the limit of $91,200). The patterns of coordinated spending by the House congressional campaign committees are remarkably similar. Table 6-3 gives each national party committee's coordinated expenditures since 1996.

Coordinated expenditures are treated somewhat differently for Senate races and House races owing to the enormous variation in the size of the constituencies. In House races, the number of constituents is approximately the same across districts by design, and changes in district populations are adjusted each decade following reapportionment and redistricting. Because each senator represents an entire state, the same cannot be said for Senate races. Therefore, each election cycle the FEC calculates a state-coordinated expenditure limit as either the state's current voting-age population (VAP) times two cents ($.02) times a cost of living adjustment (COLA), or double the limit for coordinated expenditures in a U.S. House race, whichever is greater.[56] In 2012 eight states were limited to a minimum of $91,200, and the maximum limit of $2,593,100 was in California.[57] These limits represent the share for national party spending and state party spending and can thus be doubled if each party organization decides to exercise its rights to do so (rare since the advent of independent expenditures). Of the thirty-three Senate races in 2012, the DSCC spent $9.3 million in sixteen races coordinated with its senatorial candidates, in expenditures ranging from $5 to $2,650,000. The NRSC made coordinated expenditures in only twelve of the thirty-three races. In total, the NRSC spent $7.7 million on coordinated expenditures, which ranged from $12,000 to $1.6 million.

Since 2004 both the DNC and the RNC have been permitted to make coordinated expenditures on behalf of their presidential candidates with the candidate's knowledge and consent. As noted above in the discussion of the national committees and presidential candidates, in 2012 the RNC, using its Presidential Trust, spent $21,533,007 for Romney. The RNC also made an additional $697,827 in coordinated expenditures in eleven U.S. House races. The DNC spent $20,929,764 coordinated with Obama but only $3,123 in two U.S. House races. Neither the RNC nor the DNC made coordinated expenditures in U.S. Senate contests in 2012.

Independent Expenditures

Since the 1998 election cycle, political party committees have been able to make unlimited hard-money independent expenditures.[58] Since the 1976 *Buckley* v. *Valeo* decision, individuals and PACs have been able to spend as much as they can legally amass to advocate for or against a candidate's

Table 6-3. *Coordinated Expenditures by Party Committees, Election Years, 1996–2012*[a]
2012 dollars

	1996	1998	2000	2002	2004	2006	2008	2010	2012
Democratic National Committee	9,785,990	8,238,623	18,064,824	441,602	19,537,756	411,798	6,822,526	383,612	20,785,956
Democratic Senatorial Campaign Committee	12,420,615	11,865	169,543	231,874	5,339,485	6,601,331	4,075,610	11,391,946	9,354,010
Democratic Congressional Campaign Committee	8,774,127	4,197,000	3,480,088	2,253,121	3,108,437	2,708,682	1,771,160	3,916,097	5,348,667
Republican National Committee	34,468,265	5,480,373	32,460,827	18,018,216	19,614,875	3,319,334	26,499,853	1,116,583	22,306,014
National Republican Senatorial Committee	858,294	47,261	229	705,620	9,530,978	10,012,325	1,631,795	18,233,458	7,706,227
National Republican Congressional Committee	10,864,262	7,298,842	4,929,203	747,330	3,869,211	1,835,401	3,646,396	6,423,814	4,716,307
Total Democrat	33,435,527	26,165,138	28,934,143	8,747,745	41,327,085	21,091,435	19,348,376	26,206,275	39,335,834
Total Republican	47,044,649	22,022,679	41,243,085	20,792,052	34,648,275	16,093,773	33,765,186	28,563,396	36,314,906

Sources: Federal Election Commission, "National Party Committee Data Summaries (1/1/11–12/31/12)" (www.fec.gov/press/summaries/2012/ElectionCycle/NatlPartyYE.shtml). Conversion factors from Robert Sahr (http://oregonstate.edu/cla/polisci/individual-year-conversion-factor-tables); 2012 amounts calculated by authors.

a. The totals for each party include state and local coordinated expenditures, which are not shown.

election. The only stipulations are that the spending entity (individual, PAC, or party organization) cannot coordinate in any way with the campaign being helped and that the party or PAC expenditure must be from disclosed and limited contributions (hard money). For the past several cycles, the party committees have set up separate offices just to conduct independent expenditure campaigns so that the regular staff of the party organizations is in no way involved with the independent expenditure arm.[59]

Independent expenditures are reported as being spent either in favor of the party's candidate or against that candidate's opponent. Any entity that makes an independent expenditure must report its intent to do so to the FEC forty-eight hours before the campaign action begins. This is a post-BCRA provision designed to give fair warning to the opposition that an "attack" is on its way.

If the party organization is going to have to give up coordination in order to make independent expenditures, then conventional wisdom holds that it might as well use this distance to make independent expenditures that are more difficult for the candidate to make without experiencing unintended negative consequences. So it is rare that party organizations' independent expenditure ads advocate for their candidate. The DCCC made only five independent expenditures in support of its own party's candidate in 2012, and only in races where it also spent something on coordinated expenditures. The highest pro-candidate independent expenditure was $658,304. As table 6-4 shows, the DCCC spent $60.5 million on independent expenditures in 2012, less than it had the previous three election cycles.

In 2012, in terms of independent expenditures against the opposing candidate, the DCCC made no independent expenditures in 18 of the 114 races where the DCCC made some other expenditure. The DCCC made independent expenditures against opposing candidates in 96 races, though the magnitude of the spending varied widely. In 46 races, the DCCC spent less than $100,000 for independent expenditures. It spent between $100,000 and $500,000 in 15 races and between $500,001 and $1 million in nine others. This left 29 races in which the DCCC invested more than $1 million, and the amount spent in coordinated expenditures in 24 of these was considerable.

Although the Supreme Court extended the right of independent expenditures to party committees in 1996, with the case involving the Colorado Republican Party, the surge in party use of independent expenditures

Table 6-4. *Independent Expenditures by Party Committees, Election Years, 1996–2012*[a]
2012 dollars

	1996	1998	2000	2002	2004	2006	2008	2010	2012
Democratic National Committee	0	0	0	0	146,213,204	−26,314	1,177,095	16,302	0
Democratic Senatorial Campaign Committee	2,029,315	1,632,394	177,333	0	22,752,758	48,550,649	77,419,302	43,654,527	52,556,798
Democratic Congressional Campaign Committee	0	0	2,577,759	1,514,861	44,874,434	73,094,821	87,037,774	69,140,881	60,545,679
Republican National Committee	0	0	0	637,755	22,032,394	15,971,158	56,992,951	0	42,394,347
National Republican Senatorial Committee	14,205,603	273,499	356,800	0	24,287,723	21,984,356	41,562,125	27,269,378	32,455,514
National Republican Congressional Committee	0	0	731,733	3,199,231	57,416,851	93,461,467	32,931,291	48,674,286	64,653,293
Total Democrat	2,156,486	1,810,018	3,095,428	3,194,563	214,586,310	122,066,708	165,943,964	113,017,754	113,751,224
Total Republican	14,937,117	444,590	1,354,223	4,040,309	107,136,871	132,024,459	132,900,402	80,145,282	140,417,126

Sources: Federal Election Commission, "National Party Committee Data Summaries (1/1/11–12/31/12)" (www.fec.gov/press/summaries/2012/ElectionCycle/NatlPartyYE.shtml). Conversion factor from Robert Sahr (http://oregonstate.edu/cla/polisci/individual-year-conversion-factor-tables); 2012 amounts calculated by authors.

a. The totals for each party include state and local independent expenditures, which are not shown. The 2006 total for the Democratic National Committee is negative owing to adjustments made after the original expenditures were reported from the 2004 presidential race.

came in 2004 as a substitute for the soft-money expenditures the party committees had been making, starting in 1996 and ending in 2002. According to the data presented in table 6-4, the party committees in the aggregate spent about $4.5 million in independent expenditures in 2000 and $7.2 million in 2002, but in 2004 they collectively spent $322 million. The amounts have not risen to that level since 2004, with the party committees spending a total of $254.2 million in independent expenditures in 2012. Party committees have found ways to raise the hard money necessary to fund concentrated independent expenditures since 2004. In a sense, the independent expenditures of 2004–12 have replaced the soft-money expenditures of 1998–2002.[60]

The NRCC spent $64.7 million on independent expenditures in 2012, more than in the past two elections (see table 6-4). The NRCC made nine pro-candidate independent expenditures in contrast to the DCCC's six. For independent expenditures against opposing candidates, the NRCC made only fifty such expenditures, compared with the DCCC's ninety-six. In no instance did the NRCC spend less than $100,000 on a negative independent expenditure, compared with the forty-six races in which the DCCC behaved this way. The NRCC spent between $100,000 and $500,000 in ten races and between $500,001 and $1 million in eleven others. This left twenty-nine races in which the NRCC invested $1 million or more in 2012; in eight of these races, the independent expenditures exceeded $2 million.

Independent expenditures vary much more widely in senate races for the same reason coordinated expenditures do, as mentioned above. The DSCC spent nearly $53 million on independent expenditures in thirteen senate races, ranging from a low of $278,846 in the New Mexico senate race to a high of $7,881,089 in the Virginia senate race. The NRSC spent just over $32 million on independent expenditures in nine targeted senate races. The lowest independent expenditure was in the Ohio senate race ($990,553), and the highest was in the Virginia senate race ($5,768,873). As might be expected, the races with the largest independent expenditures were about the same in both parties; Virginia and Wisconsin led the way. However, the senate race that saw the most spending in 2012—the Massachusetts contest between Republican incumbent Scott Brown and Democratic challenger Elizabeth Warren—was conspicuously absent from both parties' independent expenditure lists because the parties honored the candidates' request that outside spenders stay out of their race.

The DNC and the RNC had very different approaches to their independent expenditures in the 2012 election cycle. The DNC did not make any independent expenditures. Although the DNC had not used this spending option often in the past, the zero number is unexpected. The RNC spent $2,497,699 for positive independent expenditures for Romney and $41,131,576 in negative independent expenditures against President Obama. This independent expenditure spending is separate from spending on hybrid advertising between the RNC and the Romney campaign. In hybrid advertising, two organizations split the cost of airing ads, "which aren't considered specific to the presidential race because they include phrases like 'Obama and his allies.'"[61] The *Washington Times* estimated that the RNC spent $5 million with the Romney campaign on hybrid ads, mostly on Spanish-language television stations. Hybrid advertising permits the party and candidate to split the costs of the ad and still get the lower candidate rates for these ads.[62]

Major Party Investments: The 2012 Virginia Senate Race

More than $82 million from all sources was spent in the U.S. Senate race in Virginia. Democratic incumbent U.S. senator James Webb, who had defeated Senator George Allen (R) in 2006, declined to run for reelection. In 2012 Allen decided to run for his former seat. His Democratic challenger was former governor (and DNC chair) Tim Kaine. Together, the candidates spent $31.3 million: $17.9 million by Kaine and $13.4 million by Allen.

Overall, $51.4 million was spent in outside money in this race. Both senatorial committees spent more in the Virginia senate race than any other senate race in 2012. The DSCC spent more than $9 million: $1,119,199 in coordinated expenditures on Kaine's behalf and $7,881,089 in negative independent expenditures against Allen. The NRSC spent more than $6.9 million: $1,136,192 in coordinated expenditures on Allen's behalf and $5,768,873 in negative independent expenditures against Kaine. Of the remaining $36.4 million in expenditures, $22.3 million was spent by partisan Super PACs, with additional spending by 501(c) organizations. American Crossroads, Crossroads GPS, and Independence Virginia PAC (Sheldon Adelson) spent $16.2 million against Kaine. The Majority PAC spent $6.1 million against Allen. Kaine won the race by six percentage points in perhaps the most closely watched and closely polled 2012 senate race.

The Limits of Party Power: The 2012 Massachusetts Senate Race

The most expensive U.S. Senate race in 2012 was one in which the parties did not play a direct role—the Massachusetts contest between Scott Brown and Elizabeth Warren. Brown spent $35 million, and Warren spent $42 million, for a total of $77 million, the most spent by any general election candidate. The seat had previously been occupied by Senator Ted Kennedy. After Kennedy's death in 2009, Scott Brown won the seat in an upset special election. Warren's challenge to Brown had enormous significance for several reasons. First, Brown's 2010 victory was won with the help of the campaign team who had helped Mitt Romney secure the Massachusetts governor's seat in 2002. After its successful 2010 win with Brown, Romney used this team to run his national presidential campaign, which was headquartered in Boston. Second, Warren was no ordinary quality challenger, but a crusader for consumer protections against big businesses, especially banks, in the aftermath of the global financial crisis of 2008. Warren came up with the idea of a consumer protection bureau created in legislation to address shortcomings in the oversight of the financial system. She was expected to be President Obama's nominee to run the bureau, but senate Republicans made it clear that Warren should not expect to be confirmed. Her revenge was to run "outside" the Senate by running to fill a seat in it.

Early in January 2012, Senator Brown suggested to Warren that both candidates sign a pledge to discourage outside money, because he feared the consequences of prolonged outside campaigns against him. Capitol Hill newspaper *Roll Call* reported that

> Warren, the presumptive Democratic nominee, and Brown signed a pledge to pay a penalty if any third-party group advertised on their behalf or against their opponent. The agreement says that the candidate who benefits from the third-party advertising would pay 50 percent of the cost of the advertising buy to a charity of his or her opponent's choice. . . . The agreement attempts to limit the advertising activity of corporations, Super PACs, 527s, and the state and national party committees. Early indications were that national parties were willing to play ball.[63]

As the numbers show, this is indeed what happened. As a result of the Brown-Warren agreement, parties did not spend money to help their senate candidates in Massachusetts, and neither did Super PACs. Are candidates indeed in the driver's seat, as so many have argued? In other cases in which parties were not asked to leave the race alone, all six party committees spent in competitive races, though not always treating each race the same. Both House committees left their incumbents pretty much to their own devices, trying instead to give their challengers an extra boost. Since the Democrats gained ground in both houses of Congress and retained the White House, we can say the Democratic Party fared rather well. On the other hand, Republicans retained control of the House while their party was losing the presidential race and certain key senate races, so it is clear that they also did well in a difficult year.

Conclusion

Parties have indeed adapted to the changed campaign finance landscape and have remained relevant and useful. Contemporary American parties have developed innovative fundraising and spending practices that allow them to effectively pursue winning in a relatively restrictive campaign finance environment. For example, the advent of Super PACs that can raise and spend unlimited amounts from virtually any source puts the parties at a relative disadvantage. Party committees must raise their funds within a framework of contribution limits and can accept funds only from individuals, PACs, candidates, and other party committees, while Super PACs may also accept unlimited contributions directly from corporations and labor unions.

Parties have also found themselves competing directly with their presidential nominees in a post-public-money era that finds presidential candidate organizations and party organizations pursuing the same donors at the same time. The parties have responded to such challenges by, for instance, increasing joint fundraising, which helps both their candidates and themselves. The parties have also worked to direct more resources to targeted races by cosponsoring hybrid ads with candidates, making the parties' and the candidates' money go further. Both parties have also invested significant resources to develop, refine, and most effectively use lists of potential donors, volunteers, and voters.

Moreover, in recent years, many observers have begun to view the parties as broader coalitions beyond formal party committees—as a party network or "web."[64] Given that most traditional PACs and virtually all Super PACs and 501(c) organizations identify with one party or the other, their efforts to elect candidates are not at cross purposes. For example, the major Super PACs are behaving like shadow party organizations. The parties still seem to be setting the strategic agenda, since Super PAC campaign activity follows the lead of political party targeting. If political party financing is the only rubric by which parties are judged in the 2012 elections, then we must conclude that their influence is waning. But instead, if political party organizations orchestrate the actions of the broader network, then their influence remains robust.

Notes

1. Adam Liptak, "A Drop in the Bucket," *Columbia Law School Magazine* (Fall 2010) (www.law.columbia.edu/magazine/54665/a-drop-in-the-bucket). The fundamental misunderstanding about corporations is that they are all profit-generating, public stock–issuing entities. This is clearly not the case in general for corporate bodies and in particular for those involved in campaign activism. Corporate entities in the 2012 campaigns tend not to be profit-bearing and privately held.

2. R. Sam Garrett, *Super PACs in Federal Elections: Overview and Issues for Congress,* Report R42042 (Congressional Research Service, April 4, 2013), pp. 7–11.

3. Rachel Louise Ensign, "The New Rules for Political Donations," *Wall Street Journal,* April 30, 2012 (http://online.wsj.com/article/SB1000142405270230381 6504577319723511631462.html).

4. Federal Election Commission, "Candidate and Committee Viewer" (www.fec.gov/finance/disclosure/candcmte_info.shtml).

5. Joint fundraising figures from Center for Responsive Politics: 2008 figures from "Joint Fundraising Committees" (www.opensecrets.org/pres08/jfc.php); 2012 figures from "Joint Fundraising Committees" (www.opensecrets.org/=pres 12/jfc.php).

6. Anthony Corrado, "Financing the 2008 Presidential General Election," in *Financing the 2008 Election*, edited by David Magleby and Anthony Corrado (Brookings, 2011), p. 127.

7. Center for Responsive Politics, "Joint Fundraising Committees," January 6, 2010 (www.opensecrets.org/pres08/jfc.php).

8. See discussion of joint fundraising in the 2008 presidential election in Corrado, "Financing the 2008 Presidential General Election," pp. 139–41.

9. *Colorado Republican Federal Campaign Committee* v. *Federal Election Commission*, 518 U.S. 604, 116 S.Ct. 2309 (1996).

10. Jim Wilson, "Final Rules on Coordinated and Independent Expenditures," *Federal Election Commission Record* 29, no. 1 (2003): 14 (www.fec.gov/pdf/record/2003/jan03.pdf).

11. Center for Responsive Politics, "2012 Presidential Race" (www.open secrets.org/pres12/index.php).

12. Center for Responsive Politics, "Joint Fundraising Committees."

13. Fredreka Schouten, "Obama Doubles as DNC Fundraiser in Chief," *USA Today*, May 24, 2011, p. 2a (www.hispanicbusiness.com/2011/5/24/obama_doubles_as_dnc_fundraiser_in.htm).

14. Eliza Newlin Carney, "RNC Troubles Will Linger: Steele's Successor Will Face Debt, Fundraising, and Structural Problems," *National Journal*, December 6, 2010 (www.nationaljournal.com/columns/rules-of-the-game/steele-s-successor-at-rnc-will-face-unenviable-task-20101206).

15. Center for Responsive Politics, "Joint Fundraising Committees."

16. Center for Responsive Politics, "2012 Presidential Race."

17. Dave Cook, "Republican Phone Sex Scandal, Fundraising Challenge Add to RNC Woes," *Christian Science Monitor*, April 1, 2010 (www.csmonitor.com/USA/2010/0401/Republican-phone-sex-scandal-fundraising-challenge-add-to-RNC-woes).

18. Peter H. Stone, "GOP Rainmaker Rides High," *National Journal*, May 8, 2010, p. 6.

19. Federal Election Commission, "2012 Coordinated Party Expenditure Limits," May 30, 2012 (www.fec.gov/info/charts_441ad_2012.shtml).

20. Reid Wilson, "Paul Ryan to Head Presidential Trust," *Hotline On Call* (blog), *National Journal*, September 23, 2011 (www.nationaljournal.com/blogs/hotlineoncall/2011/09/paul-ryan-to-head-presidential-trust-2); Peter Hamby, "RNC Reserves Vital Cash for Eventual GOP Nominee," *Political Ticker* (blog), *CNN Politics*, March 29, 2012 (http://politicalticker.blogs.cnn.com/2012/03/29/rnc-reserves-vital-cash-for-eventual-gop-nominee/).

21. Rick Wiley, political director of the Republican National Committee, interview by David Magleby, February 11, 2013.

22. See Center for Responsive Politics, "Donor Lookup," 2013 (www.open secrets.org/indivs/).

23. *McCutcheon v. Federal Election Commission*, 572 U.S. ___(2014).

24. Robert Barnes and Matea Gold, "Supreme Court Case Could Give Wealthy Donors More Latitude in Elections," *Washington Post*, October 3, 2013 (www.washington post.com/politics/supreme-court-case-could-give-wealthy-donors-more-latitude-in-elections/2013/10/03/26a66d82-2ad4-11e3-b139-0298 11dbb57f_story.html).

25. Robin Kolodny, *Pursuing Majorities: Congressional Campaign Committees in American Politics* (University of Oklahoma Press, 1998).

26. Democratic Congressional Campaign Committee, "House Democrats Poised to Roll Back the Tea Party Wave," November 5, 2012 (http://dccc.org/news room/entry/house_democrats_poised_to_roll_back_the_tea_party_wave); Alex

Isenstadt, "DCCC Leads NRCC in Money Race," *Politico*, September 20, 2011 (www.politico.com/news/stories/0911/63992.html).

27. Rob Jesmer, executive director of the National Republican Senatorial Committee, interview with David Magleby, February 12, 2013.

28. Center for Responsive Politics, "Donor Lookup."

29. Rick Wiley, political director of the Republican National Committee, interview with David Magleby, March 31, 2013.

30. Paul S. Herrnson, *Party Campaigning in the 1980s* (Harvard University Press, 1988).

31. Craig Timberg and Amy Gardner, "Democrats Push to Redeploy Obama's Voter Database," *Washington Post*, November 20, 2012.

32. Kenneth Vogel and Ben Smith, "RNC Weighs Outsourcing List to New Group," *Politico*, May 17, 2011 (www.politico.com/news/stories/0511/55147.html).

33. Rachel Leven, "GOP Chairmen Fail to Cut NRCC Checks," *The Hill*, June 12, 2012 (http://thehill.com/homenews/house/232161-gop-chairmen-failing-to-cut-checks-to-nrcc).

34. Josh Lederman, "Many Dems Haven't Paid Party Dues," *The Hill*, March 21, 2012 (http://thehill.com/homenews/campaign/217189-many-dems-havent-paid-their-dues-).

35. Cameron Joseph, "Romney Opens Wallet for GOP Lawmakers," *The Hill*, May 22, 2012 (http://thehill.com/homenews/campaign/229015-romney-opens-wallet-for-gop-lawmakers).

36. Federal Election Commission, "FEC Summarizes Campaign Activity of the 2011–12 Election Cycle," press release, April 19, 2013 (www.fec.gov/press/press 2013/20130419_2012-24m-Summary.shtml).

37. David Magleby, "Political Parties and the Financing of the 2008 Election," in *Financing the 2008 Election*, edited by Magleby and Corrado, p. 225.

38. Stewart Powell, "GOP Raids Dems' Donor List, and It Pays Off for Cornyn," *Houston Chronicle*, September 6, 2010 (www.chron.com/news/houston-texas/article/GOP-raids-Dems-donor-list-and-it-pays-off-for-1711968.php); Luke Rosiak, "Bain Capital Is Largest NRCC Donor," *Inside Politics* (blog), *Washington Times*, October 16, 2012 (www.washingtontimes.com/blog/inside-politics/2012/oct/16/bain-capital-largest-nrcc-donor/).

39. "Dinner with President Obama for Obama Victory Fund–Joint Fundraising Committee," *Political Party Time 2012*, Sunlight Foundation (http://political partytime.org/party/30569/).

40. Barnes and Gold, "Supreme Court Case Could Give Wealthy Donors More Latitude in Elections.

41. Data from Federal Election Commission, "Candidate and Committee Viewer," Campaign Finance Disclosure Portal, 2013 (www.fec.gov/finance/disclosure/candcmte_info.shtml).

42. Ibid.

43. Rachel Leven, "Obama Campaign Rolls Out Swing-State Fund," *Ballot Box* (blog), *The Hill*, December 20, 2011 (http://thehill.com/blogs/ballot-box/presidential-races/200521-obama-reelect-adds-to-fundraising-arsenal-with-swing-state-victory-fund).

44. David Drucker, "Mitt Romney's Fundraising Boost Stems from Unique Tactic," *Roll Call*, July 30, 2012 (www.rollcall.com/issues/58_13/Mitt-Romneys-Fundraising-Boost-Stems-From-Unique-Tactic-216525-1.html).

45. Data from Federal Election Commission, "Candidate and Committee Viewer," 2013 (www.fec.gov/fecviewer/CandCmteTransaction.do).

46. Drucker, "Mitt Romney's Fundraising Boost Stems from Unique Tactic."

47. Ibid.

48. Lisa Riley Roche, "Romney Victory Fund Sharing Cash with Four States but Not Utah," *Deseret News*, May 31, 2012 (www.deseretnews.com/article/865556748/Romney-Victory-fund-sharing-cash-with-four-states-but-not-Utah.html?pg=all).

49. Jesmer, interview.

50. See "Freshman Class JFC: Transfers to Authorized Committees" (www.fec.gov/finance/disclosure/candcmte_info.shtml).

51. Rachel Leven, "GOP Freshmen Form Joint Fundraising Committee," *Ballot Box* (blog), *The Hill*, December 5, 2011 (http://thehill.com/blogs/ballot-box/house-races/197183-gop-freshmen-form-joint-fundraising-committee).

52. Federal Election Commission, "FEC Announces 2011–2012 Campaign Cycle Contribution Limits," press release, February 3, 2011 (www.fec.gov/press/20110203newlimits.shtml).

53. The twelve races for 2012 were Arizona, Hawaii, Indiana, Maine, Massachusetts, Montana, Nebraska, Nevada, North Dakota, Pennsylvania, Wisconsin, and Virginia. Only Democrats gave contributions to candidates in the Michigan and Missouri races, and only Republicans contributed to Pennsylvania, Maine, and Massachusetts.

54. Nathaniel Persily, "The Law of American Party Finance," in *Party Funding and Campaign Financing in International Perspective*, edited by Keith Ewing and Samuel Issacharoff (Portland, Ore.: Hart Publishing, 2006), pp. 213–40.

55. Calculated by author from tables 2 and 3 of National Party 24-Month Data Summaries: (1/1/11–12/31/12), Federal Election Commission (www.fec.gov/press/summaries/2012/ElectionCycle/24m_NatlParty.shtml).

56. Federal Election Commission, "Coordinated Party Expenditure Limits for 2012 General Election Senate Nominees," 2013 (www.fec.gov/info/charts_441ad_2012.shtml#Senate).

57. The eight states were Alaska, Delaware, Montana, North Dakota, Rhode Island, South Dakota, Vermont, and Wyoming (www.fec.gov/info/charts_441ad_2012.shtml#Senate).

58. *Colorado Republican Federal Campaign* v. *Federal Election Commission*, 518 U.S. 604 (1996).

59. Shira Toeplitz, "NRCC Names First Female to Lead Independent Expenditure Arm," *Roll Call*, March 21, 2012 (www.rollcall.com/issues/57_113/NRCC_Names_First_Female_to_Lead_Independent_Expenditure_Arm-213261-1.html?pg=1).

60. David B. Magleby and Quin Monson, eds., *The Last Hurrah? Soft Money and Issue Advocacy in the 2002 Congressional Elections* (Brookings, 2004); David B. Magleby, *The Other Campaign: Soft Money and Issue Advocacy in the 2000 Congressional Elections*, edited by David B. Magleby (Lanham, Md.: Rowman and Littlefield, 2003).

61. T. W. Farnam, "Obama's Sept. Spending Doubles That of Romney," *Washington Post*, October 21, 2012, p. A7.

62. Emily Miller, "Obama's Cash Crunch: RNC Has the Edge in a Key Monetary Battle," *Washington Times*, October 26, 2012, p. B2.

63. Joshua Miller, Shira Toeplitz, and Abby Livingston, "At the Races," *Roll Call*, January 24, 2012 (http://congressional.proquest.com/congressional/docview/t63.d44.2568817711?accountid=14270).

64. Gregory Koger, Seth Masket, and Hans Noel, "Partisan Webs: Information Exchange and Party Networks," *British Journal of Political Science* 39, no. 3 (2009): pp. 633–53.

SEVEN *Interest Groups*

DAVID B. MAGLEBY AND JAY GOODLIFFE

When it comes to raising and spending money in elections, there are three main players: candidates, political parties, and interest groups. However, as discussed in earlier chapters, there is some crossover among these three groups; for example, interest groups play a crucial role in helping candidates and party committees fund their activities. Interest groups as a category include business and labor organizations, trade associations, ideologically oriented groups, single-issue groups, and even individuals who want to participate beyond conventional candidate and party committee contributions. Interest groups operate separately from candidates and parties but also are major underwriters of candidates and parties through campaign contributions. In this chapter we examine both modes of interest group participation.

As they have long done, interest groups played an important role in financing the 2012 election. As discussed by Anthony Corrado in chapter 2, court rulings and administrative decisions expanded the ways in which interest groups could engage in electioneering. Super PACs were the most important expansion in interest group participation in 2012. These independent-expenditure-only committees first formed in the 2010 election cycle, following the *Citizens United* v. *Federal Election Commission* Supreme Court decision in early 2010 and the D.C. Circuit Court of Appeals *SpeechNow.org* v. *Federal Election Commission* decision soon thereafter, as well as the related Federal Election Commission (FEC) advisory opinions.[1] Given the timing of these decisions and advisory opinions, only 83 Super PACs formed before the 2010 election.[2] In the

2011–12 election cycle, the number of registered Super PACs rose to 1,310, of which 424 spent more than $1,000 and 81 spent more than $1 million.[3]

Contributing to Super PACs, which are relatively new on the political scene, is another way to influence federal elections. As discussed in earlier chapters, much of the Super PAC activity in 2011–12 was an extension of particular presidential campaigns, and taken as a whole, Super PACs spent $388 million in the presidential race and $244 million on congressional contests. Some Super PACs at both the presidential and congressional levels are organized by former party leaders. For example, American Crossroads, whose leadership includes Republican strategist Karl Rove, spent $105 million on independent expenditures in 2011–12.[4] We categorize Super PACs later in this chapter, but the often close connection between candidates, congressional leaders, party leaders, and Super PACs helps explain why they have been part of several chapters in this volume. Under law, they are supposed to operate independently of candidates and party committees, and therefore, they are a primary focus of this chapter.

Interest groups (and individuals) can form groups whose primary purpose is not to elect or defeat a candidate but who are still able to raise and spend money in federal elections. These varied groups are called Section 501(c) organizations, named after the section of the Internal Revenue Code that defines them. Social welfare organizations are organized under Section 501(c)(4), labor groups under 501(c)(5), and trade associations under 501(c)(6). Charitable organizations, organized under Section 501(c)(3), may not advocate in candidate elections. There are also Section 527 organizations that are primarily organized to influence elections.[5] Unlike donors who contribute to PACs and Section 527s, donors to 501(c) groups are not required to be disclosed. However, the expenditures of these groups are disclosed to the Internal Revenue Service (IRS), the Department of Labor in the case of labor unions, and, when expenditures are made to influence elections, the FEC.

Instead of supporting or opposing candidates and campaigns through Super PACs, corporations may have contributed to other organizations that require less disclosure. Early in the 2012 general election campaign, the *New York Times* reported that "large corporations are trying to influence campaigns by donating money to tax-exempt organizations that can spend millions of dollars without being subject to the disclosure requirements that apply to candidates, parties and PACs."[6] ProPublica's analysis of campaign ad spending in 2012 found that "more money is being spent on TV advertising in the presidential race by social welfare nonprofits, known as 501(c)(4)s for their section of the tax code, than by any other type of independent group."[7]

Interest Groups as Major Funders of Candidates and Party Committees

Interest groups have a variety of options for financing federal election–related activities. The first option has been available since the passage of the Federal Election Campaign Act (FECA) as amended in 1974. Two of these options have developed over the past two decades. First, interest groups can contribute to candidates and party committees through political committees, organized under FECA, that report to the FEC. These committees are known as political action committees, or PACs. Second, groups can spend unlimited amounts on communications to their members or employees. These expenditures are disclosed and reported to the FEC as internal communications. Third, in federal elections PACs can spend money raised in limited contributions that is independent of the candidates and party committees. These expenditures are generally labeled independent expenditures. The FEC defines independent expenditures as "spending by individuals, groups, political committees, corporations or unions expressly advocating the election or defeat of clearly identified federal candidates. These expenditures may not be made in concert or cooperation with, or at the request or suggestion of, a candidate, the candidate's campaign, or a political party."[8]

Since 2010, groups have a fourth mode of participation available to them. They can form committees that will make only independent expenditures and that do not contribute to any candidate or party committee. These independent expenditure-only committees are also known as Super PACs. Groups with an existing PAC may also designate an affiliate that will make only independent expenditures. Anthony Corrado discusses these "hybrid" Super PACs in chapter 2. For clarity, we sometimes label PACs that make contributions to candidates or party committees and make independent expenditures from limited contributions "traditional PACs" to distinguish them from the new Super PACs. A fifth way individuals and groups can seek to influence elections is to form or join others in a group organized under Section 501(c) of the Internal Revenue Code as discussed previously.

Interest groups are not limited to any single mode of organization, so many organize under more than one of these types. For example, in 2012, American Crossroads, a large Super PAC, also had an associated 501(c)(4), Crossroads Grassroots Policy Strategies (GPS).[9] Similarly, the League of Conservation Voters (LCV) had a traditional PAC that made campaign contributions, the League of Conservation Voters Action Fund; the League of Conservation Voters Inc., a 501(c)(4) that made independent expenditures; and a Super PAC, the League of Conservation Voters Victory Fund, which made independent expenditures.[10] These three groups spent $50 million to elect and defeat particular federal candidates.

Traditional PACs

For most interest groups, the preferred way to participate in financing elections has been through PACs. Organized labor is credited with inventing PACs: United Mine Workers president John L. Lewis established the first PAC, the Non-Partisan Political League, in 1936, as part of the newly formed Congress of Industrial Organizations (CIO).[11] When the CIO merged with the American Federation of Labor (AFL), the Committee on Political Education (COPE) was formed, and it became the model for later PACs.[12] The business community followed, and today 45 percent of PACs are business or trade association related, while 5 percent are unions.[13]

There are two general types of traditional PACs. The FEC calls the first type of PAC "separate segregated funds." These kinds of PACs may solicit funds only from individuals associated with or connected to the sponsoring organization, which include corporations, trade associations, and labor unions. As of 2012, there were 1,854 registered corporate PACs, 724 connected to trade associations, and 305 PACs related to labor unions. Ideological or issue groups constitute the second type of PAC; the FEC labels these "nonconnected committees." These PACs may raise funds from the general public.[14] Besides ideologically or issue-focused PACs, nonconnected PACs may be formed by members of Congress or other political leaders. Nonconnected PACs must pay administrative expenses out of contributions to the PAC, while sponsors of corporate, union, or trade association PACs may pay the administrative costs of the connected PAC. As of 2012, there were 2,955 nonconnected PACs.[15] In the 1970s, corporate PACs experienced the greatest growth. In the past ten years, nonconnected PACs have seen the highest growth, partially

Figure 7-1. *PAC Contributions to Congressional Candidates and Congressional Candidate Expenditures by Election Cycle, 1975–76 to 2011–12*

Millions of 2012 dollars

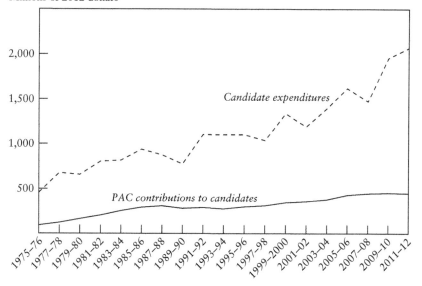

Source: 1972–2008 congressional data from *Financing the 2008 Election*, edited by David B. Magleby and Anthony Corrado (Brookings, 2011), 2010–12 data from Federal Election Commission (www.fec.gov) and Center for Responsive Politics (www.opensecrets.org).

driven by the increase in leadership PACs.[16] In the 2012 election, corporate PACs spent the most money: $343 million.[17]

As discussed in chapter 1, under FECA, contributions to candidates from a PAC are limited to a maximum of up to $5,000 for the primary election and $5,000 for the general election phase of an election cycle. PAC contributions, unlike individual contributions, were not increased under the Bipartisan Campaign Reform Act (BCRA), nor were they indexed to inflation.

Over time, PAC contributions in inflation-adjusted dollars have increased in most years but not as much as overall spending by congressional candidates and party committees. Figure 7-1 plots total PAC contributions to congressional candidates for 1976 through 2012, as well as total expenditures by congressional candidates for this same period in 2012 dollars.

Figure 7-2. *PAC Contributions to Congressional Candidates by Election Cycle, 1979–80 to 2011–12*

Millions of 2012 dollars

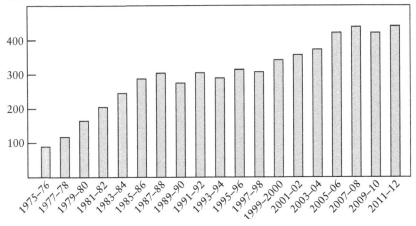

Source: Harold W. Stanley and Richard G. Niemi, *Vital Statistics on American Politics, 2009–10* (Washington: Congressional Quarterly Press), p. 92; Federal Election Commission, "2011–12 Election Cycle Data Summaries through 12/31/12" (www.fec.gov/press/summaries/2012/ElectionCycle/PACYE.shtml).

Contributions from PACs to congressional general election candidates have gradually risen since 1976, with only occasional declines (see figure 7-2). In 2011–12 PACs contributed $419 million to congressional candidates, up from $388 million in 2007–08. Over this same time period, congressional candidates' campaign expenditures have risen more sharply, and there are more ups and downs in their expenditure rates. Thus in terms of candidate receipts, PACs played a lesser role in 2012 than they did from 1976 to 1990. For example, congressional candidates spent less in 2008 than in 2006 or 2010, returning to a pattern seen in 1978, 1982, and 1988, when congressional candidates spent more in midterm than in presidential election years. The 2011–12 election cycle saw an all-time high in congressional candidate expenditures of $1.76 billion (see table 1-2, p. 18).

Since 2000, the most active PAC in terms of dollars contributed to federal candidates has been the National Association of Realtors, which has contributed a cumulative amount of $18.61 million since the 2000 election. Of the top five PACs in contributions to candidates in the past four presidential elections, four have been business-related groups: the National Association of Realtors, the National Auto Dealers Association,

Table 7-1. *Top PAC Contributors to Federal Candidates,*
by Recipient Party, 2011–12

PAC Name	Total[a] (dollars)	Democrats (percent)	Republicans (percent)
National Association of Realtors	3,885,102	44	55
National Beer Wholesalers Association	3,373,500	41	58
Honeywell International	3,208,524	41	58
Operating Engineers Union	3,153,539	84	15
National Auto Dealers Association	3,064,000	28	72
American Bankers Association	2,729,350	20	79
AT&T	2,525,500	35	64
American Association for Justice	2,497,500	96	3
Credit Union National Association	2,474,600	47	51
International Brotherhood of Electrical Workers	2,440,400	98	2
American Federation of State, County, and Municipal Employees	2,276,140	99	1
Lockheed Martin	2,256,500	41	59
Machinists and Aerospace Workers Union	2,188,500	98	1
Plumbers and Pipefitters Union	2,098,600	94	5
Every Republican Is Crucial	2,086,000	0	99
American Federation of Teachers	2,079,644	99	0
Teamsters Union	2,062,910	95	4
Boeing	2,020,500	44	56

Source: Compiled from Federal Election Commission data.
a. Totals include subsidiaries and affiliated PACs, if any.

the National Beer Wholesalers Association, and the National Association of Home Builders. The other six of the top ten PACs in money given since 2000 are labor unions (International Brotherhood of Electrical Workers; International Brotherhood of Teamsters; American Federation of State, County, and Municipal Employees (AFSCME); United Automobile Workers; Laborers' Union; and International Association of Machinists and Aerospace Workers), with all but the Teamsters being part of the AFL-CIO.[18]

Table 7-1 lists the top-spending PACs in contributions to federal candidates in 2011–12 and the percentage of each PAC's contribution that went to Democrats or Republicans. Most of the these PACs were from business or trade associations. The National Association of Realtors contributed the most to congressional candidates in 2011–12. Other trade associations with active PACs in 2011–12 were beer wholesalers, auto dealers, bankers, and credit unions. Some of the most active PACs came from publicly traded corporations such as Honeywell International, the third most active PAC, as well as AT&T and Lockheed Martin.

How do the most active PACs allocate their contributions between the two parties? With the exception of the credit union group, these business and trade association groups allocated nearly two-thirds (63 percent) of their campaign contributions to Republicans. The Credit Union National Association gave 51 percent to Republicans and 47 percent to Democrats (and the remainder to independents who caucus with Democrats). More than a third of the top twenty contributing PACs in 2011–12 were labor unions. The labor PAC that gave the most to candidates during that cycle was the Operating Engineers Union. The seven top union PACs gave 95 percent of their contributions in 2011–12 to Democrats. Only one of the top twenty PACs in campaign contributions in 2011–12 was not from business or labor; it was the Every Republican Is Crucial (ERIC) PAC, a leadership PAC affiliated with House majority leader Eric Cantor— which, not surprisingly, gave 100 percent to Republican candidates.[19]

Although there is partisan competition between PACs by type of PAC—labor versus business—there is near uniformity in the allocation patterns. Across virtually all PACs, the preference is to give to House incumbents and to rarely support House challengers. This long-standing pattern continued in 2012.[20] Figure 7-3 plots PAC contributions to incumbents, challengers, and open-seat candidates for the House general elections from 1996 to 2012.

In 2011–12, PACs continued their long-standing pattern of allocating more than four-fifths of their contributions to House candidates, with the remainder going to Senate candidates. Because PAC contributions are limited to $5,000 in the primary election and $5,000 in the general election, the larger number of House candidates helps explain this difference. Republican House candidates received more in PAC contributions than Democratic House candidates (56 versus 44 percent). Of the $340 million in PAC contributions to House candidates in 2011–12, 84 percent went to incumbents, with Republican incumbents getting 89 percent of contributions given to GOP candidates and Democratic incumbents getting 77 percent of all PAC contributions given to Democrats.

The pattern of giving to incumbents was not as strong in the Senate in 2012. Democratic Senate candidates received slightly more in PAC contributions than Republican Senate candidates in 2011–12 (53 versus 47 percent). Senate Democratic incumbents received 71 percent of PAC contributions to candidates from their party, whereas Senate Republican

Figure 7-3. *PAC Contributions to U.S. House General Election Candidates, 1996–2012*

Millions of 2012 dollars

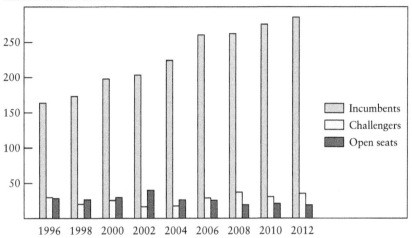

Source: Federal Election Commission, "PAC Contributions to Candidates" (www.fec.gov/press/press_archives.shtml).

incumbents received 49 percent of PAC contributions to their party's candidates. In 2011–12 Senate contests, PACs that gave to Republicans invested more in open-seat candidates and challengers. This reflects the fact that the 2012 Senate races were waged largely in contests with Democratic incumbents. For example, in 2012, Democrats had fifteen incumbents (plus independent Bernie Sanders, who caucuses with them) who sought reelection to Republicans' seven. Most PAC contributions go to congressional candidates, not to presidential candidates or party committees.[21] In 2012 PACs contributed $1.9 million to presidential candidates; Obama received $15,000, and the remainder went to Republican candidates.[22]

Internal Communications

Interest groups are allowed to spend unlimited amounts of money communicating to their organizations' members or companies' employees.[23] These communications are viewed by employers, unions, and other membership organizations as important because the source is personally connected to the recipient of the message. The Business-Industry Political Action Committee (BIPAC) has been a leader in direct communications to business employees. Darrell Shull, its chief operating officer, notes that, based on research in 2012, the committee knew "that younger voters are highly receptive to private sector messages that come from credible sources." Among the most credible sources, Shull reports, are employers.[24]

Important to the success of these communication efforts is that the group has established a pattern of communicating with its members before election-related communications are sent, rather than relying on just one "issue alert" or communication about the election.[25] Internal communications constitute just 1 percent of expenditures by traditional PACs.[26] In federal races in 2012, roughly $20 million was spent on internal communications, just under what was spent in 2008, and $9 million less than what was spent in 2004, which was the high point in the period since 1980. Presidential election internal communications dropped from $24 million in 2004 to $16 million in 2008 and to $7.7 million in 2012. Spending on internal communications in congressional races was higher in 2012 than in any election since 1980, with roughly $5 million in reported internal communications in House contests and the same amount in Senate contests. This still constitutes less than 1 percent of all interest group expenditures in House and Senate races.[27] Internal communications are more likely to be reported as being in support of candidates rather than against candidates (see table 7-2). Groups can both make a campaign contribution to a candidate and communicate directly to employees or members about candidates.

Independent Expenditures by Traditional PACs

Interest groups can also seek to influence the outcome of federal elections through independent expenditures. In the landmark 1976 *Buckley* v. *Valeo* decision, the Supreme Court struck down the limits on individuals, corporations, and unions that spend independently of the parties and candidates. For political committees that spend independently, the contribution limits remained in place. Thus an individual could contribute up to $5,000 per year to a PAC (see table 1-1, p. 6). The PAC in turn could spend unlimited amounts raised in this way as independent expenditures. The court in *Buckley* did not alter the long-standing restriction that corporations and unions could not use general treasury funds for election advocacy. This restriction on general treasury funds, dating back to the Tillman Act of 1907 for corporations and to the Taft-Hartley Act of 1947 for unions, was later reversed in the *Citizens United* v. *Federal Election*

Table 7-2. *Internal Communication Costs, Presidential Election Years, 1980–2012*

Millions of 2012 dollars

Year	Presidential candidates		House Candidates		Senate Candidates	
	For	Against	For	Against	For	Against
1980	5.5	1.6	2.2	0.3	0.8	0.1
1984	10.2	0.1	2.2	0.1	1.3	0.0
1988	3.8	0.2	2.1	0.0	2.3	0.04
1992	6.8	0.1	3.7	0.02	3.1	0.1
1996	3.5	0.4	3.9	0.7	2.5	0.07
2000	14.4	0.8	4.7	0.3	3.0	0.1
2004	29.2	0.0	2.2	0.01	3.4	0.006
2008	17.0	2.2	2.4	0.004	1.0	0.002
2012	7.7	2.7	4.2	0.4	4.0	1.0

Source: Federal Election Commission (ftp://ftp.fec.gov/FEC).

Commission and *SpeechNow.org* v. *Federal Election Commission* decisions and subsequent administrative rulings.[28]

The *Buckley* v. *Valeo* decision held that individuals could also make unlimited independent expenditures. In prior election cycles, individuals have on occasion made independent expenditures. The largest individual independent expenditure before 2012 was $2 million made by Stephen Adams in 2000 and again in 2004.[29] Most independent expenditures have been made by groups. When groups make independent expenditures on their own, without turning to a Super PAC, they employ political professionals to make those expenditures, much as they would if they were candidates. Groups are not constrained in their independent expenditures as to how much they can allocate to a particular contest, as PACs are in their direct contributions to candidates' campaign committees. Thus the independent expenditures may reveal which contests the groups feel most strongly about: for example, the Service Employees International Union (SEIU) spent $3.6 million in independent expenditures against Mitt Romney. Table 7-3 lists the ten groups that spent the most in conventional independent expenditures in 2011–12. Conventional independent expenditures are the funds used by PACs for these independent expenditures that were drawn from limited contributions to the PAC. In contrast, Super PACs, new to presidential elections in 2012, can raise unlimited funds. We discuss Super PACs in greater detail later in this chapter.

Table 7-3. *Interest Groups That Spent the Most in Independent Expenditures with Traditional PAC Funds, 2011–12*[a]

		For Democrats and against Republicans		For Republicans and against Democrats	
Organization name	Grand total (dollars)	Total (dollars)	Percent	Total (dollars)	Percent
National Rifle Association	16,554,005	205,483	1	16,348,522	99
Service Employees International Union	16,374,940	16,374,940	100	0	100
American Federation of State, County, and Municipal Workers	12,449,381	12,449,381	100	0	0
Senate Conservatives Fund	3,546,738	0	0	3,546,738	100
National Association of Realtors	3,391,843	960,400	28	2,431,443	72
Conservative Majority Fund	3,024,846	0	0	3,024,846	100
National Education Association	2,677,430	2,099,780	78	577,650	22
National Right to Life	2,642,497	8,727	<.05	2,633,770	100
Government Integrity Fund	2,431,748	0	0	2,431,748	100
Republican Majority Campaign	2,360,392	0	0	2,360,392	100

Source: Compiled from Federal Election Commission data.
a. Totals include independent expenditures made by local affiliates of each organization.

When we compare independent expenditures by interest groups in 2011–12 with the 2000, 2004, and 2008 election cycles, we find that two groups were very active over these four election cycles: the National Rifle Association was one of the top three spenders, and National Right to Life was one of the top ten spenders in independent expenditures in all four cycles. In addition, the SEIU and AFSCME were top ten spenders in 2004, 2008, and 2012. After dropping out of the top ten in 2008, the National Education Association returned in 2012. In 2012 several newer organizations were among the top ten spenders, such as the Conservative Majority Fund (an anti-Obama group known for its birth certificate demands)[30] and the Senate Conservatives Fund (Jim DeMint's leadership PAC).

Independent Expenditures by Super PAC

The 2011–12 election cycle marked the first presidential election in which individuals or groups could give unlimited contributions to a Super PAC. This capacity to raise unlimited contributions from individuals and groups distinguishes Super PACs from traditional PACs. For some, giving millions to a Super PAC would be less time consuming than managing all that goes into making an independent expenditure: finding the consultants, hiring lawyers, reporting to the FEC, and so on.

Given that donors in 2012 had more visible and active entities to which they could contribute, was there increased competition among these entities for the donors' contributions? To what extent did the outside groups, the Super PACs, and the Section 501(c) organizations draw funds away from candidates or party committees? Party committee officials consistently acknowledged that there was greater competition for contributions from large donors in 2012, in part owing to the addition of Super PACs. Rob Jesmer, the executive director of the National Republican Senatorial Committee in 2011–12, stated, "We live in a much more competitive environment now because of the advent of Super PACs, and so there's somewhat more donor confusion."[31]

For a donor who wants to contribute more than BCRA's limits allow, a Super PAC affords that opportunity, and the connection to the candidate may provide an added incentive to participate in this way as well. Other donors may prefer to give to a Section 501(c) organization because it allows them to remain anonymous. Still others may feel strongly about an issue and want to give to a group such as the Human Rights Campaign or Planned Parenthood. But for donors focused on a particular contest, the likely order of contributions is first the candidate, then the party committee, then the Super PAC. Donors who are motivated by ideology or a particular issue might be drawn to a PAC or Section 501(c) organization in lieu of the party committee and Super PAC. Examples include pro-choice, pro–traditional marriage, and environmental groups and the NRA.

What impact did Super PACs have on traditional PAC independent expenditures? In 2012 independent expenditures in congressional campaigns by traditional PACs declined slightly compared with 2010, dropping from $55 million to $52 million. (We compare congressional campaigns to take into account presidential campaign spending, which obviously occurred only in 2011–12.) Meanwhile, independent expenditures by Super PACs in congressional campaigns increased from $63 million in 2010 to $233 million in 2012.[32] For example, the traditional PAC of the National Association of Realtors spent $3.6 million on independent expenditures in congressional campaigns in 2012, down from the $6 million it spent on independent expenditures in congressional campaigns in 2010. However, the Realtors association increased its Super

PAC independent expenditures on congressional campaigns from $1.1 million in 2010 to $3.2 million in 2012.[33]

Just as PAC contributions to candidates have a distinct partisan slant, so too with the spending patterns of top independent expenditure groups. Unions, which were three of the largest independent spenders in 2011–12, spent 78 to 100 percent of their independent expenditures for Democrats or against Republicans. Business organizations spent independently for Republicans and against Democrats with a range of 100 percent of the time for the National Federation of Independent Business (NFIB) to 72 percent for the National Association of Realtors. Top ten issue organizations, such as the National Rifle Association and National Right to Life, spent all of their independent expenditures for Republicans and against Democrats.

In the 2010 election, the registered Super PACs collectively spent $93 million.[34] The Supreme Court decisions that allowed for the formation of Super PACs were handed down at the beginning of 2010, leaving little time for organization. The Super PAC that spent the most in 2010 was American Crossroads, cofounded by the Republican operative Karl Rove. American Crossroads spent $21.7 million in independent expenditures, and its affiliated 501(c)(4), Crossroads GPS, spent $15.4 million.[35] With Crossroads and other Super PACs such as Club for Growth, Karl Rove and other operatives saw 2010 as a chance to build infrastructure and experiment with different methods. As former FEC commissioner Michael Toner stated, "2010 was a warm-up cycle, a warm-up because *Citizens United* didn't really come down until the early part of that year, and there was a lot of experimentation that took place in 2010, and a number of these PACs were quite active in 2010—American Crossroads, it would be a good example on the conservative side, Common Sense 10 on the progressive side."[36]

As John Green discusses in chapter 3, Super PACs played an important role in the 2012 presidential primaries. As Newt Gingrich threatened Mitt Romney's lead in the polls before the Iowa caucuses, Restore Our Future (the Super PAC that supported Mitt Romney) broadcast advertisements attacking Gingrich. One report stated that 45 percent of the ads broadcast in Iowa were against Gingrich.[37] Later in the primaries, Super PACs hindered Romney. Foster Friess donated $1 million to the Red White and Blue Fund, a Super PAC that supported Rick Santorum. The ads the Super PAC ran in Iowa helped Santorum finish a very close second (as tallied on election night in the caucuses) and stay in the race longer.[38] Santorum was later declared to have been the winner of the Iowa caucuses. And Sheldon Adelson and his wife donated $20 million to Winning Our Future, a Super PAC that supported Newt Gingrich.[39] This allowed Gingrich to survive the initial primaries and stay in the race longer and required Romney to spend money that could have been used against Obama once Romney had secured the nomination. That Super PAC also started the attacks on Romney's tenure at Bain Capital; similar attacks were later the focus of the Obama campaign and its allied Super PAC, Priorities USA. Overall, Super PAC spending on advertising exceeded candidate spending in the presidential primaries. By April 22 (when Romney was the presumptive nominee), outside groups had spent $77.5 million, and candidates had spent $28.1 million.[40] It is a widely shared view among political professionals in both parties that Super PACs kept Gingrich and Santorum in the race longer than they would have been able to stay based only on what they raised as candidates.[41] Rick Wiley, the political director of the Republican National Committee (RNC), stated, "Rick Santorum probably would not have gotten this far in this race had it not been for his Super PAC. . . . Newt Gingrich is another great example of the same thing."[42] But it is also the case that Romney benefited from the attacks on his opponents mounted by Restore Our Future. As Matt Rhoades, Romney's campaign manager, said, "During the primary the Super PACs were good for Mitt Romney and bad for Mitt Romney."[43] Rhoades singled out the South Carolina primary as one in which Super PACs damaged the Romney candidacy. Bill Burton, a senior strategist for Priorities USA, observed, "I don't think that Mitt Romney would have been the nominee if it weren't for Restore Our Future."[44]

In 2012 Super PACs were important to the financing of congressional elections. Some Super PACs were closely aligned with particular candidates, other Super PACs had strong endorsements from House or Senate leadership, and still others were more broad-based partisan Super PACs, most notably American Crossroads.[45]

Several Super PACs associated with congressional leaders were active in 2012. Majority PAC (Senate Democratic majority leader Harry Reid) supported Senate Democrats, House Majority PAC (House Democratic minority leader Nancy Pelosi) supported House Democrats, Congressional Leadership Fund (Republican House Speaker John Boehner) supported House Republicans, and Young Guns Action Fund (Republican House majority leader Eric Cantor) also supported House Republicans. Another Super PAC identified with Reid, American Bridge 21st Century, did opposition research for Majority PAC and other progressive Super PACs. Super PACs on both sides formed alliances with other Super PACs. For example, Planned Parenthood worked with House Majority PAC in ten House races, and the League of Conservation Voters worked with the Center for Wildlife, Sierra Club, Environment America, Natural Resources Defense Council, and National Wildlife Action Fund in the New Mexico Senate race.[46] Individually focused Super PACs also operated in congressional contests; for example, Senator Orrin Hatch (R-UT) and Representative Howard Berman (D-CA) had the support of specific Super PACs in 2012.[47]

The most important and visible manifestation of these Super PACs was in television advertising. The Wesleyan Media Project, which tracks television advertising in every U.S. media market, estimates that presidential candidates spent $24 million on TV ads in the 2012 caucuses and primaries, with Mitt Romney spending the most at $14.1 million. Interest groups, including Super PACs, spent much more than the candidates did on TV ads during the 2012 presidential nomination contest. They spent $77 million, or more than triple what the candidates spent. The Mitt Romney–aligned Super PAC alone spent $31 million.[48] The spending of outside groups in 2012 was frequently commented on in the media.[49]

The Obama-aligned Super PAC, Priorities USA Action, played an important role in negative advertising in early summer 2012, especially with attacks on Romney's core competency, job creation. As noted, these themes had already been part of the GOP nomination contest.[50] Harold Ickes, who played an important role in organizing and fundraising for Priorities USA, observes, "We . . . can say things that the campaign can't say. We are even free to do other things, and I think that our anti-Romney, especially the Bain ads, some polling evidence . . . indicates that it was effective and it was early."[51] Glen Bolger, who did polling for Romney's Super PAC, Restore Our Future, viewed the strategy of the Obama campaign and the Super PAC as seeking to "impugn Mr. Romney's character and question his ability to play his strong suit, which was somebody who could create jobs."[52] Both nominees' Super PACs remained active in battleground states through the general election.[53]

In the general election, candidate and party spending dwarfed Super PAC spending, but Super PAC spending remained important. As Candice Nelson observes in chapter 4, Priorities USA's attacks on Mitt Romney for his business dealings at Bain Capital in the summer before the nominating conventions weakened Romney on one of his potential strengths, handling the economy. With Romney short on primary election funds to fend off late challengers, other Republican Super PACs attempted to fill the gap, but they were still outspent two to one during this period.[54] In the opinion of Romney's pollster, these funds were used to "define Romney on their [Priorities USA Action's] terms."[55]

Table 7-4 shows the independent expenditures of the top twenty most active Super PACs in the 2011–12 cycle. Two of the three highest-spending Super PACs were associated with presidential campaigns: Restore Our Future (Romney) and Priorities USA (Obama). In addition, Winning Our Future, the seventh highest-spending Super PAC in 2012, supported Newt Gingrich's presidential campaign. Both the Romney- and Gingrich-supporting Super PACs show substantial spending against other Republican primary opponents. Three of the top ten Super PACs supported Republicans across different races: American Crossroads, FreedomWorks (associated with the Tea Party and Dick Armey), and the Ending Spending Action Fund (associated with J. Joe Ricketts). Majority PAC and House Majority PAC supported Democratic Senate and House candidates, respectively. The last two Super PACs in the top ten were associated with traditional interest groups: Club for Growth (supporting Republicans) and SEIU (supporting Democrats).

For the Super PACs that ranked eleventh to twentieth in total spending, we again find some candidate-specific groups (Santorum-aligned Red White and Blue Fund), interest groups (Planned Parenthood), and unions (AFL-CIO). But some of these Super PACs were created to influence specific nonpresidential races. The Texas Conservatives Fund spent in the Texas Senate primary against Ted Cruz and for David Dewhurst. The Independence Virginia PAC spent money in the Virginia Senate general election against Tim Kaine and for George Allen.

As Super PACs came into existence, there was much speculation about how active corporations would be in funding them. Since corporations could contribute to Super PACs directly from their treasuries (executives could already contribute individually), critics worried that corporations could flood campaigns. Senator Russ Feingold said, "It is possible that the Court's decision will not just take us back to a pre-McCain-Feingold era, but back to the era of the robber baron in the 19th century. That result should frighten every citizen of this country."[56] In his 2010 State of the Union address after *Citizens United*, President Obama criticized the ruling, claiming it would "open the floodgates for special interests—including foreign corporations—to spend without limit in our elections."[57]

Table 7-4. *Independent Expenditures by the Top Twenty Super PACs, 2011–12*
Dollars

Organization name	Grand total	Total for Democrats	Total against Democrats	Total for Republicans	Total against Republicans
Restore Our Future	142,097,336	0	88,572,350	13,919,902	39,605,084
American Crossroads	104,746,670	33,084	95,844,402	8,493,968	375,216
Priorities USA Action	65,205,743	0	0	0	65,205,743
Majority PAC	38,152,864	3,651,229	0	0	34,501,635
House Majority PAC	30,714,650	865,034	0	0	29,849,616
FreedomWorks for America	19,636,548	42,870	7,079,203	11,306,234	1,208,241
Winning Our Future	17,007,762	0	5,000	12,970,828	4,031,934
Club for Growth Action	16,585,075	15,000	4,244,957	3,060,031	9,265,087
Service Employees International Union	15,189,094	12,867,337	0	5,679	2,316,078
Ending Spending Action Fund	13,250,766	0	6,674,460	6,452,125	124,181
Congressional Leadership Fund	9,450,223	0	9,450,223	0	0
Independence USA PAC	8,365,650	5,113,573	431,356	2,080,923	739,798
Women Vote!	8,034,944	1,763,590	92,900	0	6,178,454
Now or Never PAC	7,760,174	0	5,361,639	2,111,775	286,760
Red White and Blue Fund	7,529,554	0	0	6,739,158	790,396
AFL-CIO Workers' Voices PAC	6,362,019	3,266,956	0	602	3,094,461
Texas Conservatives Fund	5,872,431	0	0	0	5,872,431
Planned Parenthood Votes	5,039,082	966,350	0	0	4,072,732
Independence Virginia PAC	4,921,410	0	4,921,410	0	0
Young Guns Action Fund	4,722,335	22,100	3,896,480	354,780	448,975

Source: Center for Responsive Politics, "Super PACs," March 20, 2013 (www.opensecrets.org/pacs/superpacs.php?cycle=2012).

However, contrary to what many believed and feared, corporations, especially publicly traded corporations, were not major funders of Super PACs in 2012. One reason frequently cited in our interviews for this limited involvement was that corporations do not want to risk offending their customers by contributing to partisan candidate elections. As Bill Miller, a senior vice president of the Business Roundtable, stated, "The downside risk of being overt in your explicit political goals is not something that 90-something percent of corporate CEOs want to be involved in. . . . All you have to do is look at the Target example and Minnesota Forward and say, do corporations really want to go and stick their neck out in an overt way and risk boycotts and petitions and all of those things? No, they don't."[58] Miller was referring to a $150,000 contribution made by the Target Corporation to a committee, Minnesota Forward, that supported a Republican gubernatorial candidate in 2010. The contribution sparked protests by Democrats and gay rights groups, and Target later apologized for the contribution.[59]

During the Republican presidential primaries, less than 1 percent of the candidate-aligned Super PAC receipts came from publicly traded corporations.[60] Super PACs received 12 percent of their funds from for-profit businesses and even less from labor unions (4 percent).[61] The business that made the largest contribution from its general funds ($10.6 million) was Specialty Group, a Tennessee real estate company that donated to FreedomWorks. The union that made the largest contribution was United Auto Workers, which gave $14 million to the Super PAC that supported Obama (Priorities USA) and Democratic Senate and House candidates (Majority PAC and House Majority PAC), as well as its own Super PAC.[62]

The major source of funds—70 percent—for Super PACs in 2012 was individuals, many of them wealthy individuals whose contributions came in part from publicly or privately held corporations. We have linked the FEC individual contributions to Super PACs (and other committees), which allows us to report all contributions to Super PACs from donors who gave the committee more than $200. This allows us to link together donations by the same donor to different committees (or to the same committee at different times). Table 7-5 lists the twelve individuals who gave the most to Super PACs in 2011–12. These figures are aggregate contributions and, where noted, are to more than one Super PAC.

The top individual contributors to Super PACs were Sheldon Adelson and his wife, Miriam, who together gave $88.4 million in 2011–12. Much of the Adelsons' wealth comes from the Las Vegas Sands Corporation, in

Table 7-5. *Top Individual Contributors to Super PACs, 2011–12*
Dollars, unless otherwise indicated

Name	Aggregate Amount Donated to Super PACs	Number of Super PACs Donated to	Aggregate Amount Given to Other Committees/ Candidates
Miriam Adelson	44,575,000	6	2,525,000
Sheldon Adelson	43,825,000	8	3,675,000
Harold Simmons	25,000,000	4	800,000
Bob Perry	22,900,000	6	1,400,000
Fred Eychaner	13,800,000	4	300,000
J. Joe Ricketts	12,700,000	2	0
Michael Bloomberg	12,050,000	2	50,000
James Simons	9,500,000	3	163,338
John Childs	4,125,000	4	76,800
Robert Rowling	3,635,000	3	44,135
Jeffrey Katzenberg	3,125,000	3	106,300
Steve Mostyn	3,003,850	1	101,100

Source: Compiled from Federal Election Commission records of donations linked and aggregated by donors.

which Adelson holds a controlling interest. Adelson initially contributed to Gingrich's Super PAC, but once Gingrich conceded, he contributed to Romney's Super PAC. The Adelsons also contributed to the Young Guns Action Fund and American Crossroads and reportedly to conservative 501(c) organizations.[63] In general, top Super PAC donors contribute to more than one Super PAC, and they also contribute to parties and candidates.

Another way to look at Super PAC funding is to look at the number of donors to the Super PAC overall and the number of million-dollar donors. Table 7-6 provides these data for the top Super PACs in 2011–12. Here again, we use the FEC data of individual donations that we have linked and aggregated to the level of the donor.

Among the top raising Super PACs, FreedomWorks raised about $5 million, and had the most donors: 2,995. The largest donor was William Dunn, a futures trader. None of the FreedomWorks donors gave $1 million. The average donor gave $1,695 (which could have been multiple donations aggregating to $1,695). The Super PAC with the fewest donors—one—was the Independence USA PAC (associated with New York City mayor Mike Bloomberg), which raised just over $12 million. The UAW Education Fund's single donor was the UAW International Union. Not surprisingly, the Romney- and Obama-affiliated Super PACs were among the top five Super PACs in numbers of donors. Both of these

Table 7-6. *Number of Donors and Million-Dollar Donors for Top-Raising Super PACs, 2011–12*

Super PAC	Total $ raised	Number of donors	Mean $ amount contributed	Number of donors, by $ amount contributed		
				$1,000,000 or more	$500,000– 750,000	$100,000– 250,000
Restore Our Future	123,393,328	1,441	85,630	25	19	137
American Crossroads	91,014,749	1,569	58,008	16	13	52
Priorities USA Action	63,408,859	2,083	30,441	29	13	36
Winning Our Future	23,807,264	149	159,780	3	3	3
Majority PAC	21,952,854	259	84,760	3	4	43
House Majority PAC	18,926,027	641	29,526	2	5	19
Club for Growth Action	17,609,987	1,739	10,127	6	3	15
Ending Spending Action Fund	13,839,250	16	864,953	1	2	0
Independence USA PAC	12,004,235	1	12,004,235	1	0	0
UAW Education Fund	11,406,000	1	11,406,000	1	0	0
American Bridge 21st Century	9,687,390	166	58,358	1	0	20
Congressional Leadership Fund	7,707,500	53	145,425	3	0	3
Planned Parenthood Votes	6,268,410	133	47,131	1	2	15
Young Guns Action Fund	5,786,450	34	170,190	2	0	4
Independence Virginia PAC	5,172,500	13	397,885	2	0	0
Texas Conservatives Fund	5,095,050	67	76,046	1	1	13
FreedomWorks for America	5,077,756	2,995	1,695	0	1	5
Women Vote!	4,479,056	690	6,491	0	0	9

Source: Compiled from Federal Election Commission records of donations linked and aggregated by donors.

Super PACs had more than twenty-five donors who gave $1 million or more. Their mean aggregate donor contributions were about $86,000 for Restore our Future and about $30,000 for Priorities USA.

In our interviews with Super PAC leaders, a common refrain was that donors to Super PACs were encouraged to "max-out" in their contributions first to the candidates and then to the party committees, and only afterward to give to Super PACs. As Navin Nayak, a senior vice president of campaigns at the LCV, said regarding U.S. Senate donors in 2011–12, the "candidate is first fundraising for himself. Once those donors have maxed out to them, they want those donors to give to the DSCC [Democratic Senatorial Campaign Committee] at their maximum level. And once they're done with that, they're going to be asking those donors to give to Majority PAC."[64] Only after donating through those three avenues are candidate-centered donors likely to look for more issue-based Super PACs such as the LCV Super PAC.[65]

Conventional wisdom holds that outside groups are best suited to attack advertising, while candidates are better suited to defining themselves positively and responding to attacks. In addition, party committees are better suited to get-out-the-vote (GOTV) efforts than are Super PACs, and candidates are best suited to creating positive messages, making the case for their candidacy, and responding to attacks from the opponent and allied groups.

The Wesleyan Media Project tracked the tone of television advertisements in both the primary and the general election season. During the campaign primaries (January 1, 2011, to April 22, 2012), 86 percent of the interest group television advertising in the presidential races was negative. In contrast, 53 percent of candidate television advertising was negative in the same time period. Compared with the 2008 campaign primaries, where only 25 percent of the interest group television advertising was negative, interest groups aired more than ten times as many ads, making up almost 60 percent of all presidential advertising. Most of the increase in ads and negativity can be attributed to Super PACs.[66] This trend of negativity continued in the general election campaigns. From June 1, 2012, to the election, 85 percent of the interest group television advertising in the presidential race was negative, while 54 percent of candidate television advertising was negative.[67]

In both the presidential primaries and the general election contest, Super PACs were the workhorses in delivering negative messages. Gingrich's supporting Super PAC, Winning Our Future, attacked Romney as a "corporate 'raider' whose firm 'destroyed the dreams of thousands of Americans' by buying up companies and firing its workers. [It produced a] film titled 'King of Bain: When Mitt Romney Came to Town.'"[68] Santorum's supporting Super PAC (Red White and Blue Fund) attacked Romney for leaving "Massachusetts with 'over $1 billion' in debt after his term as governor. The ad [run by the Super PAC] also claims that the Massachusetts healthcare reform bill Romney signed into law while governor was the 'blueprint' for President Obama's healthcare reform law."[69] During this period, Romney's Super PAC, Restore Our Future, also took the offensive against Gingrich "for having 'more baggage than the airlines,' for being fined by Congress for ethics violations, for his position on illegal immigration, even for admitting that he has made mistakes on the campaign trail."[70] Restore Our Future also attacked Santorum for his "votes, while he served in the U.S. Senate, to raise the debt ceiling five times and his past support for billions in 'wasteful spending,' a reference to congressional earmarks."[71]

Some Super PACs that supported Obama involved themselves in the Republican primaries, most notably Priorities USA, which ran an ad attacking Romney on the auto bailout days before the Michigan primary, quoting a Romney op-ed titled, "Let Detroit go bankrupt."[72] Similarly, the Obama campaign ran an ad before the Michigan primary on the same theme.[73]

But Obama-linked Super PAC Priorities USA entered the fray in earnest only after Romney was the presumptive standard bearer. As of May 31, Priorities USA had spent $5.8 million in independent expenditures. By election day, it would spend $64.6 million.[74] Its early summer ads attacking Romney's core strength as a "jobs creator" were in many ways reminiscent of the attacks by an outside group, Swift Boat Veterans for Truth, who attacked John Kerry's reputation as a Vietnam War hero in the period immediately after the Democratic convention in 2004. Then, as in 2012, the candidate under attack offered only a muted response. Kerry later acknowledged that "failing to respond more quickly and aggressively to the 'Swift Boat Veterans for Truth' had been a mistake." Kerry and top aides "attributed the Democrat's narrow loss to President Bush, in part, to the attacks."[75] Being "swift boated" has become common parlance among campaign consultants, and the widely shared view is that the person under attack needs to respond aggressively.[76]

In one ad, Priorities USA connected Bain Capital's closure of a steel plant—which led to a loss in employees' health insurance—to a worker's wife's death from cancer. The Romney response to the Priorities USA attack on Bain and his record as a "job creator" was surprisingly quiet; the campaign merely called the ad a diversion. Other Republicans and fact-checkers (and some Democrats) criticized the ad.[77] The Obama campaign also criticized the ad. As David Axelrod, the campaign senior strategist, said, "That was not an ad from the Obama campaign, it was an ad from a Super PAC. We made clear that we didn't think that was appropriate to accuse Romney of somehow being responsible for that woman's death. . . . I should point out that that ad ran exactly one time in this whole big country, and partly I suppose because we made our disapprobation known publicly."[78]

The underlying message of the Priorities USA attack on Romney was that he was a heartless businessman, detached from ordinary people and uncaring about their lives.[79] Mike Lux of Progressive Strategies saw Romney being defined in this way as "absolutely critical to us winning this race."[80] This narrative was later reinforced by Romney's comments at a Florida fundraiser for large donors: "There are 47 percent who are with [Obama], who are dependent upon government, who believe that they are victims, who believe the government has a responsibility to care for them, who believe that they are entitled to health care, to food, to housing, to you-name-it. . . . My job is not to worry about those people. I'll never convince them they should take personal responsibility and care for their lives."[81]

The Super PACs that opposed President Obama also pursued negative messaging, but they faced a different challenge. Americans already had established views of the president, and many of the critical undecided or swing voters generally liked Obama and had voted for him. Glen Bolger, a 2012 pollster for both Crossroads and Restore Our Future, noted that in 2012, the Obama campaign "had a much easier time of defining Mitt Romney who, like John Kerry, wasn't particularly well defined when he became the nominee," whereas Romney and his allies were running against "an incumbent who is obviously extraordinarily well known and well defined."[82]

Why did Super PACs choose not to defend Romney during June and July, when the Bain and other attacks were helping shape the public perception of Romney? The answer is that the Super PACs assumed that positive candidate definition was something the candidate campaign would pursue. As Rick Wiley stated, "It's hard for Restore Our Future, for instance, to go up and defend Romney's business model. . . . I think the campaign has to respond to that."[83]

Figure 7-4. *Total Dollars Raised by Restore Our Future, by Day and Amount, 2011–12*

Thousands of dollars

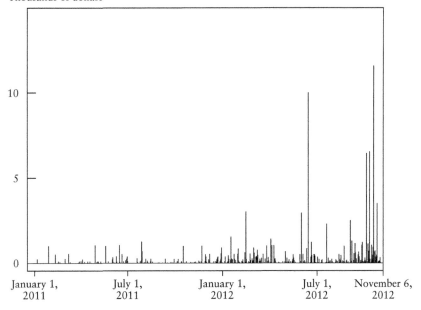

The timing of outside money spending in 2012 was important. Figure 7-4 illustrates daily contributions received by Restore Our Future over the election cycle. Larger spikes represent larger donations on that day.

The Romney Super PAC received more than one-third of its money in the last two months of the campaign. The large spike in June represents two $5 million donations from Sheldon and Miriam Adelson. This pattern is similar daily to donation patterns for all Super PACs, as illustrated in figure 7-5. Thus one reason so much of the spending was late in the election cycle was that the money donated to Super PACs came later in the cycle. For example, more than $40 million was donated to Super PACs on October 19, with more than $31 million of that from Sheldon and Miriam Adelson.

One consequence of the timing of the contributions to Super PACs is that the committees were delayed in making ad buys in some cases and therefore paid a higher rate for the ads. Postelection analyses of ad-buying strategies commented on the greater efficiency of the Obama campaign's

Figure 7-5. *Total Dollars Raised by Super PACs, by Day and Amount, 2011–12*

Thousands of dollars

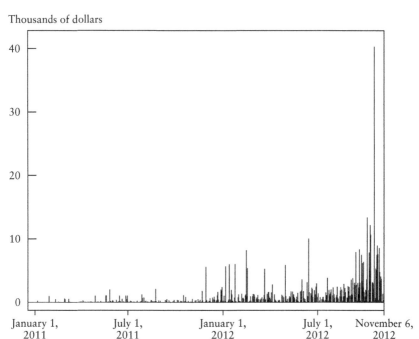

ad buys as compared with the Romney campaign's week-to-week ad-buying strategy.[84] The Romney campaign's weekly ad-buying strategy also made more complicated and expensive the ad-buying strategy of Romney's allied groups. Interest groups build their strategy around what the candidate's campaign is doing, determining target states and media markets, in part, on where the candidate will be advertising. Not knowing more than a week in advance where the candidate was going to be advertising increased the cost and reduced the options of Romney's allied interest groups.

A great deal of outside group spending (independent expenditures, Super PAC expenditures, 501(c) expenditures reported to the FEC, and so forth) in congressional races was for television ads. This was especially the case for U.S. Senate contests, which garnered more outside group spending ($270 million) than House races ($203 million).[85] Outside groups constituted 27.5 percent of ads aired in Senate races, compared to 17.9 percent of all House ads.[86] The 2012 contests that attracted the most outside money are listed in table 7-7.

Table 7-7. *Top Outside Spending in Senate and House Races, 2011–12*
Dollars

Race	Total	For Democrats	Against Democrats	For Republicans	Against Republicans
Senate					
Virginia Senate	36,482,705	2,078,749	22,239,318	1,647,555	10,517,083
Wisconsin Senate	31,631,648	2,469,186	9,959,504	3,767,843	13,546,847
Ohio Senate	29,296,771	1,821,688	15,295,684	5,621,319	6,339,313
Indiana Senate	23,556,883	357,388	8,390,952	4,436,945	9,176,798
Nevada Senate	18,913,055	746,693	9,121,605	862,791	8,127,858
Florida Senate	17,818,805	1,143,149	9,744,392	5,693,276	1,236,919
Montana Senate	16,821,830	1,645,985	7,702,776	396,179	6,810,935
Texas Senate	15,517,708	30,867	0	4,219,273	11,267,568
Arizona Senate	14,425,180	246,935	3,821,711	3,761,707	6,594,827
Missouri Senate	9,977,421	1,695,405	1,220,150	2,209,725	4,850,255
House					
Ohio District 16	6,862,010	239,562	2,743,559	97,627	3,781,262
Illinois District 8	6,280,136	124,013	4,289,172	1,397,280	469,671
Florida District 18	5,980,765	301,181	2,125,874	850,264	2,703,446
Pennsylvania District 12	5,631,133	824,989	2,221,880	1,350,242	1,234,022
Minnesota District 8	4,782,995	224,271	1,710,891	169,005	2,678,828
California District 7	4,351,450	629,597	490,000	19,832	3,212,021
California District 10	4,329,630	270,569	3,108,578	107,100	788,173
Florida District 10	4,273,936	2,188,637	1,151,745	39,135	894,419
Iowa District 4	4,253,995	531,191	1,179,309	188,923	2,156,806
New York District 18	4,223,250	237,002	1,367,333	1,222,393	1,396,522

Source: Center for Responsive Politics, "2012 Outside Spending, by Race" (Senate) (www.opensecrets.org/outsidespending/summ.php?cycle=2012&disp=R&pty=N&type=S); Center for Responsive Politics, "2012 Outside Spending, by Race" (House) (www.opensecrets.org/outsidespending/summ.php?cycle=2012&disp=R&pty=N&type=H).

Some large donors to outside groups on the Democratic side in 2004 were not as heavily involved in 2008 and 2012 as they had been previously. Most notably, George Soros, who contributed $23.7 million to various organizations in 2004, decreased his contributions to $5 million in 2008 and $2.8 million in 2012. Another major donor, Peter Lewis, contributed $23.2 million in 2004 but gave less than $1 million in 2008 and nothing in 2012.[87] Will some of the large donors to Republican outside groups in 2012 scale back their contributions as heavily in 2016? Adelson has said he is willing to again double his donation in 2016,[88] and David Koch, another large GOP donor, has said, "We're going to study what worked, what didn't work, and improve our efforts in the future. We're not going to roll over and play dead."[89]

The level of candidate support for Super PACs varied in 2012. From early on, most GOP contenders signaled their strong support of their allied Super PAC. Some candidates such as Mitt Romney appeared at some of their Super PAC fundraisers, while not explicitly doing "the ask" for money to the Super PAC. Romney also hosted retreats for major donors in Park City, Utah, and New York City, with one of the purposes being that donors wanted "to be part of this tight-knit Romney finance team."[90] Others, including Newt Gingrich and Rick Santorum, showcased the support of major Super PAC donors. For example, in February, the Gingrich campaign gave a briefing to donors, including Sheldon Adelson, at the Adelson-owned Venetian Hotel.[91] Foster Friess traveled with the Santorum campaign and appeared on stage with him the night Santorum won the Missouri primary.[92] Barack Obama's support of Priorities USA was, in comparison, muted. He had not courted large donors during his first term and had been critical of their role in elections in his 2008 campaign.[93] Unlike Romney, Santorum, and Gingrich, he did not appear at Priorities USA Action fundraising events, a contrast that one senior official claimed was "by design."[94]

The perception that Super PACs receive strong support from candidates raises the question of just how independent the Super PACs really are. Paul S. Ryan, senior counsel of the Campaign Legal Center, stated, "The entire legal theory underpinning the existence of Super PACs is that the money they are raising and spending cannot corrupt candidates because they have no relationship with candidates. In reality, we've seen in the past few years that many Super PACs are joined at the hip with candidates."[95] The close connection of major Super PAC donors to the candidate supported by the Super PAC was a recurrent pattern in 2012.

In general, Super PACs can be categorized into two broad groups: those linked to preexisting interest groups and new entities that are not connected to existing PACs or interest groups. Examples of the former include ideological groups such as Women Vote! (EMILY's List) and Planned Parenthood Votes; business groups such as the National Association of Realtors; environmental groups such as the LCV; and unions. The Super PACs that are not outgrowths of existing interest groups include American Crossroads, American Bridge, Senate Majority PAC, and House Majority PAC. Other examples of Super PACs that are not linked to existing interest groups are candidate-specific Super PACs such as Priorities USA, Restore Our Future, and Red White and Blue Fund.

Super PACs have become specialized as to function, whether that specialty is television and radio ads, voter mobilization, or even opposition research. Take, for example, the American Bridge 21st Century Super PAC, which provides opposition research for other progressive Super PACs.[96] Rodell Mollineau, president of American Bridge, said, "We share our information, our research, our tracking footage with other PACs, other third-party expenditure groups such as, in this last cycle, Priorities USA, Majority PAC, House Majority PAC, labor, anyone who has a third-party apparatus. Our research serves as the backbone for their polling memos, and for . . . how they're going to go about their attack or their critique."[97] In 2012, the Republicans lacked a similar entity, relying instead on political consulting firms to provide their opposition research. But in the wake of the 2012 election came the announcement of the formation of a new group, America Rising, to provide Republican-leaning Super PACs with this resource.[98]

Ideological Super PACs such as Club for Growth, FreedomWorks, and Campaign for Primary Accountability focus largely on primary elections. On the Democratic side in 2012, there were congressional Super PACs that focused on U.S. Senate races (Majority PAC) and some that focused on House contests (House Majority PAC). There were also multiple Super PACs that focused on electing Republican House candidates (Congressional Leadership Fund and Young Guns Action Fund, the latter of which was closely aligned with Majority leader Eric Cantor).[99] There was no specific Republican Senate Super PAC, but American Crossroads and the affiliated 501(c)(4) group, Crossroads GPS, spent $62 million in Senate and House races.[100] The Super PACs were major players in presidential battleground states and in competitive U.S. Senate and U.S. House contests.

Section 501(c) Groups

It has long been the case that groups organized under the IRS code for tax purposes could also engage in political activity so long as this was not their primary purpose.[101] For example, labor unions fall under Section 501(c)(5) of the Internal Revenue Code, and trade associations such as Americans for Job Security are organized under section 501(c)(6). The most common of these groups is a more diverse group of social welfare organizations, organized under section 501(c)(4). This latter category generated the most interest and attention in 2012 as the numbers of these groups grew and as they collectively began to rival Super PACs in expenditures. How much election activity constitutes less than a group's primary purpose is not specified. Charles R. Spies, the counsel for and treasurer of Restore Our Future, stated, "The IRS has not given a clear or bright line answer of what constitutes primary purpose. I think there are differing views, ranging from 51 percent to 60 percent or 70 percent."[102] Some groups are organized under Section 501(c)(3), and contributions to these groups are tax deductible. But Section 501(c)(3) groups may not engage in partisan political activity. Our discussion of Section 501(c) groups therefore includes only Section 501(c)(4), 501(c)(5), and 501(c)(6) groups.

Section 501(c) organizations report some of their spending to the FEC when they expressly advocate for the election or defeat of a candidate (independent expenditures) or when they advocate for a particular issue that identifies a candidate near an election (electioneering communications). In 2012 Section 501(c) groups reported $336 million in express election advocacy expenditures, which was much higher than the $69 million spent in 2008 or the $11 million spent in 2004.[103] Table 7-8 presents the spending reported to the FEC by the twenty top-spending Section 501(c) organizations in 2011–12.

It is important to note that these 501(c) groups also engage in political activity that is not reported to the FEC but is reported to the IRS and the Department of Labor. These reports, however, are annual reports and are generally not available until months after election day. Some organizations have been tracking IRS Form 990, and when possible, we have used their data. One other source of data is interviews conducted with leaders of 501(c) groups. Based on all of these data sources, we estimate that 501(c) groups spent $640 million on the 2012 election.

For some of the groups for which we have data from persons involved with the group, the amounts reported to the FEC are much lower than those provided in our interviews. For example, Crossroads GPS reported to the FEC that it spent $71 million in 2011–12, but Spies told us that it spent $300 million[104] (from which we subtracted the $117 million spent by its affiliated Super PAC, American Crossroads, to estimate $183 million in spending by Crossroads GPS). In arriving at this estimate, we examined databases from the Center for Responsive Politics, the Sunlight Foundation, and ProPublica.[105] In some instances, annual reports to the IRS were reviewed and added to one or more of these groups' tallies of outside groups. None of these groups, however, have been actively track-

Table 7-8. *Top-Spending 501(c) Organizations in the 2012 Election*[a]
Dollars

Organization	Amount
Crossroads GPS	71,181,940
Americans for Prosperity	36,352,928
US Chamber of Commerce	35,657,029
American Future Fund	25,415,969
Americans for Job Security	15,872,864
Americans for Tax Reform	15,794,552
American Action Network	11,689,399
League of Conservation Voters	11,229,498
Americans for Responsible Leadership	9,793,014
NRA Institute for Legislative Action	8,607,876
Patriot Majority USA	7,013,886
Planned Parenthood Action Fund	7,013,886
60 Plus Association	4,615,892
National Association of Realtors	4,606,898
Republican Jewish Coalition	4,595,666
VoteVets.org	3,190,540
Young Guns Network	2,874,481
CitizenLink	2,574,666
NFIB The Voice of Free Enterprise	2,168,004
Center Forward	2,057,089

Source: Center for Responsive Politics, "2012 Outside Spending, by Group" (www.opensecrets.org/outsidespending/summ.php?cycle=2012&chrt=V&disp=O&type=U).

a. Dollar amounts as reported to the Federal Election Commission, excluding 501(c)(5) groups.

ing labor union Section 501(c)(5) spending. We therefore are relying on the estimates provided by Brandon Davis at the Service Employees International Union.

One reason for the formation of many new 501(c) groups was the fact that it is so difficult to track how much these groups raise and spend because names of contributors to 501(c) groups are not reported, the reporting of expenditures by 501(c) groups does not coincide with the election schedule, and groups themselves determine which of their expenditures are related to an election. Nonetheless, some individuals involved with 501(c) groups self-disclose, and we can estimate expenditures through advertising buys and other indicators. In most instances, the reported 501(c) spending was much greater than what the affiliated Super PAC reported. For example, American Action Network's Super PAC spent $10.8 million, whereas its affiliated 501(c)(4) spent $44.2 million. In other cases it was the reverse. As stated above, we estimate that $640 million was spent by Section 501(c) groups in 2011–12. We see this as a conservative estimate because we only added to the FEC reported data in cases where we had interview data, which was a small fraction of all Section 501(c) groups. In many cases, we also identified press reports that confirmed what we were told in our interviews.[106] If we were to assume that other organizations have a similar ratio of disclosed to undisclosed 501(c) spending, then our estimate of 501(c) spending is $1.017 billion.[107]

When asked why some people prefer to contribute to a 501(c) organization rather than to a Super PAC, the answer was consistently "because they want anonymity."[108] This desire for anonymity extends not only to individuals but also to corporations, unions, and other entities. Fred Wertheimer, the president of Democracy 21, asserted, "Everyone says corporations are not spending money directly. Why should they? They can give it to someone else and do it without any fingerprints."[109] Charles Spies said, "The big difference probably with the 501(c)(4)s or 501(c)(6)s and Super PACs is publicly traded corporations [that contribute more to 501(c)s]."[110] Rodell Mollineau, the president of American Bridge Super PAC, noted that some donors give to 501(c) groups not to hide their ideology but so they would not be solicited by other organizations for money.[111] Some observers have speculated that much of the reported $100 million raised and spent by the Chamber of Commerce, a Section 501(c)(6) organization, came from corporations.[112]

527 Groups

Although they were the forerunner of Super PACs, 527 groups could not expressly advocate the election or defeat of any candidate. As a result, most 527 groups influenced elections through voter mobilization and issue advocacy campaigns. With the introduction of Super PACs and the growth in their activity, 527 groups have decreased in importance, but some groups were still active in the 2012 election. Table 7-9 lists the 527 groups that raised over $1 million.

Most of the 527 groups that were active in 2012 were formed in previous election cycles. Even with the advent of Super PACs, 527s continue because unlike Super PACs they can make contributions and because they can participate in nonfederal elections. For example, ActBlue started in 2004 as an Internet fundraising "middleman" for Democrats, "more an on-line banking hub than an electioneering entity."[113] ActBlue has a PAC as well as a 527. The group states that its 527 is intended for nonfederal activities,[114] though many of its 527 expenditures are used to benefit fed-

Table 7-9. *Top Ten 527 Organizations by Receipts, 2011–12*[a]

Dollars, unless otherwise indicated

Organization	Total receipts	Expenditures	Federal PAC	Partisan classification
ActBlue	16,731,798	14,626,209	x	Democratic
College Republican National Committee	13,635,610	14,156,096		Republican
EMILY's List	10,123,976	9,894,653	x	Democratic
Citizens United	9,815,160	9,305,909	x	Democratic
Service Employees International Union	9,609,566	10,872,872	x	Democratic
Int'l Brotherhood of Electrical Workers	8,084,621	6,768,467	x	Democratic
Plumbers and Pipefitters Union	6,380,541	5,796,679	x	Democratic
RightChange.com	5,136,240	5,206,186	x	Republican
Gay & Lesbian Victory Fund	4,801,801	7,175,540	x	Democratic
GOPAC	3,998,204	4,482,304	x	Republican

Source: Center for Responsive Politics, "Top 50 Federally Focused Organizations" (www.opensecrets.org/527s/527 cmtes.php?level=C&cycle=2012).

a. The data are based on records released by the Internal Revenue Service on Monday, March 4, 2013. The partisan classifications were determined by the authors based on each group's stated intent, the partisan orientation of the group's contributors (if data available), and newspaper accounts of the group's activity.

eral candidates and the Democratic Party.[115] The College Republican National Committee was organized as a 527 in 2001.[116] It emphasizes young-voter mobilization, and most of its expenditures in 2012 went to media and mailings.[117] It appears that group preferences largely determine whether groups organize as a federally registered Super PAC under the FEC or as a Section 527 group under the IRS.

Group Cooperation and Coordination

As the number of groups actively campaigning for or against candidates has increased, and as the amount of money they spend has grown, so too has the need for them to cooperate and coordinate. Although candidates cannot legally coordinate with Super PACs, with other PACs that make independent expenditures, or with Section 501(c) organizations, these groups can and do communicate and coordinate their activities with one other. Since the 2004 election, more than twenty progressive groups have regularly met and coordinated at meetings organized by a group named America Votes. America Votes, initially organized as a 527, raised more than $3 million in 2004. It formed an affiliated Super PAC in 2011. In 2012 America Votes had twenty-seven groups, including unions, environmental groups, prochoice groups, and Super PACs who met regularly in Washington, D.C., and it had similar groups working together at the state level in nineteen states as well. In addition to sharing plans for targeting states and contests, America Votes participants share plans about the timing of advertising and about where they will be conducting voter activation. Many of the America Votes participating groups also used data from Catalist, employed the Voter Activation Network (VAN), and analytic tools shared by groups that participate in the Analyst Institute. America Votes has helped participating groups be more effective and has fostered a cohesive team effort. [118] The Sierra Club's national political director, Cathy Duvall, saw America Votes as especially important because it provides "access and tools" to smaller organizations.[119] Others also praised the coordinating role played by America Votes, especially in key races. In 2012, for example, some groups were not comfortable with U.S. Senate candidate Heidi Heitkamp's issue positions on their group's core issues. Such information allowed groups that were comfortable with Heitkamp to ramp up activity, while others picked up the resulting slack in other states. More broadly, Karin Johansen, who in 2012 managed the campaign of Democrat Tammy Baldwin in the Wisconsin Senate race, but who has also worked for party committees and interest groups in the past, described the involvement of groups in 2012 as "a much more sophisticated process than it used to be."[120]

Republicans did not have an equivalent convener of allied groups in 2008, but they did organize one in 2012. One of the instigators was Karl Rove, the former chief strategist for the George W. Bush 2000 and 2004 campaigns and a senior adviser to President Bush from 2001 to 2009, who was also instrumental in the creation of American Crossroads. The coordinating group, nicknamed the Weaver Terrace Group after Mr. Rove's home on that street where the group first started meeting, now allows Republicans to regularly gather and communicate in similar ways as the Democrats do at the America Votes table. Steven Law, president and chief executive officer of American Crossroads, stated that the purpose of the Weaver Terrace Group is "to share information and encourage people to pull the oars in the same direction, to the extent that we could. That was very much an idea that not only did he [Rove] come up with, but he initiated." At the first meeting of the group, Rove stated, "We're not allowed to talk to the [candidate] campaigns, but we can talk to each other; why don't we do so?"[121]

To date, Republican outside groups do not seem to be as unified in supporting this model of communication and cooperation. For example, the Koch brothers–funded Americans for Prosperity does not participate. As Kenneth P. Vogel reported in *Politico*, "Americans for Prosperity's . . . president Tim Phillips attended a couple of the meetings in 2010, but told *Politico* he bowed out because the focus was more on electing Republicans than pushing fiscally conservative policies. 'We feel more comfortable talking about issue efforts, but I'm not sure those meetings have that as much, so it doesn't make sense for us to go to them.'"[122]

The cooperation on the Democratic side includes sharing not only information about strategy, targets, and timing but also information about voters. This exchange is facilitated by Catalist, a stand-alone business enterprise not connected to the Democratic Party or any particular candidate or group. The initial investors purchased a bond to fund the business and stand to profit from the investment with a capped interest payment. Laura Quinn, one of the founders of Catalist, stated that Catalist is owned by a trust and "was built as a utility," with "profits committed to more research and development."[123] Catalist features a large data file with individuals' names, addresses, past turnout patterns, consumer data, party registration, and so forth. The file also has consumer data on a range of items such as magazine subscriptions and cars owned.

In the 2012 election cycle, no outside group equivalent to Catalist existed on the Republican side. Many observers agree that this was a substantial disadvantage for Republican allied groups and candidates. After the election, a pro-Republican group modeled after Catalist was announced; the Data Trust is headed by former RNC official Anne Hathaway and the committee's former chair Mike Duncan.[124] A separate database, Themis, funded by the Koch brothers, has also been announced.[125]

Evidence that the infrastructure for outside group campaign activity has grown extends beyond voter lists to opposition research. As mentioned earlier, pro-Democratic groups now share an opposition research resource, which has both a Super PAC (American Bridge 21st Century) and a 501(c)(4) named American Bridge 21st Century Foundation. Although party committees have long conducted opposition research for candidates and party committees, the outside groups and party independent expenditures groups did not have such an organization until 2011, when American Bridge was formed to provide research for campaign strategy, polling, and advertising. A good example of the role of

American Bridge is the Todd Akin race in Missouri in 2012, where the group sent out a "talking direct mail piece" that "highlighted [Akin's] 'legitimate rape' comments."[126]

Conclusion

Interest groups in 2012 continued to play their long-standing role of helping finance congressional candidates through PAC contributions. Moreover, PACs continued their long-standing practice of giving heavily to incumbents. Contributions from PACs to presidential candidates pale in comparison with PAC activity in congressional elections.

Interest groups have also long been active in electoral activity not directly linked to candidates. In 2012 that outside activity grew substantially in the form of Super PACs and Section 501(c) groups. Some interest groups retained their use of conventional independent expenditures funded through limited and disclosed contributions. Some groups, especially membership organizations such as unions, actively communicate to their members or employees. These internal communications are not limited in terms of the amount that can be spent on them, and they are viewed as being credible because the source of the communication is known and trusted.

From 1996 through 2002, interest groups played an expanded role in elections through unlimited contributions of soft money to parties and through ads targeted to particular races that were indistinguishable to voters from electioneering messages.[127] Spending on these issue ads was unlimited, and donors were not required to be disclosed because these ads were deemed to not be electioneering communications. In 2002 BCRA banned party soft money and redefined electioneering communications to limit "issue advocacy." The soft-money ban remains unchanged, but recent court rulings have expanded what groups may do in campaigns.

A large amount of outside money was spent through Section 527 groups in 2004, but that activity was greatly diminished in 2008. In 2010 the landscape of outside money was altered by *Citizens United* and *SpeechNow.org*, which allowed unlimited contributions for independent expenditures. As we have argued in this chapter, Super PACs were important in prolonging the GOP presidential nomination process in 2011–12 and in defining candidates in negative ways. Donors who prefer anonymity were able to accomplish many of the same objectives by giving to Section 501(c) groups.

The net effect of Super PACs and Section 501(c) groups was a higher level of outside group activity in 2012 than was the case in 2008. In the presidential election, the model of influence was the largely candidate-specific Super PAC. Outside money was also important in congressional elections. This was also not new. In some respects, Super PACs linked to congressional party leaders are reminiscent of party soft money in 1998–2002, with clear connections between donors and congressional party leaders. Outside money was also important in 2010 and 2012 in congressional nomination contests in the Republican Party.

After the 2012 election, as happened after 2004, spending by outside groups that supported the losing side led to speculation about a possible future decline in such activity. However, it is unlikely that activity by outside groups will decline in the future. Some large donors have indicated that they intend to remain active in funding outside groups, and other large donors have announced plans to become more active in party nomination contests.[128] It is likely that presidential candidates in the future will generally encourage Super PACs, and candidate-specific Super PACs in congressional contests are likely to become more prevalent.

Notes

1. *Citizens United* v. *Federal Election Commission*, 558 U.S. 310 (2010); *SpeechNow.org* v. *Federal Election Commission*, 599 F.3d 686 (D.C. Cir. 2010); Federal Election Commission, Advisory Opinion 2010-09 (Club for Growth), July 22, 2010 (http://saos.nictusa.com/aodocs/AOpercent202010-09.pdf); Federal Election Commission, Advisory Opinion 2010–11 (Commonsense Ten), July 22, 2010 (http://saos.nictusa.com/aodocs/AOpercent202010-11.pdf).

2. Center for Responsive Politics, "Super PACs," 2010 (www.opensecrets.org/pacs/superpacs.php?cycle=2010).

3. These numbers come from the FEC website. The total number of registered Super PACs comes from the committee master file for 2012 (Federal Election Commission, "cm12," 2013 [ftp://ftp.fec.gov/FEC/2012/]). Data on spending come from the committee summary file (Federal Election Commission, "2012 Committee Summary," 2013 [www.fec.gov/data/CommitteeSummary.do?format=html &election_yr=2012]). In both cases, we consider Super PACs to include committees of type O, V, and W. For committees of type V and W (so-called Carey committees or hybrid PACs), we include only the contributions and expenditures from their noncontribution (that is, Super PAC) accounts. Note that the summary file has fewer such committees, as it covers only those groups that report spending

(even if they report no spending, as many groups did), whereas the master file includes all registered groups.

4. Federal Election Commission, "Independent Expenditure–Only Committees," 2013 (www.fec.gov/press/press2011/ieoc_alpha.shtml).

5. Internal Revenue Service, "Common Tax Law Restrictions on Activities of Exempt Organizations," 2013 (www.irs.gov/Charities-&-Non-Profits/Common-Tax-Law-Restrictions-on-Activities-of-Exempt-Organizations). Any political organization that files with the FEC is officially organized under Section 527. However, we follow the common parlance of identifying a 527 as a group primarily organized to influence elections not through express advocacy but through issue advocacy and voter mobilization (Center for Responsive Politics, "527 Basics" [www.opensecrets.org/527s/basics.php]).

6. Mike McIntire and Nicholas Confessore, "Tax-Exempt Groups Shield Political Gifts of Businesses," *New York Times*, July 7, 2012 (www.nytimes.com/2012/07/08/us/politics/groups-shield-political-gifts-of-businesses.html?pagewanted=all &_r=0).

7. Kim Barker, "How Nonprofits Spend Millions on Elections and Call It Public Welfare," *ProPublica*, August 18, 2012 (www.propublica.org/article/how-non profits-spend-millions-on-elections-and-call-it-public-welfare).

8. FEC, "Independent Expenditure–Only Committees."

9. Center for Responsive Politics, "American Crossroads," 2012 (www.open secrets.org/outsidespending/detail.php?cmte=C00487363&cycle=2012); Center for Responsive Politics, "Crossroads GPS," 2012 (www.opensecrets.org/outside spending/detail.php?cmte=C90011719&cycle=2012).

10. Center for Responsive Politics, "League of Conservation Voters," 2012 (www.opensecrets.org/outsidespending/detail.php?cmte=League+of+Conservation +Voters&cycle=2012).

11. Thomas T. Spencer, "'Labor Is with Roosevelt': The Pennsylvania Labor Non-Partisan League and the Election of 1936," *Pennsylvania History* 46, no. 1 (1979), p. 3.

12. Frank J. Sorauf, *Money in American Elections* (Glenview, Ill.: Scott, Foresman, 1988), p. 73.

13. Compiled from Federal Election Commission data (see especially www.fec.gov/press/summaries/2012/ElectionCycle/24m_PAC.shtml). We include corporate and trade organizations and corporations without stock in this tally. We do not include nonconnected PACs (among them, MoveOn.org but also Deloitte PAC), membership PACs (EMILY's List but also PricewaterhouseCoopers PAC), and cooperative PACs (Growth and Prosperity PAC, the leadership PAC of Representative Bachus, but also American Crystal Sugar Company PAC).

14. Federal Election Commission, "Quick Answers to PAC Questions" (www. fec.gov/ans/answers_pac.shtml).

15. Compiled from Federal Election Commission data.

16. Federal Election Commission, "PAC Count: 1974 to Present," 2013 (www.fec.gov/press/summaries/2011/2011paccount.shtml).

17. Federal Election Commission, "2012 Full Election Cycle Summary Data," 2013 (www.fec.gov/press/summaries/2012/ElectionCycle/PACYE.shtml).

18. AFL-CIO, "AFL-CIO Unions," 2013 (www.aflcio.org/About/AFL-CIO-Unions).

19. In 2012 ERIC PAC contributed $2,040,000 to House Republicans and $45,000 to Senate Republicans. Center for Responsive Politics, "Every Republican Is Crucial PAC Contributions to Federal Candidates," 2012 (www.open secrets.org/pacs/pacgot.php?cmte=C00384701&cycle=2012).

20. David B. Magleby and Candice J. Nelson, *The Money Chase: Congressional Campaign Finance Reform* (Brookings, 1990), pp. 54, 83–84.

21. Marian Currinder, *Money in the House: Campaign Funds and Congressional Party Politics* (Boulder, Colo.: Westview, 2008), pp. 52–53.

22. Compiled from Federal Election Commission data.

23. "All corporations are permitted to communicate with their *restricted class* whenever they so choose, and labor unions may likewise communicate with their members. A corporation's restricted class is defined as its stockholders and its executive or administrative personnel and their families. . . . Similarly a corporation could invite a candidate to appear before its restricted class and endorse the candidate in connection with the event. . . . Communications with the restricted class generally are not regulated by the FEC, but internal communications costing more than $2,000 per election that expressly advocate the election or defeat of a candidate must be reported. The exemption for communications with members has been used by labor unions for voter registration drives, telephone banks to turn out the vote on election day, and candidate endorsements. Such communications may be expressly partisan in nature, but they can be directed only to a union's members or to a corporation's restricted class, *not* to the general public." Anthony Corrado and others, *The New Campaign Finance Sourcebook* (Brookings, 2005), pp. 58–59.

24. Darrell Shull, chief operating officer of Business-Industry Political Action Committee, interview by David Magleby, April 3, 2013.

25. Bernadette Budde, senior vice president for candidate advocacy, Business-Industry Political Action Committee, interview by David Magleby, December 12, 2012.

26. Compiled from Federal Election Commission data.

27. Compiled from Federal Election Commission data.

28. *Citizens United* v. *Federal Election Commission; SpeechNow.org* v. *Federal Election Commission;* FEC, Advisory Opinion 2010-09 (Club for Growth); FEC, Advisory Opinion 2010-11 (Commonsense Ten).

29. Compiled from Federal Election Commission data.

30. Jeremy Ashkenas, and others, "PAC: Conservative Majority Fund," *New York Times* (http://elections.nytimes.com/2012/campaign-finance/pac/conservative-majority-fund).

31. Rob Jesmer, executive director of the National Republican Senatorial Committee, interview by David Magleby, February 12, 2013.

32. FEC, "2012 Full Election Cycle Summary Data"; see especially "Independent Expenditure Summary Data for Congressional Candidates" (www.fec.gov/press/summaries/2012/ElectionCycle/IE_ECYE.shtml).

33. Compiled from Center for Responsive Politics, "National Assn of Realtors: Outside Spending Summary," 2012 (www.opensecrets.org/outsidespending/detail.php?cycle=2012&cmte=C00488742); Center for Responsive Politics, "National Assn of Realtors Congressional Fund," 2010 (www.opensecrets.org/outsidespending/detail.php?cycle=2010&cmte=C00488742); Center for Responsive Politics, "National Assn of Realtors," 2012 (www.opensecrets.org/outsidespending/detail.php?cmte=C00030718&cycle=2012); and Center for Responsive Politics, "National Assn of Realtors," 2010 (www.opensecrets.org/outsidespending/detail.php?cmte=C00030718&cycle=2010).

34. Not all Super PACs were active. See Federal Election Commission, "2012 Full Election Cycle Summary Data" (www.fec.gov/press/summaries/2012/ElectionCycle/PACYE.shtml), especially "PAC Financial Activity" (www.fec.gov/press/summaries/2012/ElectionCycle/file/pac_financial_activity/PAC1_2012_24m.pdf).

35. Federal Election Commission records.

36. Michael Toner, cochair of the election law and government ethics practice at Wiley, Rein, and Fielding, interview by David Magleby, December 20, 2012.

37. Kevin Liptak, "Nearly Half of Iowa Ads Attack Gingrich," *Political Ticker* (blog), *CNN Politics*, December 30, 2011 (http://politicalticker.blogs.cnn.com/2011/12/30/nearly-half-of-iowa-ads-attack-gingrich/).

38. Kenneth P. Vogel, "3 Billionaires Who'll Drag Out the Race," *Politico*, January 12, 2012 (www.politico.com/news/stories/0112/71358.html).

39. Nicholas Confessore, "'Super PAC' for Gingrich to Get $5 Million Infusion," *New York Times*, January 23, 2012 (www.nytimes.com/2012/01/24/us/politics/super-pac-for-gingrich-to-get-5-million-infusion.html); Aaron Blake, "Adelsons Give Gingrich Super PAC Another $5 million," *The Fix* (blog), *Washington Post*, April 23, 2012 (www.washingtonpost.com/blogs/the-fix/post/adelsons-give-gingrich-super-pac-another-5-million/2012/04/23/gIQAlqNmbT_blog.html).

40. Kantar Media/CMAG, with analysis by the Wesleyan Media Project; Erika Fowler, "Presidential Ads 70 Percent Negative in 2012, Up from 9 Percent in 2008," May 2, 2012 (http://mediaproject.wesleyan.edu/2012/05/02/jump-in-negativity/), table 2.

41. Dan Balz, *Collision 2012: Obama vs. Romney and the Future of Elections in America* (New York: Penguin Group, 2013).

42. Rick Wiley, political director of the Republican National Committee, interview by David Magleby, February 11, 2013.

43. Institute of Politics, John F. Kennedy School of Government, Harvard University, *Campaign for President: The Managers Look at 2012* (Lanham, Md.: Rowman and Littlefield, 2013), p. 195.

44. Ibid., p. 142.

45. On the connections between Majority Leader Reid and the Majority PAC and between Speaker Boehner and the Congressional Leadership Fund and American Action Network, see Nicholas Confessore, "New Super PAC Forming to Back G.O.P. Majority," *New York Times*, October 14, 2011 (http://query.ny times.com/gst/fullpage.html?res=9401E6D61738F937A25753C1A9679D8B63); on the connection between House Majority Leader Pelosi and House Majority PAC, see Kim Severson, "Former Governor Sanford and Rival Debate in House Race," *New York Times,* April 29, 2013 (www.nytimes.com/2013/04/30/us/ politics/sanford-and-colbert-busch-debate-in-house-race.html?_r=1&); on the relationship between House Majority Leader Cantor and the Young Guns Action Fund and Young Guns Action Network, see Nicholas Confessore, "New G.O.P. Help from Casino Mogul," *New York Times*, June 16, 2012 (www.nytimes.com/ 2012/06/17/us/politics/sheldon-adelson-injects-more-cash-into-gop-groups. html).

46. Deirdre Schifeling, national organizing and electoral campaign director of the Planned Parenthood Action Fund, and Justine Sessions, director of advocacy media for Planned Parenthood, interview with David Magleby, April 4, 2013; Navin Nayak, senior vice president of the League of Conservation Voters, interview by David Magleby, March 4, 2013.

47. Dan Eggen, "Congressional Incumbents Start Attracting 'Super PACs': The Influence Industry," *Post Politics* (blog), *Washington Post*, November 30, 2011 (http://articles.washingtonpost.com/2011-11-30/politics/35283501_1_majority-pac-american-crossroads-fec). Committees active in these two races included Committee to Elect an Effective Valley Congressman, for Howard Berman (D-CA) (House); and Strong Utah, for Orrin Hatch (R-UT) (www.opensecrets. org/pacs/superpacs.php).

48. Travis N. Ridout, Michael M. Franz, and Erika Franklin Fowler, "When Are Interest Group Ads More Effective?," paper presented at the Annual Meeting of the American Political Science Association, Chicago, Ill., September 2013.

49. Jeanne Cummings, "Super-PACs Kept Romney-Obama Even in $1 Billion Ad Race," *Bloomberg*, November 1, 2012 (www.bloomberg.com/news/2012-11-02/super-pacs-kept-romney-obama-even-in-1-billion-ad-race.html).

50. Sean Sweeney, senior strategist at Priorities USA, interview by David Magleby, February 11, 2013.

51. Harold Ickes, president of Priorities USA and cofounder of the Ickes and Enright Group, interview by David Magleby, December 12, 2012.

52. Glen Bolger, cofounder and partner of Public Opinion Strategies, interview by David Magleby, March 19, 2013.

53. Neil King Jr., "Romney Super PAC Plans Ad Blitz in Battleground States," *Washington Wire* (blog), *Wall Street Journal*, May 2, 2012 (http://blogs.wsj.com/washwire/2012/05/02/romney-super-pac-plans-ad-blitz-in-battleground-states/); Chris Cillizza, "Priorities USA Action Reserves $30 Million in Fall Ad Time," *The Fix* (blog), *Washington Post*, August 1, 2012 (www.washingtonpost.com/blogs/the-fix/post/priorities-usa-action-reserves-30-million-in-fall-ad-time/2012/08/01/gJQAhlNrPX_blog.html).

54. Paul Blumenthal, "Super PACs, Outside Money Influenced, but Didn't Buy the 2012 Election," *Huffington Post*, November 7, 2012 (www.huffingtonpost.com/2012/11/07/super-pacs-2012-election-outside-money_n_2087040.html).

55. Neil Newhouse, cofounder of Public Opinion Strategies, interview by David Magleby, December 27, 2012.

56. "Statement of U.S. Senator Russ Feingold on *Citizens United* v. *Federal Election Commission*," press release and Senate speech, October 21, 2009 (www.democracy21.org/uploads/percent7B674F1A22-67FC-4FED-8D3C-03A8217A00CBpercent7D.PDF).

57. Barack Obama, "Text: Obama's State of the Union Address," *New York Times*, January 27, 2010 (www.nytimes.com/2010/01/28/us/politics/28obama.text.html?pagewanted=all); Barack Obama, State of the Union Address, January 27, 2010, White House Office of the Press Secretary (www.whitehouse.gov/the-press-office/remarks-president-state-union-address).

58. Bill Miller, senior vice president of Business Roundtable, interview by David Magleby, January 22, 2013.

59. Tom Scheck, "Target Apologizes for Donation to MN Forward," *Minnesota Public Radio*, August 5, 2010 (http://minnesota.publicradio.org/display/web/2010/08/05/target-apology-donation).

60. Matt Bai, "How Much Has Citizens United Changed the Political Game?," *New York Times*, July 17, 2012 (www.nytimes.com/2012/07/22/magazine/how-much-has-citizens-united-changed-the-political-game.html?pagewanted=all&_r=0).

61. Blair Bowie and Adam Lioz, "Billion-Dollar Democracy: The Unprecedented Role of Money in the 2012 Elections" (www.demos.org/sites/default/files/publications/BillionDollarDemocracy_0.pdf), pp. 7–8.

62. Center for Responsive Politics, "2012 Top Donors to Outside Spending Groups," 2012 (www.opensecrets.org/outsidespending/summ.php?cycle=2012&disp=D&type=O&superonly=S).

63. Peter H. Stone, "Sheldon Adelson to Lavish $71 Million in Casino Money on GOP Super PACs, Nonprofits," *Huffington Post*, June 16, 2012 (www.huffingtonpost.com/2012/06/16/sheldon-adelson-to-lavish_n_1600149.html).

64. Nayak, interview.

65. Ibid.

66. Erika Fowler, "Presidential Ads 70 Percent Negative in 2012, Up from 9 Percent in 2008," May 2, 2012, Kantar Media/CMAG, with analysis by the Wesleyan Media Project (http://mediaproject.wesleyan.edu/2012/05/02/jump-in-negativity/).

67. Erika Franklin Fowler and Travis N. Ridout, "Negative, Angry, and Ubiquitous: Political Advertising in 2012," *The Forum* 10, no. 4 (2013): 51–61.

68. Michael Isikoff, "Pro-Gingrich Super PAC to Air Anti-Romney Video," *NBC News*, January 7, 2012 (www.nbcnews.com/id/45911039/ns/politics-decision_2012/t/pro-gingrich-super-pac-air-anti-romney-video/#.UZ-01tVnA6c).

69. Daniel Strauss, "Santorum Super PAC Airs Ad in Illinois Attacking Romney on Healthcare, Economy," *The Hill*, March 15, 2012 (http://thehill.com/video/campaign/216253-santorum-super-pac-airs-ad-in-illinois-attacking-romney-on-healthcare-economy).

70. Nicholas Confessore and Jim Rutenberg, "Group's Ads Rip at Gingrich as Romney Stands Clear," *New York Times*, December 30, 2011 (www.nytimes.com/2011/12/31/us/politics/restore-our-future-attack-ads-harm-gingrich-in-iowa.html?_r=0).

71. Kevin Bohn, "Romney Super PAC Attacks Santorum over the Economy," *Political Ticker* (blog), *CNN Politics*, March 27, 2012 (http://politicalticker.blogs.cnn.com/2012/03/27/romney-super-pac-attacks-santorum-over-the-economy/).

72. Mitt Romney, "Let Detroit Go Bankrupt," Opinion Pages, *New York Times*, November 18, 2008 (www.nytimes.com/2008/11/19/opinion/19romney.html?_r=0); CNN Political Unit, "Obama Super PAC Takes on Romney in Michigan Ad," *Political Ticker* (blog), *CNN Politics*, February 22, 2012 (http://politicalticker.blogs.cnn.com/2012/02/22/obama-super-pac-ad-takes-on-romney-in-michigan/).

73. Laura Meckler, "Obama, Super PAC Air Ads in Michigan on Auto Bailout," *Washington Wire* (blog), *Wall Street Journal*, February 23, 2012 (http://blogs.wsj.com/washwire/2012/02/23/obama-super-pac-air-ads-in-michigan-on-auto-bailout/).

74. Various monthly Federal Election Commission reports (http://images.nictusa.com/cgi-bin/fecimg/?C00495861).

75. James Rainey, "Kerry Takes on $1 Million 'Swift Boat' Challenge," *Los Angeles Times*, November 17, 2007 (http://articles.latimes.com/2007/nov/17/nation/na-kerry17).

76. Michael Kinsley, "To Swift-Boat or Not," *Time*, June 12, 2008 (www.time.com/time/magazine/article/0,9171,1813974,00.html).

77. Devin Dwyer, "Ad Tying Romney to Cancer Death Airs 'In Error,'" *Political Punch* (blog), *ABC News*, August 14, 2012 (http://abcnews.go.com/blogs/politics/2012/08/ad-tying-romney-to-cancer-death-airs-in-error/).

78. Institute of Politics, University of Chicago, "A Conversation with David Axelrod," *YouTube*, November 29, 2012.

79. Bolger, interview.

80. Mike Lux, cofounder and president of Progressive Strategies, interview by David Magleby, January 14, 2013.

81. David Corn, "Secret Video: Romney Tells Millionaire Donors What He REALLY Thinks of Obama Voters," Politics, *Mother Jones,* September 17, 2012 (www.motherjones.com/politics/2012/09/secret-video-romney-private-fundraiser).

82. Bolger, interview.

83. Wiley, interview.

84. Tom Hamburger, "Romney Spent More on TV Ads but Got Much Less," *Washington Post*, December 11, 2012 (http://articles.washingtonpost.com/2012-12-11/politics/35767760_1_romney-campaign-officials-obama-ampaign-ad-strategy).

85. Center for Responsive Politics, "2012 Outside Spending, by Race," 2012 (www.opensecrets.org/outsidespending/summ.php?cycle=2012&disp=R&pty=N& type=A).

86. Michael M. Franz, "Interest Groups in Electoral Politics: 2012 in Context," *The Forum* 10, no. 4 (2013): 62–79.

87. Center for Responsive Politics, "2012 Top Donors to Outside Spending Groups," 2012 (www.opensecrets.org/outsidespending/summ.php?cycle=2012& disp=D&type=V); Center for Responsive Politics, "Top Individual Contributors to Federally Focused 527 Organizations, 2008 Election Cycle," 2008 (www.open secrets.org/527s/527indivs.php?cycle=2008); Center for Responsive Politics, "Top Individual Contributors to Federally Focused 527 Organizations, 2004 Election Cycle," 2004 (www.opensecrets.org/527s/527indivs.php?cycle=2004).

88. Nick Wing, "Sheldon Adelson Vows to 'Double' Donations to GOP after Huge 2012 Election Failure," *Huffington Post*, December 5, 2012 (www.huffing tonpost.com/2012/12/05/sheldon-adelson-gop_n_2244070.html).

89. Kenneth P. Vogel, "Koch World Reboots," *Politico*, February 20, 2012 (www.politico.com/story/2013/02/koch-world-reboots-87834.html).

90. Matt Waldrip, deputy national finance director of Romney for President, Inc., interview by David Magleby, March 12, 2013.

91. Maggie Haberman and Alexander Burns, "Adelson, Newt, Donors Convene at Venetian in Vegas," *Burns and Haberman* (blog), *Politico*, February 3, 2012 (www.politico.com/blogs/burns-haberman/2012/02/adelson-newt-donors-convene-at-venetian-in-vegas-113469.html).

92. Jim Rutenburg, "Santorum Upsets G.O.P. with Three Victories," *New York Times*, February 7, 2012 (www.nytimes.com/2012/02/08/us/politics/ minnesota-colorado-missouri-caucuses.html?pagewanted=all&_r=0).

93. Bill Burton, quoted in Institute of Politics, *Campaign for President: The Managers Look at 2012*, p. 163.

94. Bob Bauer, partner, Perkins Coie, and general counsel for Obama for America, interview by David Magleby, March 21, 2013.

95. Quoted in Michael Beckel, "Did GOP Congressman Make Illegal Super PAC Solicitation?" Center for Public Integrity, February 7, 2013 (www.public integrity.org/2013/02/07/12165/did-gop-congressman-make-illegal-super-pac-solicitation).

96. The Democrats were first to create a Super PAC that conducted opposition research. American Bridge was formed on November 23, 2010 (according to FEC filings), and in 2012 it raised $12.5 million. Following the 2012 election, Republicans created America Rising, with Romney's 2012 campaign manager Matt Rhoades, the Republican National Committee research director Joe Pounder, and spokesperson Tim Miller, RNC deputy communications director leading the organization. Rachel Weiner, "America Rising: Mitt Romney Staffer Starting Opposition Research Group," *Post Politics* (blog), *Washington Post*, March 21, 2013 (www.washingtonpost.com/blogs/post-politics/wp/2013/03/21/america-rising-mitt-romney-staffer-starting-opposition-research-group/).

97. Rodell Mollineau, president, American Bridge 21st Century, and Chris Harris, communications director, American Bridge PAC, interview by David Magleby, March 19, 2013.

98. Maggie Haberman, "RNC, Romney Operatives Launch Firm," *Politico*, March 21, 2013 (www.politico.com/story/2013/03/america-rising-89189.html).

99. On the Congressional Leadership Fund, see Reity O'Brien, "PAC Profile: Congressional Leadership Fund," Center for Public Integrity, October 3, 2012, updated January 23, 2013 (www.publicintegrity.org/2012/10/03/11077/pac-profile-congressional-leadership-fund).

100. Center for Responsive Politics, "American Crossroads/Crossroads GPS Recipients, 2012," 2012 (www.opensecrets.org/outsidespending/recips.php?cmte =American+Crossroads percent2FCrossroads+GPS&cycle=2012); Gregory Wallace, "Crossroads' Six Ads Hit Obama, Other Democratic Candidates," *Political Ticker* (blog), *CNN Politics*, September 18, 2012 (http://politicalticker.blogs.cnn.com/2012/09/18/crossroads-six-ads-hit-obama-other-democratic-candidates/).

101. John Francis Reilly and Barbara A. Braig Allen, "Political Campaign and Lobbying Activities of IRS 501(c)(4), (c)(5), and (c)(6) Organizations," in *Exempt Organizations: Technical Instruction Program for FY 2003*, 2003 (www.irs.gov/pub/irs-tege/eotopicl03.pdf).

102. Charles R. Spies, counsel and treasurer of Restore Our Future, interview by David Magleby, August 17, 2012.

103. Center for Responsive Politics. "Outside Spending, by Group," 2004 (www.opensecrets.org/outsidespending/summ.php?cycle=2004&chrt=V&disp=O&type=U).

104. Center for Responsive Politics, "Crossroads GPS," 2012 (www.open secrets.org/outsidespending/detail.php?cmte=C90011719&cycle=2012); Spies, interview.

105. Center for Responsive Politics, "Outside Spending," 2013 (www.open secrets.org/outsidespending/fes_summ.php?cycle=2012); Sunlight Foundation Reporting Group, "Follow the Unlimited Money" (http://reporting.sunlightfoun dation.com/outside-spending-2012/overview/); ProPublica, "Buying Your Vote" (www.propublica.org/series/buying-your-vote).

106. In estimating 501(c) spending, we started with the total spending estimates given in interviews (confirmed, if possible, in press reports), subtracted the publicly reported spending (such as independent expenditures and electioneering communications), and arrived at the estimate of unreported 501(c) spending. We added our unreported spending to the Center for Responsive Politics' spending estimate, being careful not to double-count any tabulated spending with our estimate of unreported spending, to get to $640 million. For example, Crossroads (in all of its entities) reportedly spent $300 million. Of that, $118 million was disclosed as Super PAC spending (and transfers). From various reports, the center estimates that Crossroads has spent $71 million as 501(c) spending. We conclude that Crossroads spent $111 million as a 501(c) in undisclosed spending, for a total of $182 million.

107. To calculate this, we used the ratio of disclosed spending (from the Center for Responsive Politics) to undisclosed spending (from interviews), and applied that ratio (1.9) to all of the center's disclosed spending, not counting unions ($311 million). That makes $596 million in undisclosed spending plus $311 in disclosed spending by 501(c)(4) and 501(c)(6) organizations. Add to that the estimated $110 million that unions spent through 501(c)(5) organizations, and we calculate 501(c) spending to be $1.017 billion.

108. Mollineau and Harris, interview; Brian Walsh, political director of American Action Network, interview by David Magleby, March 18, 2013; Spies, interview.

109. Fred Wertheimer, president of Democracy 21, interview by David Magleby, August 16, 2012.

110. Spies, interview.

111. Mollineau and Harris, interview.

112. Carol D. Leonnig, "Corporate Donors Fuel Chamber of Commerce's Political Power," *Washington Post*, October 18, 2012 (http://articles.washington post.com/2012-10-18/politics/35501119_1_center-for-political-accountability-political-donations-chamber) Mike Allen and Jim Vandehei, "GOP Groups Plan Record $1 Billion Blitz," *Politico*, May 30, 2012 (www.politico.com/news/stories/0512/76849.html).

113. E-mail correspondence from Anthony Corrado, September 11, 2013.

114. ActBlue, "Frequently Asked Questions" (https://secure.actblue.com/faq).

115. Center for Responsive Politics, "ActBlue: Expenditures, 2012 Cycle" (www.opensecrets.org/527s/527cmtedetail_expends.php?ein=202517748&cycle =2012).

116. College Republican National Committee, "History" (www.crnc.org/ about/history/).

117. Center for Responsive Politics, "College Republican National Cmte: Expenditures, 2012 Cycle" (www.opensecrets.org/527s/527cmtedetail_expends. php?ein=521082055&cycle=2012).

118. Schifeling and Sessions, interview.

119. Cathy Duvall, national political director at Sierra Club, telephone interview by David Magleby, February 12, 2013.

120. Karin Johansen, principal in the grassroots and government practice at Dewey Square Group, interview by David Magleby, March 18, 2013.

121. Karl Rove, cofounder and adviser to American Crossroads, interview by David Magleby, March 15, 2013.

122. Kenneth P. Vogel, "Karl Rove's Fight Club," *Politico*, March 27, 2012 (www.politico.com/news/stories/0312/74506.html).

123. Laura Quinn, founder of Catalist, interview by David Magleby, March 19, 2013.

124. Kenneth P. Vogel, "Karl Rove vs. the Koch Brothers," *Politico* (www. politico.com/news/stories/1011/65504_Page3.html).

125. Kenneth P. Vogel and Maggie Haberman, "Karl Rove, Koch Brothers Lead Charge to Control Republican Data," *Politico*, April 22, 2013 (www. politico.com/story/2013/04/karl-rove-koch-brothers-control-republican-data-903 85.html#ixzz2SvFMaMgf).

126. Shane D'Aprile, "Super PAC Hits Akin with Talking Mailer," *Campaigns & Elections*, October, 18, 2012 (www.campaignsandelections.com/campaign-insider/332062/super-pac-hits-akin-with-talking-mailer.thtml).

127. David B. Magleby, *Dictum without Data: The Myth of Issue Advocacy and Party Building*, a report of a grant funded by the Pew Charitable Trusts, November 13, 2000.

128. Fredreka Schouten, "GOP Donor Foster Friess Vows Action in 2014 Elections," *USA Today*, January 25, 2013 (www.usatoday.com/story/news/politics/ 2013/01/25/foster-friess-republican-donor-elections-gay-rights/1864685/).

EIGHT

Lessons for Reformers

THOMAS E. MANN

This is the fourth opportunity I have had to write the final chapter of the quadrennial series of studies by David Magleby and his colleagues on financing U.S. elections. These volumes extended the work of Herbert Alexander, who launched the series with an analysis of campaign finance in the 1960 presidential election[1] and carried it forward for over three decades. My charge for *Financing the 2000 Election,* and for each subsequent volume, was to reflect on what campaign fundraising and spending patterns reveal about the effectiveness of the regulatory regime and what lessons might be drawn for those seeking changes in campaign finance law and practice through legislative, administrative, and judicial means.

As I read through my chapter on the 2000 election, I found it to be a sobering reminder of the durability of the problems associated with money in politics and of the competing viewpoints on how best to deal with them. David Magleby, the editor of that volume, noted that "if the 1996 elections revealed the first widespread avoidance of federal election law strictures, the 2000 elections witnessed the near collapse of the Federal Election Campaign Act (FECA) regulatory regime."[2] The problems? Magleby identified them as "the explosive growth of funding in targeted contests, the diminishing role of public financing in presidential elections, the increasing importance of unregulated spending by parties and groups, and the loss of transparency as disclosure requirements are circumvented."[3] All of this sounds familiar a dozen years later. To be sure, the specific forms are different today. Parties operate without soft-money accounts but are major players in redistributing resources among members of Congress, they finance independent expenditures, and they have Super PACs closely aligned with congressional party leaders. Super PACs—political action committees that can receive unlimited donations from any source and spend for and against candidates and parties without serious constraint—are now the financing organizations of choice for wealthy individuals and private corporations. Public financing in federal elections is now a dead letter for all but a few marginal candidates in presidential primaries. Non-profit 501(c) advocacy organizations provide the easiest way to spend unlimited amounts while preserving the anonymity of donors.

Arguments about the best public policy responses to these problems are also painfully familiar: is the primary objective to protect free speech or to counter corruption and restrain the influence of the wealthy? On one side are those who believe that the regulation of money in campaigns is a fool's errand. Efforts to restrict campaign contributions and expenditures inevitably violate First Amendment guarantees of free speech.[4] Political money is fungible, and legal restrictions on its flow will divert it to less accountable passageways. Hence the law of unintended consequences comes into play: the intended purposes of reform will almost certainly be overwhelmed by effects not desired or anticipated.[5] In 2000 the rallying cry was "deregulate and disclose." Today, advocates of deregulation, whose agenda is centered on easing or eliminating all restrictions on campaign contributions and expenditures, often fight to remove the transparency requirements that were once a pillar of their reform agenda.[6]

On the other side are champions of full public financing of elections. The most ambitious of these proponents' schemes would limit private financing to small donations needed to qualify for public grants.[7] The experience of the last decade or so, in both federal and state elections, has trimmed this agenda to more modest dimensions, but even that is constrained by the avalanche of privately funded independent expenditures and the Supreme Court's decision to eliminate the option of providing additional public funds in response to outside spending.[8] That has led some to pursue amending the Constitution to give Congress the power to regulate contributions and expenditures in elections.[9]

Today, as in 2000, most advocates of a stronger regulatory regime operate well short of the full public financing mode. Their concerns include, but are not limited to, preventing corruption and protecting free speech. They mostly accept important arguments long advanced by deregulators:

that adequate resources are essential for engaging citizens, enabling collective political action, attracting able candidates, promoting competitive races, and fostering healthy and accountable political parties. But these proponents of reform stress the problematic features of campaign fundraising. Risks include the close connections between lobbying and campaign finance, which promote a culture of dependency among politicians, but also can involve shakedowns by public officials of those whose interests are directly affected by policymakers; the staggering time and energy invested by candidates in dialing for dollars; individual and group imbalances in the political system flowing from economic inequalities; and the vast disparities in funding available to incumbents and challengers.

Most regulatory advocates are all too aware of the obstacles they face in the judicial, legislative, and administrative arenas. They also understand how powerfully the strategic environment of each election shapes the flow of money and pushes political actors to innovate in finding new ways around the strictures of law and regulation. Many view campaign finance reform as an ongoing process of maintenance and repair, unlikely to provide any lasting solutions to their concerns but capable of restraining abuses and enhancing the quality of and respect for our democratic system.

The Contemporary Landscape

It is foolish to consider the problems of campaign finance apart from the defining features of our contemporary political life.[10] These are difficult times for American politics and governance. The two major political parties are sharply polarized and actively engaged in an aggressive permanent campaign to hold or gain the reins of power in the White House and Congress. The Republican Party has veered sharply to the right in recent decades, even more so since the election of Barack Obama and the emergence of the Tea Party movement. With the demise of its white conservative Southern wing and the election of Bill Clinton, the Democrats became more unified and clustered left of center but also more pragmatic and accommodating of differences within their caucus. This asymmetric polarization is particularly visible when a Democrat is in the White House. Republicans have become more akin to a parliamentary party, vehemently oppositional, and, pressed hard by their most extreme faction and reinforced by an array of deep-pocketed, ideologically extreme outside groups, strategically averse to collaborating and compromising with the Democrats. Some in their ranks see threats of public default and government shutdowns as legitimate legislative tools to extract policy concessions not achievable through normal bargaining.

A rough electoral parity between the parties (with control of both houses of Congress as well as the White House now up for grabs under the right conditions) combined with striking policy differences raise the stakes of elections and put a premium on party fundraising and spending in presidential and congressional general elections. The congressional party campaign committees manage a large redistribution of funds from incumbents in relatively safe seats to more competitive races. The four committees also raise large amounts of money from individuals ranging from small donors to those who contribute the maximum permitted by law, and they then direct those funds into limited coordinated spending on behalf of their candidates, party building and grassroots mobilization activities, and more-extensive independent spending campaigns, financed with the same hard-money contributions but managed by separate party staffers housed outside of party headquarters.

Some commentators and scholars bemoan the weakening of parties in the campaign finance game, especially relative to outside groups, largely because of the 2002 Bipartisan Campaign Reform Act prohibitions on party soft money and the more recent rise of Super PACs.[11] Yet the congressional party committees are major players in the biennial contests for control of the House and Senate, more so now than a generation ago, targeting key contests and spending generously on behalf of their candidates where they deem it might make a difference in the outcome. Diane Dwyre and Robin Kolodny demonstrate this clearly in chapter 6. Moreover, parties are much more than the sum of their national, congressional, and state campaign committees. Parties are less organizations than they are networks, encompassing many individuals and groups not formally affiliated with them. These include megadonors, political consultants, interest group representatives, money bundlers, media voices, traditional PACs, and even many of the outside independent expenditure–only political action committees (Super PACs) and politically active 501(c) nonprofit groups. The largest of the Super PACs (including Restore Our Future, American Crossroads, Priorities USA, Majority PAC, and House Majority PAC) are run by former officials whose entire careers have been spent laboring for their respective parties. The vast majority of the monies spent by these nonparty organizations are primarily directed toward the same contests in which the parties are devoting their resources, thus supplementing rather than competing with the party organizations. In spite of the narrow, legalistic prohibitions against coordination with parties and candidates, they are very much a part of the team. And as Magleby asserts in chapter 1, campaign finance is a team game. In this sense, parties are major players, not waifs amid outside forces, in the finance game that contributes to the partisan polarization at the root of our dysfunctional politics and governance.

The second major feature of the contemporary landscape, made explicit by Anthony Corrado in chapter 2, is the bifurcated nature of campaign finance. Campaign finance has two worlds: one in which the source and size of contributions to candidates, parties, and traditional political committees are limited and disclosure is virtually universal, the other a modern version of the Wild West, where almost anything goes. The first world of hard money remains by far the largest component of federal election campaign finance. This is crystal clear in the figures presented by Magleby in chapter 1. Individual candidates for the presidency and Congress, supplemented by party committees and traditional PACs, raise the lion's share of the money spent in federal elections. These donations are all explicitly limited by source and size and are subject to timely disclosure.

This regulated world is not immune to weaknesses and pressure points that attract the attention of critics. Presidential bundlers help solicit individual donations that collectively earn them status as major fundraisers; the transparency of these fundraiser networks largely depends on voluntary disclosure by the presidential candidate. Joint fundraising committees facilitate the ability of donors to steer substantially larger contributions to candidates than the statutory limit on individual contributions to candidates. Leadership PACs associated with the vast majority of members of Congress permit donors who have maxed out contributing to a member's campaign committee to make an additional $5,000 contribution; leadership PACs also have looser regulations on how their funds may be used. Registered lobbyists and nonregistered corporate and trade association executives can broker multiple individual and PAC donations to enhance their standing with and access to members of Congress and their staffs.

In *McCutcheon v. Federal Election Commission*, the Supreme Court recently removed one of the main pillars of hard money by overturning the limits imposed by the 1974 Federal Election Campaign Act amendments on the aggregate amount individuals may contribute to candidates, parties, and PACs over a two-year election cycle.[12] Defendants and their supporters argued that the elimination of the aggregate limit would spur supercharged joint fundraising committees that permit multimillion-dollar hard-money contributions raised with the involvement of candidates and benefiting those candidates. The early evidence suggests they may well have been correct.[13] They also worried that a far-reaching decision by the court in this case could eventually overturn the *Buckley* distinction between contributions and expenditures, potentially undermining the jurisprudential basis for the entire regulated system. The seed for that legal retrenchment may have been planted with language in the majority decision that limits the constitutional basis for regulating contributions to candidates and parties to quid pro quo corruption.[14] Plaintiffs in this case, and deregulators more generally, welcomed a reconsideration of a constitutional distinction they have long found flawed.

The other world of campaign finance is everything else. It includes money spent on federal elections not subject to the same hard-money restrictions with regard to the source and size of contributions and the full disclosure of the sources and uses of those funds. Initially, this category was defined by the court's *Buckley* decision, which prohibited restrictions on spending of personal funds by candidates in their own campaigns and on independent expenditures by individuals for or against candidates.[15] Over time it grew to include funds raised by parties ostensibly for purposes other than electing or defeating federal candidates (such as party building and issue advertising); after the explosive growth of this party soft money between 1992 and 2000 (most of which was used for candidate-specific issue ads, largely indistinguishable from traditional campaign ads), party soft money was banned by Congress, a ban that remains in place today.

This other world of campaign finance has become known as "outside money." So-called 527 political organizations blossomed in the 2004 election as a means of steering unrestricted contributions into federal campaigns in ways that presumably did not involve independent expenditures (express advocacy advertising) or electioneering communications as defined by the Bipartisan Campaign Reform Act in 2002. As traced by Corrado in chapter 2, a series of Roberts Court decisions culminating in *Citizens United* (which declared unconstitutional the prohibition on corporate expenditures in federal elections), appellate opinions drawing on those decisions, and actions and inactions by the Federal Election Commission laid the legal groundwork for a much larger, more organizationally complex world of outside funding.[16] Super PACs, formally nonconnected, independent expenditure–only political action committees, register with the commission and are subject to its disclosure regulations. However, they can accept donations of any size from any nonforeign source, including corporations, nonprofit organizations, unions, and individuals. In 2012 many of the largest Super PACs raised most of their funds from a limited number of wealthy individuals. Donors can be hidden from public view if they contribute to nonprofit advocacy organizations affiliated with Super PACs. The breakdown in disclosure is striking: the identity of the donors responsible for about a third of the $1 billion spent independently advocating federal candidates by nonparty organized groups went unreported to the Federal Election Commission in 2012.[17]

This unregulated or loosely regulated world of campaign finance accommodates unlimited and often undisclosed money in federal elections. Most of the Super PACs are formed to advance a specific candidate (mostly in presidential primary and general elections, but this is beginning to spread to Senate and House contests) or one of the two major political parties. They constitute a universe parallel to candidate and party campaigns, formally separate and independent but effectively hardwired to them, providing ample opportunity for wealthy individuals, corporations, and groups to skirt the restrictions of the regulatory regime. These outside money groups can and do communicate with one another, and candidate and party campaigns have ways to legally signal their plans, an indirect mode of coordination, which together lead to larger and more effectively integrated campaigns.

This second world of campaign finance, though markedly smaller than the first, attracts more attention because of its explosive growth, problematic disclosure, jarring presence of multimillion-dollar players, and potential impact on the integrity, accountability, and legitimacy of the political system. Money is not the root of all problems in America's dysfunctional politics and governance, but its heightened prominence and changing forms merit the attention of citizens, policy analysts, and reform activists.

Thinking about Reform

Campaign finance reform is a highly contentious subject, one that naturally arouses partisan and incumbent interests, ideological differences, and personal beliefs about the appropriate role of money in politics. To those who favor loosening or removing restrictions on the flow of money in elections, the term *reformer* is inappropriately associated only with those who seek a strengthened regulatory regime. Whether they believe it is for good or ill, reformers of all stripes agree that the most formidable obstacle to the regulation of campaign finance is constitutional. Unlike the situation in most other democracies, where limits on expenditures by candidates, parties, and independent groups and bans on paid television ads are commonplace, the scope for regulation of money and politics in America is severely constrained by the prevailing Supreme Court interpretation of the limits imposed by the First Amendment's guarantees of freedom of speech and association. That interpretation has changed over time, sometimes, as in *Citizens United*, dramatically, depending largely on the ideological composition of the Court. The replacement on the court of Sandra Day O'Connor by Samuel Alito reversed the court's 5-4 majority in this arena of constitutional law and led to a series of decisions deregulating campaign finance law. The present court is highly unlikely to reverse course, either by entertaining permissible objectives for regulating money in elections beyond quid pro quo corruption or by reconsidering its own past decisions that spawned the surge in not very independent and only partially disclosed independent expenditures by Super PACs and nonprofit advocacy organizations. If anything, recent and future cases before this court, such as *McCutcheon*, are likely to lead to further deregulation.

This confronts reformers with a limited set of options. Champions of deregulation are pleased that the choices are limited. They embrace the jurisprudence of the Roberts court on campaign finance and continue to bring cases at the state and national levels that challenge limits on contributions to candidates and parties as well as disclosure requirements. Their agenda is to hasten the collapse of the regulatory regime and move toward an unencumbered market-based system of financing election campaigns, one however that may lack key elements of transparency and citizen-based accountability typically associated with such deregulated systems.

Those dismayed by *Citizens United* and the explosion of unrestricted and partially undisclosed big money in American elections have responded in very different ways. Some have advocated a constitutional amendment removing the free speech protections of corporations and giving Congress the authority to regulate campaign contributions and expenditures. Although this proposal has no possibility of success in the foreseeable future, proponents see it as a useful device to educate and mobilize public support on behalf of campaign finance reform. Others are working to broaden the basis on which the court considers the constitutionality of various forms of campaign finance regulation. Lawrence

Lessig, for example, advocates defining the problem as dependence corruption rooted in the original intent of the framers.[18] Still others hope to rehabilitate an equality or democratic distortion rationale.[19] A number of legal scholars and political scientists whose embrace of campaign finance regulation is mostly limited to disclosure and partial public financing see this as an opportune time to ease restrictions on political parties and possibly to eliminate all contribution limits. Many others grudgingly accept the likelihood that the present deregulating regime will hold sway for the near term and direct their energies toward defending what remains of existing regulations, patching the system in ways that are deemed constitutionally permissible by the present court (especially those that increase transparency and encourage more small donors), and exploring ways in which new technologies might ameliorate the problems of money in politics by reducing the cost of campaigns. These reformers also entertain the possibility of a change in the composition of the court that shifts the majority back to those sympathetic to a somewhat more expansive constitutional space for the regulation of campaign finance.

The scholarly research base for developing and evaluating campaign finance reform proposals is surprisingly modest. An excellent new report by a working group of scholars convened by the Campaign Finance Institute and the Bipartisan Policy Center surveys the current state of knowledge and suggests new research priorities that might better inform the reform debate.[20] One of its striking findings is how little of the research conducted over the past thirty years is directly relevant to the new world in which campaigns are conducted and financed or to the policies that are being proposed and enacted to regulate it. To be sure, there is broad agreement that the independent impact of money on election outcomes and policymaking is probably overstated in the press. The level of campaign spending is as much an indicator of electoral strength as a cause of it, especially in the case of presidential candidates and congressional incumbents. Similarly, the impact of interest group contributions on policy is not clear, direct, or dispositive. But there is far too little systematic evidence on a wide range of policy-relevant questions, including the extent and conditions under which independent spending influences the outcome of elections and the policy agenda of legislators; whether parties were weakened, strengthened, or polarized by the ban on soft money and the emergence of "outside" electioneering groups; the impact of broad disclosure on the knowledge and behavior of voters and on the integrity and legitimacy of the electoral process; the costs of nondisclosure; the motivations of megadonors; the effectiveness of contribution limits in limiting rent seeking by private interests and politicians; and the impact of small donors on political participation, polarization, and representation.

Given these empirical uncertainties, it is no wonder that differences in values and ideology as well as calculations of partisan and economic interest dominate the debate. Most assertions about cause and effect are conveniently consistent with the preferences of the asserter. A continuation of divided party government virtually guarantees congressional inaction on any reform proposal of consequence as well as the perpetuation of a dysfunctional Federal Election Commission. Extreme partisan polarization and strategic hyperpartisanship mean that unified party government is a necessary, though far from sufficient, condition for decisive action. Which party controls both ends of Pennsylvania Avenue would, however, determine whether campaign finance regulation continues along its current deregulatory path or rather is redirected with strengthened disclosure and an expanded small-donor base, the latter expedited with multiple public matching funds, New York City–style.[21]

Political Parties in Campaign Finance and American Democracy

Political parties have proved themselves essential to democracies across the globe in organizing choices for low-information voters and helping elected representatives take collective action responsive to promises made, problems confronted, and public preferences expressed on election day. The legendary political scientist V. O. Key clarified those partisan linkages by distinguishing three critical dimensions: party in the electorate, party organizations, and party in government.[22] Key's ruminations decades ago are useful today in thinking about how parties are implicated in the problems of money and politics and, more broadly, of democratic accountability and governance. Contemporary parties in America are strikingly polarized at all three levels, reflecting sharp ideological differences and strategic opposition that has morphed into a kind of tribalism. This parliamentary-like character of today's parties is mismatched with a separation-of-powers constitutional system that anticipates bargaining and compromise across governing institutions and diverse interests and factions. Moreover, as discussed above, formal party organizations have given way to extensive networks of players whose interests, values, and beliefs reinforce the distinctiveness of the parties and their unusually disciplined team play. The old notion of parties as pragmatic and moderating forces amid extreme and uncompromising interests does not fit well with contemporary American politics.[23]

Whether past campaign finance reforms bear major responsibility for these developments is a matter of dispute; my own assessment is that their contribution has been modest at most. The objective behind banning party soft money was not to weaken parties but to make them less a channel for conflicts of interest between well-heeled donors and public officials. Parties have thrived in their post-soft-money world by increasing their small-donor base, more fully exploiting the possibilities of four- and five-digit hard-money fundraising, and aggressively redistributing funds from safe incumbents to competitive races; taking full advantage of the Supreme Court decision that allowed them to make unlimited independent expenditures on behalf of their candidates; using 527 organizations to finance campaign activities with big donors; and finally, jumping on the Super PAC–nonprofit advocacy organization bandwagon (unofficially to be sure). Proposals to eliminate the ban on party soft money strike me as naïve and ill-considered, especially if the objective is to mitigate extreme partisanship and improve the climate for governing. So too do efforts to sharply increase hard-money contributions to parties.

Partly because the two party teams are pretty evenly matched in this new Wild West of campaign finance, the present system will most likely endure. Liberal billionaire donors are available to match conservative ones. Democratic and Republican party networks will both continue to exploit the opportunities created by the court's deregulatory turn. Major corporate players may try to save the Republican Party from the radical turn forced by the Tea Party movement by financing their own Super PACs to intervene in primary elections.

Breaking out of the equilibrium of the new world of campaign finance will quite likely require a confluence of events: a major campaign finance scandal, a strong unified Democratic party government that is willing to act on its beliefs, if not obviously its interests, and a reconstituted Supreme Court that finds a more expansive constitutional basis for regulating money and politics. In the meantime, skirmishes on campaign finance reform will continue on the margins of the current system and without notable success. State and local government experimentation on campaign finance is probably the most that can be expected—unless and until the logjam breaks.

There is every reason to expect a continuation of current trends in the 2014 and 2016 election cycles. That means no effective limits on the ability of individuals and groups to invest in federal elections; more candidate-specific Super PACs, in presidential primaries and congressional elections; with the help of 501(c) organizations, only partial disclosure of megadonors; and increasing overall campaign spending heavily concentrated in competitive states and districts. It also means intensified efforts in small-donor fundraising linked to microtargeting and mobilizing made possible by large databases, sophisticated statistical analysis, and ever more creative uses of the Internet.

Notes

1. Herbert E. Alexander, *Financing the 1960 Election* (Princeton, N.J.: Citizens' Research Foundation, 1962).

2. David B. Magleby, ed., *Financing the 2000 Election* (Brookings, 2002), p. 238.

3. Ibid., p. 238.

4. Bradley A. Smith, *Unfree Speech: The Folly of Campaign Finance Reform* (Princeton University Press, 2003).

5. Robert K. Merton, "The Unanticipated Consequences of Purposive Social Action," *American Sociological Review* 1, no. 6 (1936): pp. 894–904.

6. See, for example, "About the Center for Competitive Politics," Center for Competitive Politics (www.campaignfreedom.org/about).

7. See, for example, "Brief History of Fair Election Victories," Public Campaign (www.publicampaign.org/briefhistory).

8. *Arizona Free Enterprise Club's Freedom Club PAC v. Bennett*, 131 S. Ct. 2806 (2011).

9. League of Women Voters, "Review of Constitutional Amendments Proposed in Response to Citizens' United" (www.lwv.org/content/review-constitutional-amendments-proposed-response-citizens-united).

10. Thomas E. Mann and Norman J. Ornstein, *It's Even Worse Than It Looks* (New York: Basic Books, 2012).

11. Raymond J. La Raja, "Richer Parties, Better Politics? Party-Centered Campaign Finance Laws and American Democracy," *Forum* 11, no. 4 (2013: 313–38).

12. *McCutcheon v. Federal Election Commission*, 572 U.S.__ 2014.

13. Eliza Newlin Carney, "Max PACs Poised to Exploit Supreme Court Decision on Campaign Finance," *CQ Weekly*, May 5, 2014 (www.cq.com/doc/weekly report-4464536?0).

14. Jeffrey Toobin, "The John Roberts Project," *Daily Comment* (blog), *New Yorker*, April 3, 2014 (www.newyorker.com/online/blogs/comment/2014/04/the-john-roberts-project-beyond-mccutcheon.html); Lawrence Lessig, "Originalists Making It Up Again: McCutcheon and 'Corruption,'" *Daily Beast*, April 2, 2014

(www.thedailybeast.com/articles/2014/04/02/originalists-making-it-up-again-mccutcheon-and-corruption.htm).

15. *Buckley* v. *Valeo.*

16. *Citizens United* v. *Federal Election Commission,* 130 S. Ct. 876 (2010).

17. Anthony Corrado, "Hiding in Plain Sight," *Committee for Economic Development,* July 2013 (http://www.ced.org/pdf/Hiding_in_Plain_Sight_July_2013.pdf).

18. Lawrence Lessig, "What an Originalist Would Understand 'Corruption' to Mean," *California Law Review* 102, no. 1 (2014).

19. Richard L. Hasen, "Is Dependence Corruption Distinct from a Political Equality Rationale for Campaign Finance Regulation? A Reply to Professor Lessig," *Election Law Journal* 12, no. 3 (2013): 305–16; Bruce E. Cain, "Is Dependence Corruption the Solution to America's Campaign Finance Problems?," *California Law Review* 102, no. 37 (2014): 37–48.

20. Michael J. Malbin and John C. Fortier, "An Agenda for Future Research on Money in Politics in the United States," Campaign Finance Institute and Bipartisan Policy Center, August 2013 (www.cfinst.org/pdf/books-reports/scholar workinggroup/CFI-BPC_Research-Agenda_Report_Webversion.pdf).

21. Michael J. Malbin, Peter W. Brusoe, and Brendan Glavin, "Small Donors, Big Democracy: New York City's Matching Funds as a Model for the Nation and States," *Election Law Journal* 11, no. 1 (2012): 3–20.

22. V. O. Key Jr., *Politics, Parties, and Pressure Groups,* 5th ed. (New York: Crowell, 1964).

23. For a contrary view, see La Raja, "Richer Parties, Better Politics? Party-Centered Campaign Finance Laws and American Democracy."

Appendix. List of Interviews

Abe Adams, senior director, Targeted Victory, and deputy digital director, Romney for President, Inc., March 19, 2013

Tiffany Adams, vice president of public affairs, National Association of Manufacturers, March 20, 2013

Sarah Badawi, development director, Americans for Campaign Reform, March 20, 2013

Kim Barker, reporter, ProPublica, July 25, 2013

Bob Bauer, partner, Perkins Coie, and general counsel, Obama for America, March 21, 2013

Bob Biersack, senior fellow, Center for Responsive Politics, August 15, 2012

John Black, director of research, National Republican Congressional Committee, December 17, 2012

Glen Bolger, cofounder and partner, Public Opinion Strategies, March 19, 2013

Blair Bowie, democracy advocate, Public Interest Research Group, August 16, 2012

Bernadette Budde, senior vice president for candidate advocacy, Business-Industry Political Action Committee, August 16, 2012; December 12, 2012

Celeste Busser, senior media strategist, National Education Association, December 18, 2013

Sean Cairncross, deputy executive director, National Republican Senatorial Committee, February 12, 2013

Guy Cecil, executive director, Democratic Senatorial Campaign Committee, December 19, 2012

Chris Chocola, president, Club for Growth, August 15, 2012

Michael Cornfield, acting director, George Washington University Graduate School of Political Management, March 18, 2013

Chuck Cunningham, director, National Rifle Association, Institute for Legislative Action, Federal Affairs, August 15, 2012

Brandon Davis, national political director, Service Employees International Union, December 19, 2012

Cathy Duvall, national political director, Sierra Club, February 12, 2013

Rob Engstrom, senior vice president of political affairs and federal relations, national political director, U.S. Chamber of Commerce, August 16, 2012; December 14, 2012

Denise Feriozzi, political director, EMILY's List, March 27, 2013

John Fortier, director of the Bipartisan Policy Center's Democracy Project, March 18, 2013

Alex Gage, founder and CEO, Target Point, December 6, 2012

Ben Ginsberg, partner, Patton Boggs, December 17, 2012

Lisa Goeas, manager of legislative affairs, National Federation of Independent Business, December 11, 2012

Ken Goldstein, president, Kantar Media CMAG, February 11, 2013

Chris Harris, communication director, American Bridge 21st Century, March 19, 2013

Guy Harrison, executive director, National Republican Congressional Committee, December 17, 2012

Dan Hazelwood, founder, Targeted Creative, February 11, 2013

Craig Holman, government affairs lobbyist, Public Citizen, March 14, 2012

Harold Ickes, president, Priorities USA, and cofounder, Ickes and Enright Group, August 15, 2012; December 12, 2012

Rob Jesmer, executive director, National Republican Senatorial Committee, February 12, 2013

Karin Johansen, principal in the grassroots and government relations practices, Dewey Square Group, March 18, 2013

Barney Kellar, communications director, Club for Growth, August 15, 2012

Sheila Krumholz, executive director, Center for Responsive Politics, August 15, 2012

Celinda Lake, president, Lake Research Partners, August 16, 2012

Linda Lipsen, CEO, America Association for Justice, December 14, 2012

Mike Lux, cofounder and president, Progressive Strategies, L.L.C., January 14, 2013

Thomas Mann, senior fellow in governance studies, Brookings, August 15, 2012

Meredith McGehee, policy director, Campaign Legal Center, February 12, 2013

Kara McKenna, political programs manager, National Federation of Independent Business, August 15, 2012

Michael Meyers, president and partner, Target Point, February 11, 2013

Bill Miller, senior vice president, Business Roundtable, January 22, 2013

Zac Moffatt, cofounder, Targeted Victory, and digital director, Romney for President, Inc., March 19, 2013

Rodell Mollineau, president, American Bridge 21st Century, March 19, 2013

Navin Nayak, senior vice president, League of Conservation Voters, March 4, 2013

Neil Newhouse, cofounder, Public Opinion Strategies, December 27, 2012

Larry Noble, president and CEO, Americans for Campaign Reform, August 14, 2012; March 20, 2013

Michael Podhorzer, political director, AFL-CIO, August 17, 2012, December 18, 2012

Trevor Potter, firm leader in political law, Caplin and Drysdale, December 18, 2012

Laura Quinn, founder, Catalist, March 19, 2013

Lee Rainie, director, Pew Internet and American Life, February 12, 2013

Steve Rosenthal, founder and CEO of America Coming Together Organizing Group, August 17, 2012; January 28, 2013

Stu Rothenberg, editor and publisher, *Rothenberg Political Report*, September 14, 2012

Karl Rove, cofounder and adviser, American Crossroads, March 15, 2013

Paul Ryan, program director and legal counsel, Campaign Legal Center, February 12, 2013

Deirdre Schifeling, national organizing and electoral campaigns director, Planned Parenthood Action Fund, April 4, 2013

Justine Sessions, director of advocacy media, Planned Parenthood, April 4, 2013

Darrell Shull, COO, Business-Industry Political Action Committee, April 3, 2013

Greg Speed, executive director, America Votes, December 18, 2012

Charles R. Spies, treasurer, Restore Our Future, August 17, 2012, December 21, 2012

Sharon Wolff Sussin, national political director, National Federation of Independent Business, August 15, 2012, December 11, 2012

Sean Sweeney, senior strategist, Priorities USA, February 11, 2013

Michael Toner, cochair, election law and government ethics practice, Wiley, Rein, and Fielding, December 20, 2012

Matt Waldrip, deputy national finance director, Romney for President, Inc., March 12, 2013

Brian Walsh, communications director, National Republican Senatorial Committee, and political director, American Action Network, February 12, 2013; March 18, 2013

Kelly Ward, political director, Democratic Congressional Campaign Committee, December 17, 2012

Fred Wertheimer, president, Democracy 21, August 16, 2012

Rick Wiley, political director, Republican National Committee, February 11, 2013; March 31, 2013

Spencer Zwick, campaign finance director, Romney for President, Inc., March 15, 2013

Contributors

Anthony Corrado
Colby College

Stephanie Perry Curtis
Brigham Young University

Diana Dwyre
California State University, Chico

Jay Goodliffe
Brigham Young University

John C. Green
Bliss Institute, University of Akron

Paul S. Herrnson
Roper Center, University of Connecticut

Michael E. Kohler
Bliss Institute, University of Akron

Robin Kolodny
Temple University

David B. Magleby
Brigham Young University

Thomas E. Mann
Brookings Institution

Candice J. Nelson
American University

Kelly D. Patterson
Brigham Young University

Ian P. Schwarber
Bliss Institute, University of Akron

Index